Working in Digital and Smart Organizations

Edoardo Ales • Ylenia Curzi
Tommaso Fabbri • Olga Rymkevich
Iacopo Senatori • Giovanni Solinas
Editors

Working in Digital and Smart Organizations

Legal, Economic and Organizational Perspectives on the Digitalization of Labour Relations

palgrave
macmillan

Editors
Edoardo Ales
Department of Economics and Law
University of Cassino and Southern Lazio
Cassino, Italy

Ylenia Curzi
Department of Economics Marco Biagi
University of Modena and Reggio Emilia
Modena, Italy

Tommaso Fabbri
University of Modena and Reggio Emilia
Modena, Italy

Olga Rymkevich
Marco Biagi Foundation
University of Modena and Reggio Emilia
Modena, Italy

Iacopo Senatori
Marco Biagi Foundation
University of Modena and Reggio Emilia
Modena, Italy

Giovanni Solinas
Department of Economics
University of Modena and Reggio Emilia
Modena, Italy

ISBN 978-3-319-77328-5   ISBN 978-3-319-77329-2   (eBook)
https://doi.org/10.1007/978-3-319-77329-2

Library of Congress Control Number: 2018942406

© The Editor(s) (if applicable) and The Author(s) 2018
This work is subject to copyright. All rights are solely and exclusively licensed by the Publisher, whether the whole or part of the material is concerned, specifically the rights of translation, reprinting, reuse of illustrations, recitation, broadcasting, reproduction on microfilms or in any other physical way, and transmission or information storage and retrieval, electronic adaptation, computer software, or by similar or dissimilar methodology now known or hereafter developed.
The use of general descriptive names, registered names, trademarks, service marks, etc. in this publication does not imply, even in the absence of a specific statement, that such names are exempt from the relevant protective laws and regulations and therefore free for general use.
The publisher, the authors and the editors are safe to assume that the advice and information in this book are believed to be true and accurate at the date of publication. Neither the publisher nor the authors or the editors give a warranty, express or implied, with respect to the material contained herein or for any errors or omissions that may have been made. The publisher remains neutral with regard to jurisdictional claims in published maps and institutional affiliations.

Printed on acid-free paper

This Palgrave Macmillan imprint is published by the registered company Springer International Publishing AG part of Springer Nature.
The registered company address is: Gewerbestrasse 11, 6330 Cham, Switzerland

Contents

1   **Introduction**   1
Olga Rymkevich and Iacopo Senatori

Part I   **The Challenges of Digitalization for Employment Relations**   9

2   **Protecting Work in the Digital Transformation: Rethinking the Typological Approach in the Intrinsically Triangular Relationship Perspective**   11
Edoardo Ales

3   **Digital Work: An Organizational Perspective**   29
Tommaso Fabbri

4   **In Favour of Machines (But Not Forgetting the Workers): Some Considerations on the Fourth Industrial Revolution**   39
Sergio Paba and Giovanni Solinas

vi   Contents

Part II   Work in the Gig Economy   65

5   **A Fair Wage for Workers On-demand via App**   67
     Emanuele Menegatti

6   **Assessment by Feedback in the On-demand Era**   93
     Alessandra Ingrao

7   **The Classification of Crowdwork and Work by Platforms:
     Alternatives and Implications**   113
     Gionata Cavallini

Part III   Industrial Relations Strategies in Industry 4.0   139

8   **Organizing and Collective Bargaining in the Digitized
     "Tertiary Factories" of Amazon: A Comparison Between
     Germany and Italy**   141
     Bruno Cattero and Marta D'Onofrio

9   **Evolution of Trade Unions in Industry 4.0: A German
     and Italian Debate**   165
     Matteo Avogaro

**Part IV   The Impact of Digitalization on the Work
     Performance**   191

10   **DigitAgile: The Office in a Mobile Device. Threats
     and Opportunities for Workers and Companies**   193
     *Roberto Albano, Sonia Bertolini, Ylenia Curzi, Tommaso
     Fabbri, and Tania Parisi*

Contents   vii

11 "Always-on": The Collapse of the Work–Life Separation
    in Recent Developments, Deficits and Counter-Strategies 223
    Rüdiger Krause

12 Into Smart Work Practices: Which Challenges for the HR
    Department? 249
    Teresina Torre and Daria Sarti

13 Conclusion 277
    Ylenia Curzi

Index 287

Notes on Contributors

Roberto Albano PhD in sociology, is an associate professor at the Department Cultures, Politics and Society of the University of Turin, where he teaches sociology and methodology of social research. His most recent research interests include cultural change in European countries, with a special focus on work values; new forms of work organization, with a special focus on autonomy and control in Industry 4.0, teleworking, smart working and co-working. He is a member of the Scientific Committee of MU.S.I.C. – Observatory on social change and cultural innovation.

Edoardo Ales is a full professor of labour law at the University of Cassino and Southern Lazio, a member of the Academic Advisory Board of the Marco Biagi Foundation (Italy), a member of the Scientific Committee and a national expert for Italy of European Centre of Expertise (ECE), and a national expert for Italy of MoveS.

Matteo Avogaro graduated with honours in law from the University of Trento (2011) with a final dissertation in labour law about the extension of workers' protections in the labour market and the main proposals of reform in the Italian and French contexts. From October 2015, he has been a PhD candidate in labour law at the University of Milan with a comparative research project on the reform of collective bargaining and of the measurement system of trade unions' levels of representation in working places. Other research interests are Industry 4.0, work–life balance and right to disconnect, workers' social security rights in the digitized era, unfair dismissals, evolution and re-organization of trade unions

x   Notes on Contributors

especially in manufacturing, and the discipline of the labour relationships in the public sector. He is also part of the editorial staff of the *Revista Brasileira de Previdência*, edited by the Federal University of São Paulo.

Sonia Bertolini is Associate Professor of Labour Sociology, Department of Cultures, Politics and Society, University of Turin (Italy).

Bruno Cattero received his PhD at the University of Göttingen (Germany), was a research fellow at the University of Göttingen and an assistant professor at the University of Frankfurt am Main, and became a professor of economic sociology and sociology of organization at the University of East Piedmont (Alessandria, Italy) in 2002. His research interests focus on comparative industrial relations and the European social model, financialization, and the new development of digitalization at the economic and organizational levels. His recent publications include "An 'Italian way to private equity'? The rhetoric and the reality", in H. Gospel et al. (eds.), *Financialization, New Investment Funds, and Labour: An International Comparison*, Oxford: OUP;: "Partecipazione, lavoro, impresa – (ri)partendo da Gallino", in *Studi Organizzativi*, 2016 (2), "Rappresentanza del lavoro e relazioni industriali a livello europeo", in F. Barbera and I. Pais (2017), *Fondamenti di Sociologia Economica*, Milano: Egea.

Gionata Cavallini is a law graduate of the University of Milan (2015). His thesis, "The employment relationships in corporate groups", received both the "Giorgio Ghezzi" and the "Carlo Russo" award for the best thesis in labour law (2016). He is the author of several articles and comments to jurisprudence in the field of labour law, published by Italian and international reviews. He participated as a speaker in several conventions and seminars, including at an international level. He is currently working on his doctoral research, concerning the techniques of qualification and the instruments of legal protection of old and new forms of self-employed work.

Ylenia Curzi is an assistant professor in the Marco Biagi Department of Economics of the University of Modena and Reggio Emilia, where she teaches Business Organization and International HRM. She received her PhD at the University of Udine. She was a visiting scholar at Cardiff Business School (Wales, UK) in 2009. Her research interests include the relationship between organizational and technological changes, work organisation and wellbeing at work.

Marta D'Onofrio obtained her Masters in Economic Sociology at the University of Eastern Piedmont, Vercelli in 2017. She is currently participating in a research project entitled "Digital Capitalism: A Comparative Case Study on Amazon".

Tommaso Fabbri is a full professor of organization and human resource management, a vice director of the interdisciplinary Doctoral School E4E "Engineering and Economics" at the University of Modena and Reggio Emilia, Italy, and a member of the Academic Advisory Board of the Marco Biagi Foundation.

Alessandra Ingrao is a research fellow in labour law at the Department of Private Law and Legal History of the University of Milan, where, in 2016, she obtained her doctoral degree. She regularly publishes in specialized academic journals, and her research interests concern technological and remote monitoring at the workplace and data protection regulation. She is a member of the Italian Association of Labour and Social Security Law and a member of the editorial board of digital journals *Labour & Law Issues* at the University of Bologna Alma Mater Studiorum and *Revista Brasileira de Previdência* at Universidade Federal of São Paulo, Brazil (UNIFESP).

Rüdiger Krause holds a chair in private law and labour law and is director of the Institute of Labour Law of the University of Göttingen. Since 2006, he has been a member of the board of the German Association of Labour Courts as representative of labour law scholars. Since 2011, he has been co-editor of the new German labour law journal *Soziales Recht*. He has written and/or edited 12 books and over 160 articles and comments on a wide range of topics in employment and labour law. His main areas of research include employment contract law, anti-discrimination law, worker privacy, termination protection law, collective bargaining, industrial action and worker participation at the German and the European level. He is a member of various national and international associations for labour law.

Emanuele Menegatti is a co-director of the bachelor degree programme in management (in English) at the School of Economics, Management and Statistics, University of Bologna. He was a visiting professor at the University of Illinois (USA), Melbourne and Curtin Universities (Australia) and Lund University (Sweden). His main fields of specialization are comparative and EU labour law. He has published in top international journals such as the *Comparative Labor Law and Policy Journal* and the *International Journal of Comparative Labour Law and Industrial Relations*. He is co-editor of the book *Italian Labour Law and Industrial Relations in Italy*.

xii   **Notes on Contributors**

Sergio Paba is Full Professor of Political Economics, Marco Biagi Department of Economics, University of Modena and Reggio Emilia (Italy).

Tania Parisi is a research fellow at the University of Turin. Her research interests concern mainly quantitative measurement of social phenomena and methods of social research, especially with regard to data collection tools and data analysis techniques. Moreover, she studies consequences on workers' life and on their identities of new forms of working—such as telecommuting and e-working—and social innovation. She recently published "What's Still Important About Work? A Longitudinal and Cross-country Analysis of Prevalent Attitudes Towards Work During the Last 40 Years", in Addabbo T., Ales E., *Well-Being at and through Work*, 2017 in Marco Biagi Foundation book series, Giappichelli ed., Eleven International Publishing, 55–96 (with Albano R.) and "L'innovazione sociale radicale", Quarta A., Spano M. (eds.), *Rispondere alla crisi. Comune, cooperazione sociale e diritto*, 2017, Ombrecorte, Verona (with Barbera F.).

Olga Rymkevich is Senior Researcher in Labour Law and Industrial Relations, Marco Biagi Foundation, University of Modena and Reggio Emilia (Italy), and Managing Editor of the *International Journal of Comparative Labour Law and Industrial Relations* (Walters Kluwer).

Daria Sarti is Assistant Professor of Organization and Human Resource Management, Department of Economics and Management, University of Florence, Italy. She is a founding member of ASSIOA (Association of Italian Organization Studies Academics).

Iacopo Senatori is Senior Researcher in Labour Law and Industrial Relations, Marco Biagi Foundation, University of Modena and Reggio Emilia (Italy).

Giovanni Solinas is a full professor of economics at the Marco Biagi Department of Economics at the University of Modena and Reggio Emilia, Italy. He has studied at the University of Cambridge, UK, and is a member of the executive board of the Marco Biagi Foundation and the Giacomo Brodolini Foundation (Italy).

Teresina Torre is Full Professor of Organization and Human Resource Management, Department of Economics and Business Studies, University of Genoa (Italy). She is Vice President of ASSIOA (Association of Italian Organization Studies Academics).

List of Figures

Fig. 12.1 SW implementation as a process of innovation and organizational change. (Source: Our representation based on Schein (1969), Zaltman et al. (1973)) 256

Fig. 12.2 The relationships activated by the HR department in the SW project. (Source: Adapted from Chen and Nath 2008) 258

Fig. 12.3 The multiple roles of HR. (Source: Adapted from Ulrich and Brockbank 2005) 259

List of Tables

Table 10.1	Employees working with computers, laptops and smartphones for at least three quarters of their working time, by country	196
Table 10.2	Employees working at least several times a week in locations other than the employer's premises, by country	197
Table 10.3	Estimated share of eWorkers in the total population of employees by country and 95% confidence intervals	197
Table 10.4	Ideal types of "Organization Personality" (OP)	200
Table 10.5	Frequency of interruptions at work (very/fairly often): comparison between ICT-intensive and non-ICT-intensive employees, by country	209
Table 10.6	Employees reporting that it is "very/fairly" easy to find time for themselves or their family during working hours, by country	210
Table 10.7	Employees whose working day is never longer than 10 hours, by country	211
Table 10.8	Index of interference of work with family life and of interference of family life with work, by country. (Scores ≥ average)	213
Table 12.1	Organizations involved in the analysis	261
Table 12.2	Main actions by the HR department during the process of SW development	265
Table 12.3	Phases of the process and the role played by the HR department	266

1

Introduction

Olga Rymkevich and Iacopo Senatori

This book is the outcome of a project bringing together a group of scholars from different disciplinary backgrounds, who have a common interest in the innovation taking place in the field of employment relations. The project, not yet completed, was developed in the Marco Biagi Foundation, a research institute at the University of Modena and Reggio Emilia (Italy), which has been experimenting with multidisciplinary and interdisciplinary studies since it was set up in 2002. These studies encompass mainly labour law, economics and organisational theory with a view to one day involving experts from a broader range of disciplines.

The choice of studying the digital transformation of employment relations arose as a natural consequence of the working environment inhabited by the editors of this book. In fact, the complex, dynamic and increasingly topical nature of this phenomenon requires innovative

---

O. Rymkevich (✉) • I. Senatori
Marco Biagi Foundation, University of Modena and Reggio Emilia,
Modena, Italy
e-mail: rymkevich@unimore.it; iacopo.senatori@unimore.it

© The Author(s) 2018
E. Ales et al. (eds.), *Working in Digital and Smart Organizations*,
https://doi.org/10.1007/978-3-319-77329-2_1

approaches that go beyond deeply rooted, narrow and often outdated stereotypes, thus opening up an interesting experimental space for multi-disciplinary and interdisciplinary studies.

From this perspective, the present volume collects a selection of papers dedicated to the problems of digitalisation of employment relations analysed from various disciplinary points of view in light of their theoretical and practical implications. Such an approach, in the view of the editors, is the best way to tackle this phenomenon in its multifaceted and controversial aspects. At the same time, it represents a unique and original feature of this volume which distinguishes it from the other publications in the field.

Arguably, the mere multidisciplinary approach might be insufficient to address all the complexities of the phenomena of digital transformation. For this reason, a further step allowing a move from a multidisciplinary reflection towards an interdisciplinary one might be instructive for the purpose of creating a sort of a "communication channel" between disciplines that do not always communicate in a fluid manner. Such an interdisciplinary exercise requires additional intense joint efforts aimed at developing shared analytical concepts and a more coherent and integrated approach. Ideally, this should make it possible to overcome short-sighted and sometimes egoistic dogmas of individual disciplines which otherwise might not be able to gain insight into the problems inevitably generated by digital transformation.

The analysis of the impact of digitalisation on employment from various disciplinary angles clearly shows its *pros* and *cons*. On the one hand, digital technology can be conceived as a means to establish more horizontal and cooperative relationships within organisations and to provide "smart" and digital workers with greater flexibility in the definition of their working schedules, enhancing self-determination in the performance of work, while providing better opportunities to match their skills with the demand for labour, given the potential decoupling of labour supply from any physical or geographical boundary. Furthermore, it entails significant potential for job creation insofar as it can lead to an increase in productivity and the development of a production system based on innovation, possibly linked to the reshoring of previously outsourced operations and the reconfiguration of business models ("selling light not light bulbs").

On the other hand, digitalisation gives rise to a challenge for the common theoretical concepts of employment relations as well as the material conditions of workers. From a labour market perspective, it entails the risks of obsolescence of jobs, especially low-skilled ones, and the de-skilling of workers as they are made more and more dependent on the input from highly sophisticated digital platforms and devices ("smart factories for dumber workers"). The final outcome of those processes may be an increase in unemployment, segregation and inequality. From a management perspective, the use of digital devices requires new patterns of job design and job evaluation, capable of instantiating additional and invisible command-and-control features in working processes, allowing the continuous real-time monitoring and evaluation of worker performance. Another effect may be a trade-off between organisational flexibility and more intensive workloads, in both qualitative (e.g. degree of cognitive effort) and quantitative (working hours) terms. All of the above may lead to a deterioration of worker health and safety along with a heightened risk of work-related stress.

Given the intrinsic weakness of employees in terms of bargaining power in relation to the employer, evidently a set of adjustment measures should be put forward at different levels. In legislative terms, stronger and more fine-tuned employee protections, looking beyond the increasingly obsolete and rigid distinction between subordinate and self-employed workers, should be proposed. Corresponding adjustments are also necessary at the organisation and HR management level. Ideally, they should be in accordance with each other (i.e. fundamental labour law principles based on respect for human rights and dignity with economic efficiency and rationality standing at the core of the economic and organisational theory). In this regard, it seems particularly instructive to analyse existing best practices relating to the adaptation of employment provisions and organisational models to the challenges of digitalisation, tackling them in a broader comparative perspective. They range from judicial responses to cases relating to the employment status of Uber drivers in the US and the UK, to the legal regulation of specific issues prompted by digital work, such as the rethinking of restrictions on the online surveillance of employees and the recent regulation on "smart work" in Italy, as well as the initiatives promoted by IG Metall in Germany.

In light of the problems outlined above, the crucial question remains how to protect the interests of all the stakeholders operating in the digital economy. Clearly, a set of innovative, integrated and far-sighted policies is needed. Of course, such policies should enhance, among other things, the role of social dialogue which in the sphere of employment relations remains a core instrument to ensure an appropriate balance of interests of the parties involved. In this regard, the key actors of industrial relations, first of all trade unions, should rethink their respective roles in the context of the digital economy in order to be able to mitigate inevitable conflicts and, at the same time, gain additional advantages afforded by Industry 4.0. This requires all the actors involved to become more flexible, more open to innovation and change and "smarter".

Against this backdrop, there is an increasing need to establish a more integrated and shared framework of knowledge on work digitalisation, build a taxonomy of the phenomena under investigation, examine their impact, delineate future perspectives and put forward a comprehensive set of original proposals. Given the complexity and rapid evolution of the phenomenon of digitalisation, more research is needed and undoubtedly an interdisciplinary approach should be increasingly privileged in future research projects. This should allow stakeholders to anticipate and react in a timely manner to the impact of digital transformation of various aspects of employment relations.

The papers in this book attempt to take an initial step in the direction of a more comprehensive in-depth understanding of the challenges entailed in the digital transformation of employment relations, whereas the last chapter outlines a scenario for the next stage of interdisciplinary research in this field.

The **first part** of the book attempts to outline a comprehensive picture of the issues of interest for the three disciplinary fields that are included in the project.

The paper by **Edoardo Ales** aims at illustrating, from a labour law perspective, the impact that digital transformation and digitalisation are having on the workplace and the work relationship. "Dematerialisation", "privatisation", "adjustment" and "enrichment" are among the keywords that, in the author's opinion, best describe the ongoing innovations and the challenges they entail for labour law. Risks and opportunities in the transition from the traditional to the new patterns are examined, and the particular emphasis is on the health and safety of workers and the classification of the work relationship.

The paper by **Tommaso Fabbri** enriches the picture with a work organisation analysis. The first part provides a number of definitions, starting with the very concept of "digital work" and a characterisation of the phenomena involved in the process of digitalisation of the employment relationship. In the second part, the author tests the main characteristics of the new employment patterns: the findings lead him to question some assumptions related to work performed in a digital environment, such as its smartness and healthfulness.

Finally, the contribution by **Sergio Paba** and **Giovanni Solinas** sheds light on the economic implications of the "Fourth Industrial Revolution". They start by looking for an appropriate definition of the phenomenon. Then they discuss its impact on employment by reviewing the relevant literature and the industrial policies developed by governments to support the digital revolution. The authors advocate the implementation of new policies, designed for this new era of technological change (such as the provision of adequate protections and benefits for independent contractors, which should not adversely affect their independence and flexibility), and argue that governments should refrain from reviving forms of protection and regulation designed for the past industrial age.

The **second part** is focused on the problems arising in the multifaceted and complex field of the gig economy. The contributions included in this part have a common legal background and address the crucial issues of remuneration, performance assessment and qualification of the work relationship.

The paper by **Emanuele Menegatti** starts from the argument that the application of a minimum wage to workers engaged by digital platforms could alleviate the economic uncertainties that such workers often struggle with and, at the same time, provide for a fairer distribution of the profits generated by the digital platforms. Given that an approach based on the classification of the employment relationship would not represent an efficient solution (since it would not lead one to consider workers in the gig economy as employees in a strict sense), the author

6   O. Rymkevich and I. Senatori

moves to a *de iure condendo* perspective. Drawing from the theory of "purposive labour law", he advocates a redistribution of employment protections towards all personal work relations.

The contribution by **Alessandra Ingrao** is focused on the widespread use, by gig economy platforms, of customer feedback systems by which users are allowed to rate and review services and goods. Applied to the performance of a personal work service, such systems represent a new model of evaluation that impacts on the remuneration, the exercise of employers' prerogatives (such as control and disciplinary power) and the protection of the personal data of workers. The author analyses the possible solutions to such problems, making reference to the provisions of the new General Data Protection Regulation of the European Union, which include some innovative protections for this kind of worker, such as the portability of personal data and the right to be exempted from decisions based exclusively on automated processes.

The paper by **Gionata Cavallini** reviews the different paths pursued by case law and the legal literature with respect to the classification of "crowdworkers" in order to clarify whether they can be entitled to full employment rights or, otherwise, whether they can achieve a minimum floor of protections outside the domain of statutory employment law. In the author's view, the most convincing solution in the given framework is to classify this particular relationship as platform-mediated self-employed work. Although this may represent a first step in the direction of a clarification of the legal status of crowdworkers and a recognition of their rights, the author argues that legislative intervention is needed to pursue a more satisfactory outcome.

The **third part** investigates how digitalisation applied to industrial processes impacts on industrial relations practices. The two papers are characterised by the use of a comparative methodology, and both try to read into the recent developments taking place in two European models—the German and the Italian—that are characterised by similar production systems as well as by very different institutional backgrounds.

The paper by **Bruno Cattero** and **Marta D'Onofrio** presents a case study that the authors conducted on the German and Italian fulfillment centres of the leading e-commerce company, Amazon, with a particular emphasis on its logistics area. In the first part, they look into the work practices implemented at the plants, concluding that the mix between high digitalisation and low automation, while preserving jobs, is a cause of deterioration of working conditions since it allows a pervasive control of work performance and an heavier workloads. The second part examines the attitude of the company towards the trade unions' claims for better conditions. The authors find that the managerial approach is barely influenced by the different institutional contexts in the two countries. On the other hand, the unions seem to have deployed different strategies to organize employees and put forward their requests: nonetheless, the outcomes have been similarly unfavourable for the employees.

Moving from a similar background analysis of the impact of digitalisation on the manufacturing sector, the contribution by **Matteo Avogaro** compares the strategies developed by two leading trade unions—the German IG Metall and the Italian FIM-CISL—to tackle the issues raised by the adaptation of working conditions to the new context, from the perspective of employees' interests. Continuous vocational training, work–life balance and job rotation (linked to the increased complexity and specialisation of tasks) represent the most challenging topics for trade union action. The author concludes that collective agreements and dialogue between social partners remain, in the modified scenario, the main instruments to balance the workers' requests and the employers' need for innovation.

The **fourth part** looks into the effects that the introduction of organisational arrangements prompted by digitalisation exert on the performance of work, particularly as far as the traditional patterns of space and time are concerned.

The paper by **Roberto Albano, Tommaso Fabbri, Ylenia Curzi, Sonia Bertolini** and **Tania Parisi** presents a definition of "smart" (or "agile") work, which is work based on the intensive use of digital devices and increasing spatial and temporal "disembedding" from the formal organisation. The authors address three research questions, focused respectively on (a) the interaction between organisational autonomy, discretion and control; (b) the relationship between digitalisation and productivity; and (c) the reconciliation of work with non-working time. The findings lead the authors to point to directions for further research concerning the collective development of autonomous rules and new organisational competences and, on the other hand, the balance between risks and benefits that the extensive use of mobile devices entails for work organisation and work–family balance.

The paper by **Rüdiger Krause** tackles, from a labour law perspective, the problem of the "encroachment" of work life on private life, encouraged by information and communication technology and the use of mobile devices as work instruments. The author asks whether current working time regulations are a suitable means to protect the interest of "always-on" employees or whether, on the contrary, deregulation could be a better answer. The analysis builds on the theoretical concept of "time porosity" and the reconstruction of the European legislation of working time. The author finds that a proper answer to the issues raised by time porosity should come from the mix between a more effective enforcement of existing regulations and action aimed at filling some regulatory gaps, concerning, for instance, the classification of stand-by work and the acknowledgement of a right to disconnect.

The paper by **Teresina Torre** and **Daria Sarti** presents the findings of explorative research aimed at investigating the implementation of smart-working arrangements and practices within organisational contexts, focusing on the role played by HR departments. The authors reject the idea of a one-size-fits-all model for effective implementation: in their view, smart working has to be designed starting from specific situations and with specific attention to the features of each organisation. They also argue that the functions of the HR department are crucial in creating the conditions for successful implementation of smart-working arrangements, including appropriate training for users and managers, prompting a cultural adaptation of the key players and building the consensus of social partners.

Part I

The Challenges of Digitalization for Employment Relations

2

Protecting Work in the Digital Transformation: Rethinking the Typological Approach in the Intrinsically Triangular Relationship Perspective

Edoardo Ales

Introduction

Digital transformation as "the profound transformation of business and organizational activities, processes, competencies and models to fully leverage the changes and opportunities of a mix of digital technologies and their accelerating impact across society in a strategic and prioritized way, with present and future shifts in mind" (i-SCOOP) has been ongoing for decades.

However, "economic and societal changes occasioned by technological developments are shaped, not just by the availability of new technologies and their features, but also by ideologies, power structures, and human aspirations and agendas. Technologies are not exogenous forces

---

E. Ales (✉)
University of Cassino and Southern Latium, Cassino, Italy

Marco Biagi Foundation, Modena, Italy
e-mail: e.ales@unicas.it

© The Author(s) 2018
E. Ales et al. (eds.), *Working in Digital and Smart Organizations*,
https://doi.org/10.1007/978-3-319-77329-2_2

that roll over societies like tsunamis with predetermined results. Rather, our skills, organizations, institutions, and values shape how we develop technologies and how we deploy them once created, along with their final impact" (Committee on Information Technology, Automation, and the U.S. Workforce 2017, 54).

On the other hand, digitalization as "the process of employing digital technologies and information to transform business operations" may be regarded as "the fastest, most striking, example yet of the adoption of what economists call a general purpose technology (GPT) – a technology like steam power or electricity so broadly useful that it reorients the entire economy and tenor of life" (Muro et al. 2017, 5).

It is self-evident that such a "profound transformation of business and organizational activities, processes, competencies and models" which brings to the "explosion of digitally enabled business models and ways of working" is going to deeply affect the arrangements and regulation of the work relationship.

Indeed, "in terms of business models, organizations of all kinds are experimenting with myriad new formats ranging from decentralized and remote work, e-commerce, internet marketplaces, online talent platforms, online supply chain management, to 'sharing' models, dynamic pricing, crowd financing, and many more" (Muro et al. 2017, 7).

"As a result, workers of every stripe – from corporate finance officers to sales people to machine operators to utility workers and Uber drivers – are spending sizable portions of their workdays running the Waze app to navigate traffic; connecting to the office by text message; managing processes through Salesforce; or running diagnostic software at the building site or at bedside" (Muro et al. 2017, 7).

The aim of this essay is to illustrate, from a labour law perspective, the impact that digital transformation and digitalization are producing in terms of dematerialization and "privatization" of the workplace, "adjustment" and "enrichment" of the work relationship, and "framing" of the provision of services.

Furthermore, the essay will analyse the transition from the traditional work relationships to the new work patterns and conclude on the idea that one should look at digital transformation and digitalization, at the same time, as opportunities or risks for workers—or both. This is definitely a challenge for labour law.

The Effects of the Digital Transformation and Digitalization on the Work Relationship: An Overview

From the list of processes recalled above, one can see that digital transformation and the digitalization of business impact on some constitutive elements of labour law, such as the workplace, the posture of the work relationship, the allocation of prerogatives and responsibilities within it and the way in which self-employment is performed. Such a statement needs to be explained.

We can start from the workplace, which, together with undertaking and establishment, is still among the most relevant notions of labour law. It indicates the physical as well as the juridical place where workers have (the right) to perform their duties. One of the effects that digitalization of business is likely to produce is the dematerialization of the workplace, pushing workers outside the undertaking or the establishment as physical places while keeping them attached to the company as economic and legal entity. The dematerialization of workplace may occur because work will be performed on a mobile device and/or because of its "privatization", in the case of work performed at home on a platform. Both modalities fall under the name of smart or agile work.

As a consequence of the dematerialization and/or "privatization", the traditional notion of workplace has to be regarded as outdated since it is based on (i) the existence of premises owned by or to be ascribed to the employer and (ii) the indispensable presence of the worker within them.

However, if digitalization makes the physical notion of workplace outdated, one may wonder whether the juridical dimension attached to it should be preserved in order to guarantee (at least some of) the rights that were (and still are) recognized to workers because of their physical presence within employers' premises.

A promising concept that could be used to categorize the juridical dimension of the workplace is that of work environment, which is not necessarily linked to employers' ownership or availability of the place where the work is performed. In fact, in light of the dematerialization and "privatization" of the workplace, every place (even the worker's place) can be looked at as a work environment.

In turn, the notion of work environment, resulting from international and EU occupational safety and health (OSH) law, immediately recalls the need to guarantee workers' physical, psychical and psychosocial integrity in the event that they are no longer operating within the employers' premises.

The reference to OSH highlights one of the main challenges that labour law will face because of the dematerialization and/or "privatization" of the workplace, i.e. the physical separation of employers from their workers (employees) with the consequence that the former will no longer be able to exercise their managerial prerogatives (directly or indirectly) in person. Physical separation affects, in particular, the power to direct and control, personally and continuously, the quality and quantity of work performed by the worker within the agreed working time.

Of course, this represents a profound change of paradigm for labour law since personal and ongoing direction and control (still) constitute the main features of the traditional structure of the employment (subordinate) relationship as well as the most effective instruments for the assessment of workers' performance in view of its remuneration.

Indeed, the physical separation of workers (employees) from their employers is not a new phenomenon for labour law if one takes into account homework, the oldest form of distance work ever. Nevertheless, within the framework of the digitalization of business, the change of paradigm triggered by the physical separation of the worker from the employer has to be carefully scrutinized since it presents itself as ambivalent: the dematerialization and/or "privatization" of the workplace may mean either more or less control.

On the one hand, digitalization, by its nature, provides the employer with the possibility to enhance control by way of IT, above all for distance work performed online. On the other hand, the employer may decide to renounce control just because of the physical separation or to accept and even trigger physical separation because ongoing control on the performance is no longer perceived as essential.

In the first case, a strengthened control on work will require a careful assessment of its modalities under existing labour law rules or under the ones to be elaborated specifically for the new forms of IT-supported control. From such a perspective, one has to remember that labour law has always looked suspiciously at distance control, at least if not approved by the controlled workers or their representatives within the undertaking. Additionally, digitalization is likely to transform the same work tools into control devices (work-control devices), thus leading to the concurrence, into the same routine, of work, control on work, control on the respect of the working time, and assessment of the performance in the view of its remuneration.

In the second case, employers might be encouraged or obliged, by the absence of suitable remote control devices, as was the case for homework, to reduce the extent to which they shape and organize work. This will lead to the enhancement of a results-oriented approach and a corresponding increase of workers' autonomy in deciding the modalities to be used in order to achieve the results expected by the employer. This could give rise to the need for an "adjustment" of the relationship between the worker and the undertaking, from a practical and juridical point of view, in terms of coordination of the work performed in an autonomous way with the functioning of the business.

Associated with the physical separation between management and labour is the reallocation of prerogatives and responsibilities deriving from the work relationship. This mainly has to do with the increasing tendency of digitalized business to rely on reputational mechanisms based on costumers' rating instead (or because of the impossibility) of assessing by itself workers' performance.

Such a reallocation of managerial prerogatives results in the empowerment and responsibilization of costumers, who, in this way, are no longer to be regarded only as end users of the product or service but also as co-managers of the workers providing them. However, in most cases, costumers cannot exercise their co-managerial prerogatives directly since the reputational mechanism, in turn, is administered by an algorithm that normalizes costumers' feedbacks according to business guidelines.

In certain cases, costumers' empowerment can be taken to the extreme, the passive consumer being transformed into a prosumer, to be understood as somebody who will participate in the design and creation of the product or service provided by the business. The empowerment and responsibilization of the costumer/consumer, as co-manager or even as prosumer, are likely to prompt the enrichment of the traditional bilateral structure of the employment relationship by the active involvement of a third party.

This kind of involvement gives rise to an intrinsically trilateral work relationship, in which the third party enters into the same commercial contract signed with the company that produces the good or provides the service agreed upon, in most cases without the explicit consent or even knowledge of the worker.

Such an intrinsically trilateral work relationship is not comparable to agency work. The latter, in fact, triangular in its results, consists of two intertwined but separated contracts, both having as specific object the utilization of the worker by a third party not bound by the employment contract that links the worker to the agency.

Digitalization of business may also lead to the dematerialization of the company. This happens with businesses that consist of making available, via app, a virtual market place in which providers and costumers can satisfy their reciprocal interests and needs under the supervision and with the guarantee of the company owning the platform.

In this way, costumers purchase a service provided by self-employed and, by rating both the service and the provider, are able to build a reputation of the latter. By doing this, costumers help each other in making the right choice on the platform. Costumers also help the platform to exclude providers who have been rated as unreliable or undesirable by a relevant number of them according benchmarks determined by the platform on the ground of (normalized) costumers' feedbacks. In fact, the guarantee of a certain standard of service is one of the most important features of the business that the company and the providers allowed into the platform carry on. On the other hand, the company is rating costumers and if they have proven themselves unreliable or undesirable, they can be denied access to the platform.

In the case just described, one cannot, at least in our view, talk about an employment relationship between the company administrating the platform and the service provider, even in the "enriched" version, as resulting from the presence of a third party. In fact, the service provider is free to join and leave the platform at any time without any constraint. It is also free to refuse the service to the costumer without paying any consequence except on its reputation on the platform, which, in turn, can react consequently even by banning the provider.

Instead of employers, platforms of this kind can be categorized, in our view, as reputational service intermediators; costumers as clients looking for a well-reputed service provider; service providers as self-employed that, in order to profit from the (reputational) services of the platform, accept to be rated and framed within it as far as the conditions of the service are concerned. In fact, they provide a service they could also provide outside the platform, maybe even under more profitable economic conditions, without benefiting, however, from the advantages offered by a widespread and well-established reputational mechanism.

Therefore, one could talk about as many self-employment relationships as the number of service agreements concluded within the framework of the platform as reputational service intermediator.

Concluding on the impact digital transformation and the digitalization of business are likely to produce on constitutive elements of labour law such as the workplace, the posture of the work relationship, the allocation of prerogatives and responsibilities within it and the way in which self-employment is performed, one can argue that labour law is only partially equipped to face it. In fact, if the notion of work environment, which should substitute the outdated one of workplace, is already well known in international, supranational and national labour legislation, many of the concepts (elaborated on above) to cope with the newest developments of digital transformation are definitely unknown to it.

We are referring to the intrinsically trilateral employment relationship resulting from the reallocation of managerial prerogatives in terms of empowerment and responsibilization of the costumer, to be seen as co-manager or even as prosumer. The same applies to the self-employment relationships as service agreements concluded within the framework of the platform as reputational service intermediator. Even the very notion of coordinated self-employment is unknown to the majority of national legal orders.

In the next two sections, we will analyse in more detail the most important issues raised by the digital transformation with reference to the basic notions of labour law we have referred to above.

Safety, Health and the Quantification of Work in a Dematerialized and "Privatized" Work Environment

A major challenge that labour law is facing because of the dematerialization and/or "privatization" of the workplace is how to guarantee a safe and healthy work environment to the worker in the event that work will be performed outside the employer's premises. In the standard setting of labour law, in which there is a coincidence between the owner of the place where the work is performed (undertaking or establishment) and the employer of the worker who performs the work, the guarantee of a safe and healthy work environment is at the employers' charge.

From a legal point of view, that guarantee is realized by the fulfilment of the so-called safety obligation. As for its object, the safety obligation is multifaceted in the sense that it focuses, from the perspectives of a preventative as well as a protective avoidance of risks, on the following:

(a) material safety: the way in which the workplace is structured and equipped by the employer and the choice of substances and agents to be used within the production process in order to avoid or reduce physical risks;
(b) organizational safety: the way in which employers shape the production processes, including the working hours and rests periods, and in which they train, inform and instruct workers in order to avoid or reduce psychophysical risks;
(c) immaterial safety: the safeguard of workers from discrimination or harassment of any kind (perpetrated by the employer or workmates) in order to avoid or reduce psychosocial risks;
(d) shared safety: the balanced participation of workers and their representatives (specialized and generalist) in the fulfilment of the safety obligation.

Labour law, actually, has already faced the need to cope with the fulfilment of the safety obligation beyond its standard setting, i.e. in the case of work performed outside employers' premises, as it happens, without claim of completeness, with homework and, more recently, telework, agency work and posting of workers or subordinate agents. Notwithstanding the common feature, these are evidently very different cases. In the first, work is performed (mainly) at the workers' place and therefore within what we have already called a "privatized" workplace. In the second, though performed outside of the employers' premises, work is executed within a workplace owned by the user firm or the contractor. In the third, every place can be the workplace.

The question, common to all of the mentioned cases, is how physical separation, together with someone else's ownership of the workplace, is influencing the distribution of the security obligation's charges among the parties, taking into account the different facets of that obligation as categorized above. The answer can be found within the duty of the employer to guarantee a safe and healthy work environment because of the existence of the employment relationship, even at someone else's workplace, at least to the extent that the owner of the latter cannot be charged of a safety obligation of his or her own.

Decisive, in such a perspective, is that the employer shall provide the worker with the necessary training, information, technical instruction and instruments needed in order to perform the tasks assigned in a safe way—in short, the organizational safety, which corresponds to that aspect of the work environment related to the so-called technical subordination of the employee towards the employer. On the other hand, the owner is, in many cases jointly and severally, responsible for the material, immaterial and shared safety of the workplace, at least if the workplace is an undertaking or establishment.

In the case of telework performed at the workers' place, the work environment the employer is responsible for shall also include the physical safety, at least to the extent it is linked to workers' technical subordination. From such a perspective, the employer cannot be held liable if the worker is injured while taking a shower during the daily break, which could be the case if the shower had been taken within the restrooms of the undertaking.

In the case of subordinated agents visiting clients at their places, the employer remains responsible for the organizational safety, though within the limit of a tempered technical subordination as typical of the kind of tasks performed by agents. On the other hand, the employer or the social security institution by which the agent should be insured will be charged with the consequences of commuting accidents, i.e. accidents that could occur to the agent while travelling from his or her place to the client and from one client to another.

A second major challenge that labour law is facing because of the dematerialization and/or "privatization" of the workplace refers to the quantification of work performed outside employers' premises. As is well known, such a quantification is crucial in order to (i) distribute work among the workers of the undertaking according to employers' necessities, (ii) keep work within the limits provided by the law from the perspective of organizational safety, and (iii) remunerate work in a proportionate way.

In the traditional setting of labour law, the yardstick for the quantification of work performance is the working hour, which has been a cornerstone of collective bargaining since its foundation. The quantification of working hours presupposes the possibility for the employer (and the employee) to fix the beginning and the end of work and to exercise the power to control that the predetermined amount of working hours has been performed within the period agreed, which, not surprisingly, is called working time. The quantification of working hours, and consequently of working time, is also crucial for defining a fair work–life balance, i.e. the period in which the human being is free from work.

Is it clear that the picture just described is challenged by the fact that work is performed outside of employers' premises and this is mainly because both parties cannot count anymore on the physical presence of the worker in the undertaking: as opportunity to control for the employer and as security against abuses for the employee. From these perspectives, working hours and working time are beneficial for both.

As for the safety obligation, also in the case of working hours, the challenge is not new to labour law. Therefore, the remarks already proposed above apply. Actually, in relation to the quantification of work, one could argue that when the dematerialization and/or "privatization" of the workplace is the product of digitalization, both parties can profit from the fact that it is likely to transform work tools into control devices (work-control devices), allowing a very accurate calculation of working hours if work is performed online. An hour-based working system of quantification of working time fits perfectly with online work if it is possible for both parties to certify the beginning and end of the connection(s). This can also help public authorities in controlling the absence of so-called "envelope wages", whereby formal employees receive part of their wage on a declared basis and the remainder on an undeclared basis.

In reality, when the dematerialization and/or "privatization" of the workplace is the product of digitalization, problems usually arise, in terms of work–life balance, if the employer asks the worker to connect at any time without predetermining the period of the day qualified as working time, though within an agreed upon number of working hours that respects the maximum established by the law. Alternatively, problems may arise in terms of organizational safety if the connection is always on and the worker has no right to disconnect. The "always-on" mode shall be regarded as a violation of the OSH regulations even if agreed to as clause of the employment contract, which will be, as for that part, null and void.

On the other hand, as already highlighted above, one of the consequences of the dematerialization and/or "privatization" of the workplace can be the shift from a time-based to a results-oriented work relationship, in which the distribution of work is based on the production of a (part of a) good or service that will be remunerated as such if certain quality and time requirements are met.

In this case, the quality and time check of the result will substitute the assessment of the performance as ongoing control on the work to be performed for the number of hours agreed to within a predetermined period (working time). This can also allow the worker a self-organized work–life balance, no longer subordinated to the employers' needs.

The Qualification of the "Digitalized" Work Relationship and Its Consequences on the Typological Approach to Workers' Protection

From the above-mentioned, one can see that the effects digital transformation and digitalization are going to produce on the work relationship are undoubtedly relevant. However, at least for subordinated work, they are also potentially contradictory.

In fact, on the one hand, they are likely to stimulate a reallocation of the managerial prerogatives in terms of employers' renunciation of performance assessment responsibilities. This may occur through the enrichment of the bilateral relationship by a third party (simple costumer or even prosumer), leading therefore to its transformation into a trilateral relationship. Alternatively, it may happen through the rearrangement of the employment relationship into a less subordinated one, because of the difficulties or the lack of employers' interest in workers' control, as derived from the dematerialization and/or "privatization" of the workplace.

On the other hand, digital transformation and digitalization, because of their capacity to convert work tools into control devices (work-control devices), may reinforce employers' control of workers, thus deepening their subordination ("boosted" subordination) even in the case of dematerialization and/or "privatization" of the workplace.

The effect that digital transformation and digitalization are going to have on self-employment seems to be more univocal. In fact, because of the role that platforms, as virtual market places, are playing in the intermediation between service providers and costumers, they are likely to stimulate a more coordinated condition of what we can call framed self-employment. According to some scholars, platforms are interfering so deeply within the provision of services that the provider has to be looked at as a subordinate worker employed by the platform. For the reasons already explained above, this does not seem to be a convincing interpretation.

To summarize, one can argue that labour law, in its traditional regulatory setting, is facing huge difficulties because of the new structural features of the work relationship as compelled by digital transformation and digitalization. Difficulties arise mainly because of the typological approach to work regulation adopted by labour law since the beginning of its existence. By typological approach, we understand the fact that decisive for the definition of the personal scope of application of labour law provisions is the imputability of the single work relationship to one of the typologies of work relationship already qualified as worth protecting under labour law.

Typologies, in turn, are qualified according to the presence of certain features predetermined by the legislature and usually detailed by the judiciary when deciding cases of fraudulent attribution by the employer of the work relationship to one less protected typology in the absence of the required features. Alternatively, when judges are called to decide borderline cases in which the imputability of the single work relationship to one typology instead of another is controversial because of the presence of non-typical emerging features.

As is well known, the typological cornerstone of labour law has to be found in the employment relationship, the main feature of which is represented by the subordination of the employee to the employer. In turn, one of the most important features of subordination is the exercise by the employer of managerial prerogatives at the agreed upon working place and during the predetermined working time, which gives rise to the subordinated physical integration of the worker into somebody else's organization.

By triggering the dematerialization and/or "privatization" of the workplace, digital transformation and digitalization are therefore likely to impact on an important feature of subordination. By stimulating the "enrichment" of the employment relationship by a third party (simple costumer or prosumer), they challenge another crucial feature of subordination, i.e. the unitary exercise of managerial prerogatives by the employer, which, in the new trilateral setting, does not occur anymore.

Consequently, one may say that the "digitalized" version of the employment relationship is likely to lose some of the essential features of subordination, as defined by the legislator and case law, thus putting at risk its very imputability to employment as legal typology.

As is well known, in many countries, the unique alternative typology provided by the legislator in order to qualify a work relationship outside of employment is self-employment. However, from the qualification of a work relationship as self-employed it derives the inapplicability of labour law, being it referred and referable, at least in its traditional setting, to employment as legal typology. The negative results for the worker are easily imaginable.

Actually, the same reasoning applies to the "digitalized" version of the self-employment relationship, the one we have already called "framed", if one understands it as entailing an activity performed in autonomy though integrated by way of immaterial coordination within someone else's organization.

Indeed, the concept of coordinated self-employment is not unheard of. Since the Seventies, the Italian legislature has recognized its relevance as legal sub-typology of self-employment aimed at qualified (for protection purposes) work relationships in which work is performed continuously within someone else's organization, not characterized by the subordinated physical integration of the worker into somebody else's organization, as just described above.

One has to admit that Italian legislation is far from being impeccable as for the qualification features of, and effective as for the protection measures on coordinated self-employment. However, it could represent an inspiring example of how legislators may face practical changes in the way work is performed while guaranteeing appropriate workers' rights without recurring to the qualification of any work relationship as employment.

Coordination of work performed in a less subordinated (in comparison with employment) or in a less autonomous (in comparison with self-employment) dematerialized organization could be regarded as a common feature of digitalized work beyond the well-established but heuristically not (in the case at hand) effective traditional legal typologies of employment and self-employment. Therefore, coordinated work, also in case continuously performed, could represent a third typology under which digitalized work of any kind could be more effectively qualified. In turn, the basic feature of digitalized work can be found in the dematerialized and/or "privatized" workplace, accompanied by the use of a digital connection with the organizer of the work.

Evidently, "boosted" subordination, as outlined above, shall be excluded from coordinated work and can be easily qualified as employment, even if performed in a dematerialized and/or "privatized" workplace, precisely because accompanied by the use of a digital connection with the organizer of the work.

The academic qualification of the digitalized work relationship as coordinated work, in itself, does not solve the problem of workers' protection and this is because of the lack of linkage between coordinated work as typology to be and labour law provisions, which, in most cases, remain attached to the qualification of the work relationship as employment. More or less recently, legislators around Europe have tried to find a solution by stretching the notion of employment as typology to work relationship in which the subordinated physical integration of the worker into somebody else's organization was not at stake or by elaborating and partially protecting intermediate categories close to employment (quasi-subordinate workers) or by protecting self-employed (mainly as service providers) who found themselves in a situation of economic dependency upon a single client.

The same Court of Justice of the European Union has taken a stance on the issue by adopting the highly controversial notion of false self-employed, to be understood as a "self-employed service provider who performs for an employer, under a works or service contract, the same activity as that employer's employed workers".[1]

In this case as well, typologies are at stake. In fact, the court, instead of admitting that the way in which a specific work is performed shall prevail on the formal and general qualification of the workers as employees or self-employed, asks the national court to ascertain that:

> "their relationship with the [employer] concerned is not one of subordination during the contractual relationship, so that they enjoy more independence and flexibility than employees who perform the same activity, as regards the determination of the working hours, the place and manner of performing the tasks assigned".

This request sounds rather humorous since the employer at stake is an orchestra and the tasks assigned are rehearsals and concerts that cannot be performed, by definition, by enjoying more independence and flexibility whatever the qualification of the work relationship.

From such a perspective, one may wonder whether a new typology could help avoiding the same problems that the existing ones are confronted with. Indeed, one may argue that the addition of a further typology will be of no help if not accompanied by an overall revision of the typological approach as such, in the direction of focusing on the way in which the work performance integrates itself within or coordinates itself with somebody else's organization. This may happen in three modalities: a subordinated, a coordinated and an autonomous one (if applicable also in the form of intrinsically triangular relationship, as outlined above).

If one accepts this interpretation, one also has to determine to what extent and in which way workers operating in each of the three modalities have to be protected. Since human beings are at stake, access to work, health and safety at work, and income from work seem to be the crucial aspects to be guaranteed to anyone, regardless of the group one belongs to. Access to work also in terms of non-discrimination, and health and safety at work in the sense of human dignity too, should be guaranteed by the law to anyone, regardless of the group one belongs to, on the grounds of public interest. As for the third, one may wonder whether the (individually or collectively or both) bargained determination of the remuneration could still be seen as the best solution or whether it should be substituted by minimum wages or rates, once again from the perspective of public interest.

From Traditional to "Digitalized" Work Pattern: Transitions as Risk, Challenge and Opportunity

The envisaged introduction of coordinated work as typology to be in order to cope with the consequences of digitalization raises the question of how the transition from traditional to "digitalized" work patters should be assessed from the perspective of workers' protection.

If transitions take place as individual, unilateral or bargained, modification of the existing work pattern, i.e. on the basis of a self-regulatory, bottom-up approach, they are likely to represent a risk for the worker who will be confronted with a new work pattern that may exclude some traditional protective features because of its very structure. In this case, the only way of redress will be the judiciary that will act as a filter, thus substituting itself for the legislator in shaping the new patterns and looking at them, however, in their pathology, as always happens by litigation as regulatory request.

On the contrary, if transitions take place as shared modification of existing work patterns (i.e. based on workers' involvement through information, consultation participation and collective bargaining), they are likely to represent a challenge, for trade unions above all. The latter will be called to shape the new work pattern and to find out the adequate instruments of protection by way of compromise with the emergent needs of employers within a given legislative framework that they can even modify if explicitly delegated by the legislator.

If transitions take place as overall rethinking of the existing typologies of work relationship (i.e. on political demand), they are likely to represent an opportunity for the legislative system in terms of responsiveness instead of regulative chasing, usually the product of litigation as a regulatory request.

Representative of society as a whole, the legislator shall remember that "economic and societal changes occasioned by technological developments are shaped, not just by the availability of new technologies and their features, but also by ideologies, power structures, and human aspirations and agendas. Technologies are not exogenous forces that roll over societies like tsunamis with predetermined results. Rather, our skills, organizations, institutions, and values shape how we develop technologies and how we deploy them once created, along with their final impact".[2]

Therefore, any legislative intervention should be human being–friendly first in the access to work, health and safety at work, and income from work perspectives, as defined above. Only after that, it could be business-tailored too in the sense that the legislative intervention shall distribute protective measures to be put at charge of the entity that profits from the work depending upon the way in which the worker is subordinated within, coordinated with, or autonomous from somebody else's organization.

Therefore, by rethinking the typological approach, we mean to focus on how work interacts with business in the perspective of emphasizing coordination as new nexus to protective measures to be put at charge of the entity that profits from the work. This should lead to an enlarged labour law that applies to "boosted" subordination, employment and coordinated work, even if in the form of intrinsically trilateral relationships.

Notes

1. CJEU, 4 Dec. 2014, C-413/13, FNV.
2. Committee on Information Technology, Automation, and the U.S. Workforce, 2017, 54.

References

Muro, Mark., Sifan Liu, Jacob Whiton, and Siddharth Kulkarni. 2017. *Digitalisation and the American Workforce,* Metropolitan Policy Program at Brookings. https://www.brookings.edu/wp-content/uploads/2017/11/mpp_2017nov15_digitalization_full_report.pdf. Accessed on 1 Dec 2017.

3

Digital Work: An Organizational Perspective

Tommaso Fabbri

Organization and Digitalization

Digitalization is basically about information and communication technologies (ICTs). In reflections about digitalization *and* organizations, the words "information" and "communications" are priorities with respect to "technologies". Let's start from "information": every single work process can be described in terms of information processing. In addition, the more pieces of information—both that feed and that are generated by the work process—are made explicit (versus remain tacit) and formalized and socialized, the more the work process is liable to digitalization. In this respect, there's a difference between service and manufacturing processes: clerical work, as an instance of the former, is mainly immaterial, and digitalization, as a requisite for automation, is easier. This is why, at present, according to the recent ILO/Eurofound Report (2017), management, professional support, clerical support and similar areas are the types of jobs where digital

---

T. Fabbri (✉)
University of Modena and Reggio Emilia (Italy), Modena, Italy
e-mail: tommaso.fabbri@unimore.it

© The Author(s) 2018
E. Ales et al. (eds.), *Working in Digital and Smart Organizations*,
https://doi.org/10.1007/978-3-319-77329-2_3

work is most diffused. But the rise of Industry 4.0 promises increasing digitalization of manufacturing processes too and possibly the digitalization of blue collar work, including some degree of substitution of people with algorithms, machines and robots. Let's turn now to "communication": given that communication is the raw material of coordination, which, in turn, is the essence of *organized* action (Barnard 1938), digitalization, from a strictly organizational perspective, is also and mainly the transformation of coordination (processes and tools) enabled by a new generation of ICTs. More precisely, previous-generation ICTs bring unprecedented communication and coordination power, both in space—because they allow powerful remote communication and coordination tools to substitute for physical proximity—and in time, because they enable augmented synchronous and a-synchronous communications and coordination.

From this standpoint, digitalization transforms the organization inasmuch as it substitutes analog and therefore, to some extent, tacit and informal rules for action and decision with digital and therefore explicit and formalized rules for action and decision. In a digitally transformed enterprise, actions and decisions, at every logical or empirical level (decision making, coordination and control, and execution), are increasingly performed *digitally*, i.e. using *digital* information, within *digital* workflows, which are hosted in corporate digital premises, which are accessible at anytime from anywhere via *digital* and mobile devices. As a result, we witness the erosion of space-time coordinates of work.

With the inevitable imprecision of socio-biological metaphors, we might depict digitalization as the upgrading of the organizational nervous system: besides traditional analog communications infrastructure, a digital infrastructure is increasingly innervating organizational processes so that communication and coordination (among people, among people and machines, and among machines) are potentially augmented in quantity and quality. And any degree of organizational digital transformation, being an increase in information-processing capacity, may enable the organization to manage more complexity, both adaptively and proactively, and therefore to be more competitive: "*Where media are primitive, coordination system is primitive*" [...] "*The more the efficiency of the communication in the organization, the higher the "tolerance for interdependence*" (March and Simon 1958).

But this won't happen automatically, despite the claim of traditional economic theory that technical progress per se makes work more productive. *"You can see the computer age everywhere but in the productivity statistics"* is a famous quote from the American economist Robert Solow (1987), who was highlighting the fact that productivity gains—the rate of increase in the ratio between the inputs and outputs of an economic activity—exhibited a downward trend in spite of large-scale and continued investment in computerization and automation. In line with Solow, the idea that the potential of new ICTs will be untapped only if organizations are made receptive in the first place—or, even better, if new technologies are adjusted to the requirements of the organization—seems to be gaining legitimacy, even among the most technological optimists and apologists (Brynjolfsson and McAfee 2014): *"Productivity gains are a corollary of the organizational changes facilitated by technological innovations rather than the technologies themselves, and will be achieved only by companies which adopt new forms of work organization at the same time as the new technologies"* (Valenduc and Vendramin 2016).

Digital Work as Autonomous Work

Digital work is work performed by means of ICTs: work actions and decisions are enabled or supported by ubiquitous digital information, accessed-to and processed-on digital devices, at anytime from anywhere. The point in digital work is that it's digital and the fact that it can be performed away from the employer's premises is just a consequence of its being digital. Since many jobs are performed away from the employer's premises without being digital (e.g. a sales representative), distant execution shall not be considered equivalent to digital work. Digital work and remote work are not synonymous. But digital work is essentially and to some extent remote—from the employer's premises, from direct supervision...—insomuch as it does not require physical interaction with the organization, thanks to a digital mediating infrastructure: in digital work, a supervisor might check the subordinate performance on the company information systems even if he or she is in the adjacent room.

A belief is held by many, especially among labor law scholars, that because of the absence of spatial and temporal constraints (i.e. because it is generally performed away from company premises and far from direct supervision), digital work is more of an autonomous type than a subordinate type of work. Organization theory rejects this widespread belief and the following tries to make this point.

What is it that makes a traditional salesperson a digital worker? The fact that the typical activities that compose the job—for example, managing multilevel relationships with existing customers, monitoring clients and markets, scouting new segments and customers, planning and executing ad hoc promotional actions, and setting and negotiating price conditions—are performed "digitally" with various mobile devices that connect him or her to the company digital layers where databases and data-analysis software are hosted. Obviously, the digitalization of the salesperson job would imply a significant formalization and standardization effort: e.g. a customer relationship management tool that stores useful data, conducts analysis, and recommends appropriate activities to be performed throughout the different moments in the development of a relationship with a customer. In such a situation, the relationship between digital infrastructure and work behaviors is symbiotic: not only are work behaviors tracked and work performance monitored in real time, but also work behaviors are designed, ex ante, at the time of the design of the digital (or digitally supported) work process. A very mature quotation from the outstanding organization scholar John Child might help us clarify the relationship between formalization, as a requisite of digitalization, and autonomy: *"...within certain limits imposed by the organization's operating situation, managers appear to have a choice between: a) maintaining control directly by confining decisions to fairly senior levels. This economizes on the need for systems of procedures and paperwork and reduces the overhead of indirect specialist personnel to operate and maintain the systems, or b) maintaining control indirectly by relying on the use of procedures, paper records, and on the employment of expert specialists to take decisions at lower levels [within the limits on discretion imposed by the indirect control]"* (Child 1972).

Digitalization is an investment in formalized procedures which are conditions and instruments for indirect control of discretionary (not autonomous) decision making. Being far away is not synonymous with being autonomous, because the physical distance is filled with standardized work procedures, which predetermine work behaviors and make them traceable, and can make control over work and subordination even stronger. To the extent that digitalization of work processes imposes their formalization and to the extent that a company's information system architecture mirrors the information flows designed by the organizational analyst/designer (or, even more frequent though irrelevant to our ends, information flows are adjusted to the architecture of the software), work behaviors can be strictly pre-determined, leaving no room for autonomy and instead imposing some degree of discretion on the worker. The nature of discretion, the fact that it is prepared by the work process designer, affects the worker's well-being, as we will see in the following paragraph.

In the apologists of digitalization discourse, the micro-organizational issue of digital workers' autonomy couples with a macro-organizational issue: the replacement of hierarchy with horizontal communication, collaboration and trust (delayering and flattened organization) and the replacement of formal organizational units with liquid work teams as basic particles of the organization (see, for example, new organizational models such as the holacracy or the teal organization). The epitome are high-tech Californian companies: "When Matt joined the business development unit of Facebook he was told: we're not political here. We're young, cool, socially networked, hip, high-technology people [...]. We're family friendly, we have fewer levels and less hierarchy, and we make decisions collegially" (Pfeffer 2013).

The idea is not at all new, and it dates back at least to the idea of Burns and Stalker (1961) of an organic system of management, a system where the structure of control, authority and communication is of network type (versus hierarchical) and where the sanctions which apply to the individual conduct derive more from the community of interest with the rest of the working organization and less from a contractual relationship between the individual and his immediate superior. But if powerless organization theories or models have always been problematic (Pfeffer 2013), let's see what happens if we put digitalization on top.

"*The replication study*"—wrote Child (1972) after re-testing the empirical taxonomy of work organizations proposed by "The Aston Group" influential study (Pugh et al. 1969)—"*suggests a modification of the Aston position in regard to centralization. [...] In the National Study [...] the positive relationship between standardization-and-formalization (rules and documentation) and centralization is not reproduced. The negative correlations [...] are more pronounced*". In other words, "*[A]s organizations **regulate more** and more behavior, so they **decentralize***" (Hinings and Lee 1971). Again, organization theory tells us that centralization/decentralization is correlated to formalization and standardization, but the direction is negative. The more rules you impose on conducts, the less you need supervisors, and supervisors of supervisors; in brief, the fewer hierarchical layers you need to perform control. So if digitalization is rooted in (some degree of) formalization, then the case might be that "[...] many of the same communication technologies and the inexpensive computing power that make horizontal collaboration easier also permit much more computer-aided monitoring of work and communication, thereby creating environments with more control and less behavioral discretion than in the past" (Pfeffer 2013). Obviously, this digital monitoring power applies irrespectively of organizational boundaries, casting doubts on the genuineness of the autonomy of many formally self-employed workers of the gig and platform economy. For sure, we are in need of criteria for defining a digital employer, and they need to be different from the existing topological ones.

Digital Work as Smart Work

In a 1946 propaganda video of motion studies,[1] produced with the cooperation of the Industrial Engineering Staffs of General Motors, its Divisions, and General Motors Institute, with the appreciation of Ralph. M. Barnes, professor of industrial engineering at the State University of Iowa, a young manager in charge of a new project named Motion Studies tries to convince a colleague and friend that, by means of rational redesign of work actions, it is possible "to produce more and more stuff with less and less effort". The apparently sneaky title of the video, "The Easier Way", is eventually redeemed when the possibility of "more production with less work" is finally, empirically demonstrated.

Digital work is often presented as a smarter way of working because it makes possible a double, "joint" benefit (Emery and Trist 1960): on one side, it allows workers to do what they have always been doing (their job) but with less effort, thanks to time and space flexibility. "Work smarter, live better" is the motto of an association of employers in northern Italy that promotes the introduction of smart work in Italian companies: the promise of smart work, they claim, is to keep you doing your job but avoiding the costs and the stressfulness of commuting and work/life conflicting. On the other side, companies benefit too from smart working because they save office space (and the costs associated) and they have happier, more motivated employees.

With organization theory in mind, this double benefit sounds like the latest update of the socio-technical principle of "joint optimization": proper organization of work is the one that jointly satisfies technical requirements (production efficiency) and psycho-social requirements (employee satisfaction and well-being). But if the adoption of new ways or methods of working is driven by technical requirements, if technical efficiency has logical and chronological priority in the design and adoption of the new working solutions, then joint optimization is not guaranteed. Again, the problem is not a new one: "Time and motion study"—wrote Katz and Kahn back in 1966 (p. 274)—"has as its aim the equalization of effort under specified working methods of work. Every increase in individual productivity therefore raises the question of whether the worker is really working harder in accordance with the specified methods, or is working smarter and has in effect changed the methods of work so that the job is less demanding. In the latter case, the logic of time study argues that the job should be retimed". And, they added few pages after, "There's a tradition among workers, and it is not without some factual basis, that management cannot be relied upon to maintain a high rate of pay for those making considerably more than the standard and that their increased efforts will only result in their being sweated".

Yet, if we look at the data published by ILO/Eurofound recently (ILO/Eurofound 2017) about workers involved in digital work—typically medium- to high-level white collar workers—we see that the productivity gains are achieved via work intensification, i.e. thanks to (1) lack of interruptions, (2) working during breaks, (3) working in evenings

36   T. Fabbri

and weekends and (4) longer working hours, including previous commuting time which is turned into working time.

Therefore, available empirical evidence suggests that digital work, instead of smartly substituiting work in the office, might easily add to it, supplementing the work already done in the company's premises.

And if the supplement is not acknowledged and formally arranged for, the "being sweated" situation prefigured by Katz and Kahn (1966) is likely to come true. Just as ILO/Eurofound fear and warn about, "It is particularly important to address the issue of supplemental T/ICTM [digital work], which could be viewed as unpaid overtime [...]" (p. 2).

Hence, digital work is smart if it combines (the same or possibly) more production with less effort, if it improves production or coordination efficiency or effectiveness all other things being equal, if it substitutes rigid analog work with discretionary (in time and space) task performance. Digital work is not smart if it supplements analog work and working methods, if it increases productivity by means of additional working effort, let alone if it is not remunerated.

Digital Work as Healthy Work

Organization theory can also shed some light on one issue that has long remained unquestioned in the shadow of some mainstream discourse that claimed and tentatively demonstrated that autonomy and discretion are universally good for employees for both their job satisfaction and occupational health. For decades, Job Design (Davis 1966) told managers that employees, in general, appreciate variety, complexity and task uncertainty to which their knowledgeable discretion can be applied. Thompson (1967), together with some other non-mainstream organization scholars, warned managers with these prudent words: *Complex organizations and their supporting social structures encourage some individuals to exercise organizational discretion at considerable personal sacrifice. [...] Where pressures for achievement are strong, and achievement is measured by the exercise of discretion, some individuals with low tolerance for uncertainty will be swept into discretionary jobs. [...] While this must remain merely a hypothesis in the absence of additional evidence, we can assert at a minimum that individuals in such situations may experience an entire career of discomfort* (p. 121). So if time and space discretion is what characterizes digital work, then we might expect that at least some employees would perceive and experience that additional (time and space) discretion as an additional stressful burden. Again, recent ILO/Eurofound research seems to support this hypothesis.

First, by acknowledging the fact that time discretion comes together with time management necessities, which therefore are shifted from management to employees, who have to learn and execute some boundary management strategy (Clark 2000): *[T]he findings provide an indication that responsibility for monitoring working time is increasingly being shifted towards the employees themselves—hence, from an individual worker's point of view, time management has become more complex* (p. 23).

Second, by finding evidence that the alleged automatic work–life balance allowed by time discretion embedded in digital work settings is not at all automatic and that relevant un-balance and interference can result from the incapacity or unwillingness of employees to manage (also) time discretion: *A relatively high share of employees carrying out T/ICTM* [digital work] *report that they [...] miss or neglect family activities due to work activities interfering with personal life, i.e. work-home interference (WHI)* (p. 29).

Third, by finding evidence that stress and perceptions of negative impact of work on health occur more often among [digital workers] compared with employees working on employers' premises.

Finally, digital transformation is a far-reaching and heavy-bearing phenomenon. Implications for organizations appear to be paramount and positive, while it is still difficult, given the current state of research, to prefigure undisputed implications on the world of work. In this situation, we wish and advocate that policy institutions and scholarly communities avoid simplifications and shortcuts and cooperate, just as we are trying to do with this volume, in the interdisciplinary understanding and designing of the future (digital) transformation of work.

Notes

1. https://www.youtube.com/watch?v=k9vIhPszb2I&feature=youtu.be&list =PLmXpKzJ467RN98agzLcAE45cqN_UygEIx.

References

Barnard, Chester Irving. 1938. *The Functions of the Executive*. Cambridge MA: Harvard Univ. Press.

Brynjolfsson, Erik, and Andrew McAfee. 2014. *The Second Machine Age: Work Progress, and Prosperity in a Time of Brilliant Technologies*. New York: W. W. Norton & Company.

Burns, Tom, and Garry M. Stalker. 1961. *The Management of Innovation*. London: Tavistock Publication Ltd.

Child, John. 1972. Organizational Structure and Strategies of Control: A Replication of the Aston Study. *Administrative Science Quarterly* 17: 163–177.

Clark, Sue Campbell. 2000. Work/Family Border Theory: A New Theory of Work/Family Balance. *Human Relations* 53 (6): 747–770.

Davis, Louis E. 1966. The Design of Jobs. *Industrial Relations* 6 (1): 21–45.

Emery, Fred E., and Eric L. Trist. 1960. *Socio-Technical Systems*. In *Management Science Models and Tecniques*, ed. C. West Churchman and M. Verhulst. Oxford: Pergamon Press.

Eurofound and the International Labour Office (2017). *Working Anytime, Anywhere: The Effects on the World of Work*, Publications Office of the European Union, Luxemburg and the International Labour Office, Geneva. https://www.eurofound.europa.eu/publications/report/2017/working-anytime-anywhere-the-effects-on-the-world-of-work. Accessed on 31 Jan 2018.

Hinings, C.R., and Gloria Lee. 1971. Dimensions of Organization Structure and Their Context: A Replication. *Sociology* 5 (1): 83–93.

Katz, Daniel, and Robert L. Kahn. 1966. *The Social Psychology of Organizations*. New York: John Wiley & Sons.

March, James G., and Herbert A. Simon. 1958. *Organizations*. New York: Wiley & Sons.

Pfeffer, Jeffrey. 2013. You're Still the Same: Why Theories of Power Hold Over Time and Across Contexts. *Academy of Management Perspectives* 17 (4): 269–280.

Pugh, Derek S., David J. Hickson, and Bob Hining. 1969. An Empirical Taxonomy of Structures of Work Organizations. *Administrative Science Quarterly* 14 (1): 115–126.

Solow, Robert. 1987. We'd Better Watch Out. *New York Times Book Review*, July 12, 1987, p. 36.

Thompson, James D. 1967. *Organizations in Action*. New York: McGraw-Hill.

Valenduc, Gerard, and Patricia Vendramin. 2016. *Work in the Digital Economy: Sorting the Old from the New*. Brussels: ETUI.

4

In Favour of Machines (But Not Forgetting the Workers): Some Considerations on the Fourth Industrial Revolution

Sergio Paba and Giovanni Solinas

Introduction

We are in the middle of what many call the Fourth Industrial Revolution (4IR). We have some idea of when and where it started, but there is still much debate about how long it will take to deliver all of the promised fruits to the economy and society. Many scholars and observers foresee a hypothetical future of jobless economies, where machines could perform not only most of the physical activities now carried out by humans but also a large part of intelligent human activities.

In these future scenarios that oscillate between utopia and dystopia, one wonders what should be done to allow everyone to benefit from the fruits of automation and the well-being promised by machines and artificial intelligence (AI). At the moment, however, of this future world that

---

S. Paba • G. Solinas (✉)
Marco Biagi Department of Economics, University of Modena and Reggio Emilia, Modena, Italy
e-mail: sergio.paba@unimore.it; giovanni.solinas@unimore.it

© The Author(s) 2018
E. Ales et al. (eds.), *Working in Digital and Smart Organizations*,
https://doi.org/10.1007/978-3-319-77329-2_4

creates wealth without human labour, we see very little, and hopefully a future of mass technological unemployment will never see the light of day.

Instead, what we have been witnessing for quite a long time are profound transformations in technology, products and production processes and, related to this, in the nature of labour and demand for skills, in the distribution of job opportunities across sectors and territories, in labour relations and in wages.

These changes create great opportunities for some but also inequalities and uncertainty for many, at least in the short to medium term. Since few seem to doubt the benefits of technology and scientific progress, the 4IR should be accompanied by policies that encourage progress but at the same time limit the negative consequences on labour, income, and quality of life. However, although there are many policies in favour of technology and machines promoted by governments in many advanced countries, far fewer, and less effective, are the policies that deal with labour and workers who are fully invested by the technological transformation in this difficult, and probably long, transitional phase of the new industrial revolution.

The aim of this paper is to give a brief account of some of the main issues related to the 4IR. We start by looking for an appropriate definition of it, in order to identify the conceptual boundaries of the phenomenon, a crucial step for assessing the policies and their impact on the economy. Second, we discuss the impact of the 4IR on employment by reviewing the results of the relevant literature, drawing some lessons for future research. Third, we review some of the industrial policies developed by governments to support the digital revolution. We finish the paper with a discussion of the main policy issues related to the workers and the labour market.

A New Industrial Revolution?

As the founder and executive chairman of the World Economic Forum (WEF), Klaus Schwab, puts it, "*we stand on the brink of a technological revolution that will fundamentally alter the way we live, work, and relate to one another. In its scale, scope, and complexity, the transformation will be unlike anything humankind has experienced before"* (Foreign Affairs Dec. 12, 2015).

Many economists, observers, industry experts and technology analysts hold a similar view. Manufacturing, in particular, is radically reshaping production processes and has a strong impact on the use of labour, the nature of work, and the geography of production. This new era of technological change is certainly opening up new opportunities of value creation and growth with innovative products and services but also is disrupting industries and sectors, causing growing social insecurity and new inequalities. The economic and social consequences of this are still unclear and hardly predictable.

But can what has been happening in the last two decades be labelled the Fourth Industrial Revolution? There is a general agreement among historians and other social scientists about the characteristics and consequences of the first three industrial revolutions.[1] All three revolutions had a strong and positive impact on the economy, at least in the long run, in terms of gross domestic product (GDP), employment, productivity, new industries and products. Can we draw the same implications for this new phase of technological change? If indeed we are in the middle of the 4IR, what is the technology or the fundamental innovation that triggered this new historical phase?

Many definitions of this new industrial revolution have been given, some are more convincing than others, many are converging to the same point, but there is still much confusion and a lot of noise and this is due in part to the role played by governments and political interests. The following is a brief survey of the most reliable definitions.

One of the first documents that clearly mentioned the new industrial revolution was a final report published in 2013 by a German working group, named *Plattform Industrie 4.0*, set up and coordinated by the federal government in Germany as part of its ambitious new industrial policy in manufacturing (*High Tech Strategy*). The working group was composed of academics, technical experts, and members from the federal government, industry, professional associations and unions. They coined the term *Industrie 4.0*,[2] which soon after became very popular worldwide. In this document, the 4IR or *Industrie 4.0* is defined as "the technical integration of Cyber-Physical Production Systems (CPS) into manufacturing and logistics and the use of the Internet of Things and Services in industrial processes" (Kagermann et al. 2013, p. 14).

Other influential definitions were later proposed: "Cyber-physical production based on the internet of things and services" (MIT Industrial Performance Center 2017, p. 2), "Digital transformation of industrial production" (OECD 2016, p. 14), "Digitalisation of manufacturing" (IfM-UNIDO 2017, p. 10) and "Application of digital technologies to the manufacturing sector" (European House-Ambrosetti 2017, p. 1).

All of these definitions are focused on manufacturing, and the digital revolution is at the heart of the technological change. The term "digital" does not actually refer to a single technology but to a bundle of *enabling* (and potentially disruptive) technologies which in some cases includes new materials. According to the definition used by the European Commission, "The Fourth Industrial Revolution [...] integrates cyber-physical systems and the Internet of Things, big data and cloud computing, robotics, artificial-intelligence based systems and additive manufacturing". The OECD speaks of a "confluence of technologies ranging from a variety of digital technologies (e.g. 3D printing, Internet of Things, advanced robotics) to new materials (e.g. bio- or nano-based) to new processes (e.g. data driven production, artificial intelligence, synthetic biology)" (OECD 2016, p. 3). The Cambridge Institute for Manufacturing speaks of "connection and integration of manufacturing systems through the convergence of digital technologies such as cyber-physical systems, cloud computing, big data, artificial intelligence, machine learning and the internet-of-things" (IfM-UNIDO 2017, p. 26).

Other, related terms are often used to describe this new era of technological development, again with a strong focus on manufacturing: "Next Production Revolution", "Smart Industry", "Smart factory or advanced manufacturing", "Industrial Internet", "Cyber-physical systems" and "AI (Artificial Intelligence)-driven automation" (OECD 2017).

Manufacturing certainly remains at the heart of the 4IR. The emphasis on manufacturing, however, is reductive. The spread of digital technology is equally revolutionizing many service sectors. Digital technologies are embedded in an increasing number of services, and digital platforms and social networks are increasingly used to favour the interactions between economic agents and between individuals. This gives rise to the creation of new sectors of activity—think of music consumption through streaming—and the radical transformation of traditional services, as in the case of commercial distribution, finance and banking, travel agencies or the taxi sector. The impact of the digital revolution on employment and business models is probably stronger in the service sector compared with manufacturing. For example, of all the occupations in the US with the highest probability of computerization listed by Frey and Osborne (2013), only 25.6% of them are related to manufacturing. According to a survey by the WEF, more than 7 million jobs will be lost in a sample of advanced countries in the period of 2015–2020 (WEF 2016); 22.4% of the total loss will be in manufacturing and production, while 66.4% will be in office and administration. In the case of Italy, the report by European House-Ambrosetti (2017) predicts that only 26% of the expected job loss in the next fifteen years will occur in manufacturing. These data suggest that the 4IR should be considered in a broader sense, encompassing all sectors of activity.

Evidence of Displacement? Lessons from the Data

The reduction in manufacturing employment is a long-standing feature of advanced economies. In the last 15 years (2000–2015), the US lost 28.6% of employment in manufacturing, Europe (15 countries) 18.6% and Japan 14.2%.[3] Clearly, robots and automation are only some of the factors that can explain this decline. The rise of China and other emerging economies as the new factories of the world changed the geography of production on a global level in the last decades. Outsourcing and offshoring activities, along with the related increase in imports within global value chains governed by large and small multinationals, have been largely discussed in the literature and are partly responsible for the change. In addition, many technical, office and administrative activities, traditionally carried out in manufacturing companies, have been progressively moved and decentralized in the tertiary sector. Parallel to the decline in manufacturing jobs, employment in professional, technical, administrative and business support services has steadily increased.

A recent report by the OECD shows that, since 2000, almost 29 million jobs have been created in OECD countries, compared with a loss of 750,000 jobs. Even in Europe (EU28), where the labour market is traditionally more rigid, more than 9.5 million people gained a job while almost 3.1 million workers lost employment (OECD 2017). Most of the increase occurred in high-skilled service sectors (professional, scientific, technical, administrative and business support activities) and other service industries such as health and education, wholesale and retail trade, and accommodation and food service activities. At the same time, manufacturing lost more than 5.5 million jobs in Europe.

Industrial robots are employed mainly in the manufacturing industry.[4] As shown by the annual report by the International Federation of Robotics (IFR 2017, p. 87), most of them are used in the automotive industry and in the electrical and electronics industry, although the relative intensity varies across countries.

In contrast, digital (information and communication technology [ICT]) capital plays a limited role in manufacturing but accounts for a substantial share of fixed capital in the information and communication sector, in the business service sector (law and accountancy, research and development, and other business services), in the finance and insurance industry, and in the wholesale and retail trade (EU-KLEMS data).

The picture sketched above has been variously interpreted. The potential impact of the 4IR on the labour market is the subject of a recent and growing literature. The debate is addressing a number of issues, such as the employment impact, the quality of work and skills demand, the dynamics of productivity and its effect on economic growth, and the distribution of income. On the employment issue, in particular, several economists have recently tried to estimate the impact of the digital revolution and AI on employment levels.

A first strand of studies focuses on the characteristics of the different jobs and tasks and, for each of them, tries to predict the degree of potential automation and therefore the probability of job displacement. The first contribution of this type is due to Frey and Osborne (2013), who estimated the probability of computerization for 702 detailed occupations in the US. The conclusion is dire: about 47% of American employees are likely to lose their jobs in the next few years. In their approach, it is assumed that each task at risk of automation corresponds to an entire workplace (*occupation-based* approach).

Less disturbing results are obtained by Arntz et al. (2016), who estimated the job automatibility for 21 OECD countries by using the Programme for the International Assessment of Adult Competencies (PIAAC) database. From the study, it emerges that an average of only 9% of the jobs would be at risk. The difference with the previous paper lies in the distinction between tasks and jobs. Even if some tasks are automated, the worker may remain essential for other tasks (*task-based* approach). With a similar approach, Berriman and Hawksworth (2017) find that up to 30% of jobs in the UK and up to 38% in the US are at high risk of automation by 2030. By adapting the methodology proposed by Frey and Osborne (2013) to the Italian data, the study by European House-Ambrosetti (2017) finds that 14.9% of jobs, roughly equal to 3.2 million workers, are likely to be replaced by machines in the next 15 years.

Another strand of studies tries to study the impact of automation on jobs by using historical and disaggregated data at regional level. In this case, the focus is on manufacturing and on robot exposure.

Acemoglu and Restrepo (2017) focus on the effects of industrial robots on jobs and wages in US local labour markets from 1990 to 2007. They distinguish the impact of robots from other factors potentially affecting employment, such as imports from manufacturing countries (China and Mexico), offshoring activities, and information technology (IT) capital. They find evidence of a significant displacement effect due to the introduction of robots in the period under analysis. In particular, their estimate of job loss is up to 670,000 employees, roughly 6.2 jobs lost (on average) for every robot introduced.

More encouraging results come from a recent study by Dauth et al. (2017). By following an approach similar to that of Acemoglu and Rastrepo, they study the impact of rising robot exposure on the equilibrium across industries and local labour markets in Germany over the period of 1994–2014. They estimate that, on average, every robot destroys two manufacturing jobs, significantly less than found by Acemoglu and Restrepo for the US, for a total loss of 275,000 German manufacturing jobs in the reference period. More interestingly, they found that this reduction in employment was fully compensated by additional jobs in the service sector of the economy. The conclusion is that robots mainly affect the composition of aggregate employment. Interestingly, the results also show that incumbent manufacturing workers are not at risk of displacement, although they have to accept lower wages in order to keep their jobs. The decline of employment in manufacturing observed in stylized data is basically driven by fewer new job opportunities for young people.

Graetz and Michaels (2015) studied the economic impact of robot density in 17 advanced countries in the period of 1993–2007. In the paper, data are collected at the country-industry level. On average, they find no evidence of adverse employment effects due to robot densification. However, technology seems to affect workers according to their skill levels. Robots are associated with a decrease in the number of hours worked by low-skilled and, partially, by middle-skilled workers, whereas the hours worked by high-skilled workers increased during the period, confirming the skill-biased nature of the technological change in the digital revolution emphasized in the literature (Acemoglu and Autor 2011, Autor and Dorn 2013).

Gregory et al. (2016) analyse the effect of routing-replacing technological change (RRTC) on absolute labour demand. Data are collected for 238 regions across 27 European countries in the period of 1999–2010. In their analysis, they take into account three channels through which technology may affect labour. These are substitution effects, product demand effects, and product demand spillovers. The last two effects are expected to compensate for the negative impact of the substitution of capital for labour in routine production tasks. The authors find a positive total labour demand effect of RRTC. Up to 11.6 million jobs have been created across Europe in the reference period.

The evidence provided by these studies is clearly not conclusive. Results vary enormously according to the methodology employed, the availability of data, or the country under analysis. Predictions about the future impact of automation seem to be particularly demanding (and it is not clear which time span is appropriate for assessing the impact of the 4IR on employment and growth). As Mokyr et al. (2015) have pointed out, "discussions of how technology may affect labour demand are often focused on existing jobs [...] but offer much less insight about the emergence of as-yet-nonexistent occupations of the future" (p. 45). To have an idea, the introduction of the personal computer in the 1980s gave rise to the creation of more than 1,500 new professions in the US labour market, such as computer programmers, web designers, and data communications technicians (OECD 2016, p. 13). These job titles were simply unthinkable before the development of the new technology. Given these considerations, perhaps it is wiser to follow Dany Rodrik's advice: making predictions is not and should not be among the economist's tasks (Rodrik 2015). However, from this literature, we can learn a number of lessons that can be useful for future research.

First, at an empirical level, it is not easy to estimate the impact of the 4IR on the labour market. How is one to measure the extent of technological change? What is the best measure to capture the basic features of the digital revolution? As we have seen, the digital revolution is associated not with a single technology but with a bundle of many enabling technologies. By automating tasks previously performed by humans, robots can clearly displace jobs. But physical robots, such as those classified by the IFR and used mainly in manufacturing plants, are just one type of job-displacing technology. "Software" robots (*Financial Times* 2017) can equally have a tremendous impact on jobs, especially white-collar jobs, in both the manufacturing and service industries. Indeed, this was the case in the last decades since the diffusion of the ICTs. So investments in ICT computing and communications equipment plus related investments in software and databases can be another useful proxy for the digital revolution.

The point is that in many (service) sectors where ICT intensity is high, employment did not decline. This suggests that although many jobs have been displaced by ICT and software, many others have been created, compensating job losses with new opportunities of employment. As emphasized by Autor (2015), automation substitutes labour, but strong complementarities between automation and labour occur that increase productivity, raise earnings, and augment demand for labour. "Technology eliminates jobs, not work".

All this suggests that focusing on manufacturing and industrial robots can be reductive. It is necessary to adopt a general equilibrium approach because compensating forces can act across different sectors of the economy.

Second, robots and ICT capital are strictly supply-side variables, but there are other more general indicators that could be employed in empirical analysis in order to assess the extent and progress of the digital revolution, particularly in cross-country comparisons. Some examples are the fixed and mobile broadband penetration, the number of internet users, the number of patents in AI technologies, research and development indicators, human-capital indicators, and quantity and quality of scientific publications (OECD 2017). These variables can be useful not only for assessing the extent of the digital revolution but also, more importantly, for evaluating the potential for innovation. This is very important because the innovative capacity of a country is crucial for the creation of new industries and services and therefore for new jobs in the future.

Third, technological change and digitalization interact with institutional and structural factors. Structural weaknesses and rigidities of each country can make the adjustment more difficult and slow. For example, the impact of robots depends on the importance of manufacturing in the economy and its industry composition. Also, the size distribution of firms matters since large firms are more likely to innovate and digitalize production (OECD 2017). Institutional arrangements, particularly in the labour market, can also affect the path and speed of the digital revolution. For example, co-determination by workers and management is a guiding principle of German corporate governance. This might explain why in Germany the diffusion of robots and digital technologies is associated with a minor loss of manufacturing employment compared with other countries.

In summary, although the 4IR started two decades ago, some of its more disrupting technologies are still far from spreading extensively across sectors and countries. Stylized data show that although the introduction of the new digital technologies is having a deep impact on some sectors and industries, its overall effect on employment has so far been fairly limited. With wide variations between countries, new opportunities of jobs in dynamic service sectors more than compensated for the loss of jobs in manufacturing.

In Favour of Machines: Policies for the Future of Manufacturing

Industry 4.0 is a very popular term in the political discourse.[5] The Germans invented it and Chancellor Angela Merkel refers to it as *"the comprehensive transformation of the whole sphere of industrial production through the merging of digital technology and the internet with conventional industry"* (Federal Government 2014). This is not just a formal recognition of a new technological revolution; it is the starting point of new industrial policies aimed at revitalizing the manufacturing sector and strengthening its competitiveness. *Plattform Industrie 4.0*, which was launched by the German government in 2011 as a part of High Tech 2020 Strategy, is the first national policy explicitly addressed at supporting digital manufacturing. Its aim is to promote the integration of CPS and Internet of Things and Services (IoTS) in the manufacturing sector (European Commission 2017). The platform does not provide direct incentives to invest in digitization, but it draws up recommendations for actions through dialogue with all of the relevant stakeholders (businesses, trade unions, science and government). It also promotes, finances and supports research, projects, and test beds carried out by companies and specialized technology centres at universities and research institutions.

Starting with Germany, almost every advanced country has developed policies and strategies to promote technological change and support the diffusion of digital technologies. There are plenty of examples, not only in Europe but also in the US, China and Japan. A detailed review of these policies is outside the scope of this work.[6] However, it is useful to highlight some general characteristics of these initiatives.

Some policies are truly consistent with the above-mentioned definitions of the 4IR; some have definitely broader goals, which have a more tenuous relation to the digital economy; others, because of the limited resources mobilized by the governments, seem just political slogans with little content and impact.

In Europe, there are basically two types of policies. The first is aimed directly at companies, with the aim of encouraging the adoption and diffusion of digital technologies in the production process. The main objective is to foster private investments that can allow companies to reap the benefits of the 4IR in order to revitalize manufacturing and make it more competitive.

The instruments are those typical of incentive policies, such as subsidized loans, tax credits, and amortization schemes. This type of policy requires strong financial support from the state. An example is *Industrie du Futur*, launched by France in 2015, to which about 10 billion euros has been allocated (European Commission 2017). The French government has recently strengthened its intervention with the *Gran Plan d'Investissement*, which earmarks 4.9 billion euros in the period of 2018–2022 to support investments in some key digital technologies and a further 9.3 billion euros to accelerate the digital transformation of public services and health.

Along similar lines, the *Industria 4.0* initiative, launched by the Italian government in 2016, provides tax incentives and other measures to support digital innovation. The estimated total cost of the program is 18 billion euros until 2020 (European Commission 2017, MISE 2017).

In the second type of policy, public support is directed mainly at providing services, allowing knowledge sharing and awareness, and financing innovative research projects for the digital transformation of production processes. Examples are *Industria Conectada 4.0* in Spain and *MADE* (Manufacturing Academy of Denmark) in Denmark, both launched in 2014.

Other countries implemented policies with a broader goal. In the UK, the *High Value Manufacturing (HVM) Catapult initiative*, which started in 2011, is basically focused on supporting innovation through the creation of a network of technology centres (UK Government 2013). However, only one of these centres is dedicated to digital technologies. *Produktion 2030* in Sweden and *Smart Industry* in the Netherlands have a similar nature but with limited funding from the state (European Commission 2017).

The active role of governments in the 4IR is a new and important factor, a strong difference with the first three industrial revolutions in which policy apparently played a limited or indirect role. By supporting the digital revolution, all governments (implicitly) believe that the 4IR will be beneficial to the economy (GDP growth, productivity, exports, and competitiveness) and society (employment, quality of life, environment, and income distribution), at least in the long run.

In Favour of Machines (But Not Forgetting the Workers): Some... 51

To quote the title of the famous book by Brynjolfsson and McAfee (2011), no government seems to be involved in "the race against machines". All are in favour of this new wave of machines and technological progress. This general optimism of governments seems to be confirmed by the last Eurobarometer survey sponsored by the European Commission (Eurobarometer 2017) and carried out in 28 member states. According to the results, more than 60% of respondents have a positive view of robots and AI. However, an even larger proportion of respondents (72%) think that robots and AI are stealing people's jobs.

Policies in favour of machines and product innovations in manufacturing (such as Industry 4.0) are usually widely accepted and politically sustainable. There is a substantial uniformity of pro-technology policies among advanced countries though with differences in the modalities and intensity of public support. Even when machines clearly substitute for labour, there seems to be no inclination towards Luddite-type ideas or practices. Trade unions and leftist parties strongly oppose the outsourcing of production as well as imports of low-cost goods due to social dumping—two of the main factors held responsible for the loss of employment in manufacturing in advanced countries. However, their attitude towards automation and technological change is much more cautious and for some good reasons.

First, although manufacturing employment is stagnant or declining in many advanced countries, manufacturing plays a crucial role for exports, research and development, innovation, and the productivity of a country. Robots and AI promise to make production and firms more efficient, a necessary step to regain competitiveness in international markets and preserve employment. This is particularly true for small to medium enterprises (SMEs), which play a relevant role in many advanced economies and often need technological upgrading.

Second, robots and AI can be complementary to labour ("co-bots") and can contribute to better working conditions. By replacing many repetitive and dangerous tasks, they contribute to increase the demand for more skilled workers, increasing the opportunities for re-training and professional advancement.

Third, there is a hope that robots can help the re-shoring of many manufacturing activities outsourced to low-cost countries in the last decades. However, this issue is highly controversial, as the debate on the new tax bill of the Trump administration clearly shows. Furthermore, this hope does not take into account that at the moment China is the country with the highest rate of growth in robot adoption.

In Europe, this positive attitude towards robots and AI is also influenced by the widespread conviction that observed unemployment (particularly in the countries of Southern Europe), much more than technological innovation, derives from the lack of coordinated anticyclical policies, fragility (if not absence) of industrial policies, etc. On the supply side, in these countries, what (if anything) is feared is a delay in the adoption of new technologies and not a too rapid run towards them. The debate on the low rate of productivity growth in Italy since the second half of the nineties is a paradigmatic case.

Hence, in many advanced countries and not only in the US, there is a serious risk of over-consensus towards policies that univocally tend to favour capital over labour. As Acemoglu observes, "We are creating huge subsidies [...] for capital and encouraging employers to use machines instead of labor" (Acemoglu, quoted in *Newsweek*, February 2018 and in Arnold 2017, Goodkind 2017).

To this regard and for various reasons, there is a marked difference between the manufacturing and the service sectors in the political consensus granted to the digital revolution by employers, workers, unions, and political actors. The resistance to a massive adoption of digital technologies seems to be stronger in the service sector than in industry. New (or potential) Luddites are certainly far more common among taxi drivers than they are in industrial workshops, as the past violent protests against Uber in Paris, Rome, Johannesburg, and many other cities all over the world have clearly shown. Widespread discontent and protests are also common among hotel workers and hoteliers against Airbnb and Booking.com, or independent bookstores against Amazon. More generally, while there is a broad consensus on the need to regulate these new economic activities based on internet and digital technologies, there is no agreement on the specific measures to be taken. It is difficult to find balance between policies in favour of competition and protection of workers' rights, and the outcome can be an illegitimate defence of rent positions. Until now, governments, local administrations, and regulatory agencies proceed on their own, often with hesitation and difficulties. While *Industry 4.0-type* policies are common to all advanced countries, policies in favour of the diffusion of digital technologies in the service sector are more fragmented and difficult to implement. An example is the public administration, where the digital transformation of public services and the dematerialization of processes through the use of digital technologies are very slow in many countries, with a pace often conditioned by the problem of generational turnover and workers' resistance.

Not Forgetting the Workers: Policy Issues

John Maynard Keynes predicted widespread technological unemployment "due to our discovery of means of economising the use of labour outrunning the pace at which we can find new uses for labour" (Keynes 1963, p. 3). In *Economic Possibilities for Our Grandchildren* (1930), he envisaged a world with no scarcity, short working hours and plenty of leisure. More recently, in the same mood, Brynjolfsson spoke of a "Digital Athens", in which robot slaves can produce all the necessary goods, leaving people time for leisure, sport, arts and entertainment. However, a Digital Athens requires radical policies.

A strand of the contemporary policy debate takes very seriously the potential for labour substitution of robots and digital technologies and tries to find policy solutions that can solve the problem at the root. Among these, a robot tax, shared robot ownership, and universal basic income (UBI) are some of the most attractive proposals.

In her draft report to the European Parliament on civil law rules in robotics, Mady Delvaux, Member of the European Parliament and member of the Committee on Legal Affairs, suggested that "the possible need to introduce corporate reporting requirements on the extent and proportion of the contribution of robotics and AI to the economic results of a company for the *purpose of taxation* and social security contributions". She added that "in the light of the possible effects on the labour market of robotics and AI, a *general basic income* should be seriously considered, and invites all Member States to do so" [emphasis added] (European Parliament 2017). Although in the final resolution the European Parliament rejected these proposals, the example testifies to the increasing attention that politicians, economists, and public opinion are dedicating to the issue of a robot tax and UBI.

The issue of taxing robots for the purpose of collecting resources to pay for the transition costs caused by disrupting technologies is highly controversial (Guerreiro et al. 2017). Bill Gates was one of the first to support the idea: "If a human worker does $50,000 of work in a factory, that income is taxed. If a robot comes in to do the same thing, you'd think we'd tax the robot at a similar level" (see interview with *Quartz*, Delany 2017). A moderate and temporary tax on robots was advocated by Nobel Prize laureate Robert Shiller (2017) with the aim of slowing down the pace of the diffusion of robots and the substitution of labour. The main argument is that this tax, as part of a broader policy to support and retrain displaced workers, not only is socially just, because the revenues can be used to address inequality and compensate for the negative externalities of robotization, but also can be more politically acceptable compared with other measures, such as UBI or a more progressive income tax.

A recent paper by two law scholars, Abbott and Bogenschneider (2018), argues strongly in favour of a mix of policy measures, including an "automation tax", with the aim to achieve "tax neutrality" between human workers and robots. The main point is that existing tax systems are designed to tax labour more than capital. This encourages firms to invest in robots and other labour-substituting technologies even when this choice is not justified by efficiency considerations. The effect is not only a loss of employment but also a potential significant reduction in revenues for the government given that most tax revenues come from workers. As the authors say, "robots are not good taxpayers". The concern about revenue loss is reinforced by the fact that the promised benefits of automation and AI in terms of productivity growth and new employment are yet to come in many advanced countries.

As we have seen earlier, many policies inspired by *Industrie 4.0* use tax and fiscal incentives to promote investments in robots and digital technologies. To avoid excessive automation, these policies should be counterbalanced by effective incentives for hiring and training workers.

However, most economists are rather lukewarm if not openly hostile to the robot tax. Many think that this proposal would have undesirable consequences. One argument is that this measure is very difficult to apply in reality. It implies a clear identification of robots that generate unemployment. Although the recommendation to grant robots a legal status advanced by the European Parliament can go in this direction, many labour-substituting digital technologies, such as so-called software robots, are even more difficult to identify. This problem of identification would give rise to a high number of legal battles and controversies.

Another point is that robots and digital technologies are not the only factors causing unemployment. Many new products or technologies can cause substantial reductions of employment in specific industries, but nobody can really think of discouraging innovation or slowing it down through fiscal policies. Lawrence Summers labelled the robot tax "a form of protectionism against progress" (*Financial Times*, March 5, 2017). The tax would have the effect of discouraging the production and the diffusion of robots, preventing not only the positive effects on productivity and growth but also the development of better products and services. Not surprisingly, similar arguments have been put forward by the IFR, the association of robot producers (IFR 2017).

Lastly, to be effective, a tax on robots should be applied on a global level; otherwise, production and investments would move to other countries with a more favourable legislation or offshore.

A variant of the robot tax is the sharing of ownership of technological assets. This idea has been advocated mainly by Freeman (Freeman 2015, see also Berg et al. 2016). The capital share is a basic determinant of income distribution. The evidence shows that this share has been steadily increasing in the last decades. Robots would drive up the capital share indefinitely, so the income distribution would tend to grow ever more uneven. The risk, however far in time, is to arrive at a situation of great inequality, called by Freeman "modern feudalism", in which a few billionaires, like the old feudal lords, possess all the wealth and dominate both the markets and the governments—definitely a scary future. The only way for workers to benefit from labour-substituting technology is *by owning* part of the capital that replaces them. As Freeman puts it, "we must earn a substantial part of our incomes from capital ownership rather than from working". The idea sounds good. However, how to realize it without major social upheavals is another story.

As we have seen, the idea of the robot tax has several weaknesses that make its practical applicability quite difficult. Another idea, which is becoming increasingly popular and which appears, albeit in questionable versions, in the political debate of some countries, is UBI for all citizens, regardless of their economic condition. According to the definition given by the BIEN (Basic Income Earth Network), the organization founded in 1986 that collects the network of supporters of the idea worldwide, "A basic income is a periodic cash payment unconditionally delivered to all on an individual basis, without means-test or work requirement".

This idea, even more radical than the tax on robots, tries to provide an overall response to the two phenomena that have characterized advanced societies in recent decades: the increasing inequalities and the increasing polarization between a small number of owners of capital and high-skilled workers and the vast majority of people with low wages and precarious jobs.

The basic idea is the following. If highly productive machines are destined to replace much of the work in the future, this on the one hand will result in a growing concentration of wealth in the hands of those who own the machines or the high skills necessary for the development of technologies. On the other hand, it will squeeze the income and wages of the majority of the population that would work less or find work, at low wages, in activities that cannot be substituted by machines. With falling wages, many people may not have sufficient resources to meet their material needs. Moreover, low incomes could cause problems of aggregate demand because the large amount of goods produced by robots and intelligent machines is likely to remain unsold. Provision by the government of a guaranteed basic income would allow everyone to have enough resources to be able to purchase goods and services necessary to live in dignity (basic necessities). It could also allow people to freely choose whether to work and what kind of work to do (e.g. by rejecting particularly under-skilled or under-paid jobs).

Clearly, the proposal, and the future scenario on which it is based, is very strong. The idea is not new and has appeared several times in the economic debate, albeit with different motivations (a documented review is contained in the BIEN website and in the book by Standing 2017). Milton Friedman, for example, advocated basic income in the form of a negative income tax from an ultra-liberal perspective as an alternative to the welfare system and to reduce the intervention of the state in the economy.

The idea of some form of universal income is supported by some economists and social scientists (Robert Reich, Van Parijs and Guy Standing), by a growing number of politicians, mainly from the left (Bennie Sanders, Jeremy Corbyn and Benoit Hamon), and by some important technology entrepreneurs, such as Elon Musk of Tesla and Facebook CEO Mark Zuckerberg.

Van Parijs and Vanderborght (2017) and Guy Standing (2017) are some of the most fervent supporters, though on the more general grounds of "social justice, freedom and security" rather than as a solution to a future of technological employment.

Attempts to apply the idea are not lacking. In June 2016, Switzerland held a referendum on the introduction of basic income for all, but the proposal was rejected by 77% of voters. In January 2017, the government of Finland launched a trial of a form of unconditional basic income, but the experiment is limited to 2,000 unemployed people. In January 2018, the Council of Europe (2018) adopted a resolution in favour of the UBI containing generic recommendations to the European Member States. Other cases of experimentation are cited for Canada, the Netherlands and some developing countries. However, these experiments have different aims and are crucially limited to specific target groups. They cannot be taken as evidence of application of UBI.

As with the robot tax, however, the reaction of most economists is generally negative. This proposal not only is very burdensome for the state but also could be insufficient to guarantee some basic goods and services to everybody, such as health and education (McAfee and Brynjolfsson 2016; Colin and Palier 2015). In principle, it could be financed by dismantling the welfare state—but this solution is politically unsustainable, especially in European countries, which are based on an extensive and well-established welfare system (Meyer 2016)—or by a strong redistribution of the income gained by the owners of the machines.

McAfee and Brynjolfsson (2016, p. 147) argue that we are not yet in a jobless economy and the programmes for UBI would be too expensive to sustain and difficult to manage. Instead, policy "should encourage employment" basically with wage subsidies. In this way, workers are incentivized to work more hours.

In a recent forum organized by the review *Intereconomics*, several economists shared their view on the topic (Intereconomics 2017). The forum concludes dryly that "no serious answers have been found to the a question of how to finance such a system, and until a workable solution is found, a UBI is simply not feasible".

Given these difficulties, some political proposals try to limit the application of the measure to specific target groups (unemployed workers, low-income families, and disadvantaged people). However, these social problems can probably be better managed with existing policy measures. If the application of UBI is not universal, it is not clear how it can address the problem of increasing mass technological unemployment.

From a different perspective, another argument against UBI is linked to the social and cultural value attributed to the work activity per se, the ethics of work. The concern is that such a measure could discourage human work and discourage active job creation policies and have profoundly negative social consequences. McAfee and Brynjolfsson (2016): "declining work-force participation is troubling not only because work provides income but also because it gives people meaning". However, from a wider perspective, this argument is highly controversial. Post-work ideas that claim the positive values of leisure are gaining ground among politicians, unions and social activists (see the interesting survey by Beckett 2018).

The theoretical debate and policy proposals discussed so far are certainly very interesting and in some ways provocative. However, the impression remains that they are rather surreal. We are still very far from a future in which machines do everything and perhaps this will never happen. A recent article in *The Economist* reports the results of a survey among high-qualified attendees at two AI conferences (*Economist*, 1 November 2017). One of the questions was about the predicted year in which all labour would be fully automated—a gloomy future of human obsolescence. The researchers thought that it would take, on average, 125 years. The most "optimistic" were the Asian researchers, who indicated 104 years, much earlier than the Americans, who thought, on average, 169 years. The most "pessimistic" researchers responded not less than 200 years. The aspect to be understood is that the 4IR is still far from being completed and this transition period will probably last a long time and entail different times and speeds from country to country. The transition period, however, is not painless.

The digital revolution brings about radical changes and disruptions. Employed workers, economic activities and existing companies (incumbents) feel increasingly threatened. The labour market, in particular, is deeply affected. It is more difficult to find a job for low-skilled workers and for young people. Stable jobs are no longer the norm for new entrants in the labour market, and the number of temporary jobs is increasing in many countries, particularly for young people. For many workers, real wages are declining.

Policies are increasingly called for to accompany this period of transition and to mitigate the negative effects of the digital revolution. However, although it is easy to find policies in favour of the machines, few policies so far have effectively addressed "the painfulness of readjustment between one economic period and another", as Keynes put it (1930). This is the most difficult and compelling challenge facing the advanced economies. In past industrial revolutions, politics had been substantially absent. Now governments cannot stand by, and the debate about what needs to be done is entirely open. What are most needed are new policies, designed for this new era of technological change while avoiding the temptation to revive forms of protection and regulation designed for an out-dated industrial age. The design of policies in favour of work is made even more complex by the fact that many workers in the digital economy present specific characteristics: they are neither employees nor contractors. They are "independent workers". They should enjoy some forms of protection and benefits, typical of the employees, but still retain independence and flexibility. Existing labour regulations are ill equipped to understand these new forms of employment. However, actual experiences are dramatically few while social costs are growing day by day.

Notes

1. The first was characterized by mechanical production facilities and began in Britain in the 1780s with the help of water and steam power. The second introduced and developed mass production with the help of electrical energy, particularly in the early twentieth century. The third began in the 1970s and was characterized by the use of electronic and IT systems that further automated production.
2. The term *Industrie 4.0* was used for the first time during the 2011 Hannover Fair (Schwab 2016).
3. Our computation based on EU-KLEMS, OECD-STAN and BLS data.

4. An industrial robot can be defined as "an automatically controlled, repro-grammable, multipurpose manipulator programmable in three or more axes, which can be either fixed in place or mobile for use in industrial automation applications" (IFR 2017, p. 32).
5. Also, "smart" is very popular. It is so popular that recently the EU, with perhaps excessive emphasis, labelled a programme Smart Anything Everywhere (SAE)!
6. A recent survey can be found in European Commission (2017).

References

Abbott, Ryan and Bret N. Bogenschneider. 2018. Should Robots Pay Taxes? Tax Policy in the Age of Automation, *Harvard Law & Policy Review*, 12:1. https://papers.ssrn.com/sol3/papers.cfm?abstract_id=2932483. Accessed 11 Feb 2018.

Acemoglu, Daron, and David H. Autor. 2011. Skills, Tasks and Technologies: Implications for Employment and Earnings. In *Handbook of Labor Economics* 4, part B:1043–1171. Amsterdam: Elsevier.

Acemoglu, Daron, and Pascual Restrepo. 2017. *Robots and Jobs: Evidence from US Labor Markets*. NBER Working Paper 23285.

Arnold, Chris. 2017. Tax Bill Favors Adding Robots Over Workers, Critics Say. *National Public Radio Inc.* (US), December 8, 2017, 5:01 PM ET. https://www.npr.org/2017/12/08/569118310/tax-bill-favors-adding-robots-over-workers-critics-say. Accessed 4 Feb 2018.

Arntz, Melanie, Gregory, Terry and U. Zierahn. 2016. *The Risk of Automation for Jobs in OECD Countries: A Comparative Analysis*. OECD Social, Employment and Migration Working Paper 189.

Autor, David H. 2015. Why Are There Still So Many Jobs? The History and Future of Workplace Automation. *Journal of Economic Perspectives* 29 (3): 3–30.

Autor, David H., and David Dorn. 2013. The Growth of Low-skill Service Jobs and the Polarization of US Labor Market. *American Economic Review* 103 (5): 1553–1557.

Beckett, Andy. 2018. Post-work: The Radical Idea of a World Without Jobs, *The Guardian*, 19 Jan 2018.

Berg, Andrew, Edward F. Buffie, and Luis-Felipe Zanna. 2016. Robots, Growth, and Inequality. *IMF Finance & Development*, September, 53:3.

In Favour of Machines (But Not Forgetting the Workers): Some... 61

Berriman, Richard, and John Hawksworth. 2017. Will Robots Steal Our Jobs? The Potential Impact of Automation on the UK and Other Major Economies. *UK Economic Outlook*, March 2017.

Brynjolfsson, Erik, and Andrew McAfee. 2011. *Race Against the Machine. How the Digital Revolution Is Accelerating Innovation, Driving Productivity and Irreversibly Transforming Employment and the Economy.* Lexington: Digital Frontier Press.

Colin, Nicolas, and Bruno Palier. 2015. The Next Safety Net. Social Policy for a Digital Age. *Foreign Affairs* 94: 4.

Council of Europe. Social Affairs, Health and Sustainable Development. 2018. *The Case for a Basic Citizenship Income.* DOC 14462. 5 Jan 2018.

Dauth, Wolfgang, Sebastian Findeisen, Jens Südekum, and Nicole Woessner. 2017. *German Robots – The Impact of Industrial Robots on Workers.* CEPR Discussion Paper 12306. http://www.cepr.org/active/publications/discussion_papers/dp.php?dpno=12306. Accessed 4 Feb 2018.

Delany, Kevin. 2017. The Robot That Takes Your Job Should Pay Taxes, Says Bill Gates *Quartz*, February 17. https://qz.com/911968/bill-gates-the-robot-that-takes-your-job-should-pay-taxes/. Accessed 4 Feb 2018.

European Commission. 2017. Digital Transformation Monitor, National Initiatives. https://ec.europa.eu/growth/toolsdatabases/dem/monitor/category/national-initiatives. Accessed 12 April 2018.

The European House-Ambrosetti. 2017. *Technology and Labour: Steering the Change.* Milan: The European House-Ambrosetti. https://www.ambrosetti.eu/wp-content/uploads/Ambrosetti-Club-2017. Accessed 4 Feb 2018.

European Parliament. Committee on Legal Affairs. 2017. Report with Recommendations to the Commission on Civil Law Rules on Robotics (2015/2103(INL)). Rapporteur: Mady Delvaux. 27 January 2017. http://www.europarl.europa.eu/sides/getDoc.do?pubRef=-//EP//NONSGML+REPORT+A8-2017-0005+0+DOC+PDF+V0//EN. Accessed 4 Feb 2018.

The Federal Government. 2014. Speech by the Federal Chancellor Angela Merkel to the OECD Conference, 19 February 2014. https://www.bundesregierung.de/Content/EN/Reden/2014/2014-02-19-oecd-merkel-paris_en.html. Accessed 4 Feb 2018.

Freeman, Richard B. 2015. *Who Owns the Robots Rules the World.* IZA World of Labor. http://wol.iza.org/articles/who-owns-the-robots-rules-the-world. Accessed 4 Feb 2018.

Frey, Carl B., and Michael A. Osborne, 2013. *The Future of Employment: How Susceptible Are Jobs to Computerization?* Oxford Martin Programme on The Impact of Future Technologies, University of Oxford. Revised in *Technological Forecasting and Social Change*. 2017. 114:254–280.

Goodkind, Nicole. 2017. Trump Tax Plan Gives Jobs Away to Robots and Will Increase Unemployment. 15 November 2017. http://www.newsweek.com/tax-plan-robots-jobs-senate-republicans-712930. Accessed 4 Feb 2018.

Graetz, Georg, and Guy Michaels. 2015. *Robots at Work*. CEPR Discussion paper 10477. https://cepr.org/active/publications/discussion_papers/dp.php?dpno=10477. Accessed 4 Feb 2018.

Gregory, Terry, Anna Salomons, and Zierahn Ultich. 2016. *Racing With or Against the Machine? Evidence from Europe*. ZEW Discussion Paper 16-053. http://ftp.zew.de/pub/zew-docs/dp/dp16053.pdf. Accessed 4 Feb 2018.

Guerreiro, Joao, Sergio Rebelo, and Pedro Teles. 2017. *Should Robots Be Taxed?*. NBER Working Paper 23806, September 2017, Revised January 2018. http://www.nber.org/papers/w23806. Accessed 4 Feb 2018.

Intereconomics. 2017. *Universal Basic Income: The Promise vs. the Practicalities* 52, March/April, No 2.

International Federation of Robotics. 2017. *Executive Summary World Robotics 2017 Industrial Robots*. https://ifr.org/downloads/press/Executive_Summary_WR_2017_Industrial_Robots.pdf. Accessed 4 Feb 2018.

Kagermann, Henning, Wolfgang Wahlster, and Johannes Helbig. 2013. *Recommendations for Implementing the Strategic Initiative INDUSTRIE 4.0. Final Report of the Industrie 4.0 Working Group*, April 2013. Acatech, Deutsche Akademie der Technikswissenschaften. http://www.acatech.de/de/publikationen/stellungnahmen/kooperationen/detail/artikel/recommendations-for-implementing-the-strategic-initiative-industrie-40-final-report-of-the-industr.html. Accessed 4 Feb 2018.

Keynes, John M. 1963. *Economic Possibilities for Our Grandchildren, Essays in Persuasion*, 358–373 (I ed. 1930). New York: W.W Norton and Co.

McAfee, Andrew, and Erik Brynjolfsson. 2016. Human Work in the Robotic Future. Policy for the Age of Automation. *Foreign Affairs*, 95:4, July/August.

Meyer, Henning. 2016. Inequality in the Second Machine Age. The Need for a Social Democratic Digital Society. *Juncture (IPPR Progressive Review)* 23: 2.

Ministero dello Sviluppo Economico – MISE. 2017. *Piano Nazionale Industria 4.0*, Roma.

Mokyr, Joel, Chris Vickers, and Nicolas Ziebarth. 2015. The History of Technological Anxiety and the Future of Economic Growth: Is This Time Different? *Journal of Economic Perspectives* 29 (3).

OECD. 2016. *Enabling the Next Production Revolution. The Future of Manufacturing and Services – Interim Report. Meeting of the OECD Council at Ministerial Level, Paris, 1–2 June 2016.* https://www.oecd.org/mcm/documents/Enabling-the-next-production-revolution-the-future-of-manufacturing-and-services-interim-report.pdf. Accessed 4 Feb 2018.

———. 2017. *The Next Production Revolution: Implications for Governments and Business.* Paris: OECD Publishing. https://doi.org/10.1787/9789264 271036-en. Accessed 4 Feb 2018.

Rodrik, Dany. 2015. *Economics Rules: The Rights and Wrongs of the Dismal Science.* New York: W.W. Norton.

Schwab, Klaus. 2016. *The Fourth Industrial Revolution.* Geneva: World Economic Forum.

Shiller, Robert J. 2017. Narrative Economics. *American Economic Review* 107 (4): 967–1004.

Standing, Guy. 2017. *Basic Income: And How We Can Make It Happen.* London: Pelican.

Summers, Lawrence. 2017. Robots Are Wealth Creators and Taxing Them Is Illogical. *Financial Times,* 5 March 2017. https://www.ft.com/content/42ab292a-000d-11e7-8d8e-a5e3738f9ae4. Accessed 5 Feb 2018.

U.K. Government. Office for Science. 2013. *The Future of Manufacturing: A new era of opportunity and challenge for the UK. Project Report.* London: U.K. Government. Office for Science. https://www.gov.uk/government/uploads/system/uploads/attachment_data/file/255922/13-809-future-manufacturing-project-report.pdf. Accessed 5 Feb 2018.

UNIDO, University of Cambridge, IfM. 2017. *Emerging Trends in Global Advanced Manufacturing: Challenges, Opportunities and Policy Responses.* Cambridge: Institute for Manufacturing. https://www.ifm.eng.cam.ac.uk/uploads/Resources/Reports/UNIDO_FINAL_VERSION.pdf. Accessed 5 Feb 2018.

Van Parijs, Philippe, and Yannick Vanderborght. 2017. *Basic Income: A Radical Proposal for a Free Society and a Sane Economy.* Cambridge, MA/London: Harvard University Press.

World Economic Forum. 2016. *The Future of Jobs. Employment, Skills and Workforce Strategy for the Fourth Industrial Revolution,* Geneva, Switzerland: World Economic Forum, January 2016. http://www3.weforum.org/docs/WEF_Future_of_Jobs.pdf. Accessed 5 Feb 2018.

Part II

Work in the Gig Economy

5

A Fair Wage for Workers On-demand via App

Emanuele Menegatti

Introduction

According to a widespread definition, the so-called gig economy refers mainly to two forms of work: crowdwork and work-on-demand via app (Eurofound 2015; Codagnone et al. 2016; Cherry 2011; De Stefano 2016a). They both involve the performance of labour-intensive services in a triangular relationship, in which workers and customers are matched by online platforms in a (relatively) new work paradigm. However, they differ regarding a very relevant element: whereas crowdwork encompasses the completion of electronically transmittable services through online platforms, work-on-demand is more connected to traditional jobs, requiring physical and localised delivery, often related to easy tasks, such as driving, cleaning, and personal services. This difference is reflected in the diverse size of the labour market of reference, potentially global for crowdworkers and just local for workers on-demand via app (WsDA).

E. Menegatti (✉)
University of Bologna, Bologna, Italy
e-mail: e.menegatti@unibo.it

© The Author(s) 2018
E. Ales et al. (eds.), *Working in Digital and Smart Organizations*,
https://doi.org/10.1007/978-3-319-77329-2_5

This article will focus only on work-on-demand through digital app, which is far more interesting from a labour law perspective for two reasons. First of all, since it involves local labour markets, platform activities can be dealt with through national labour laws. In fact, many workers in different countries have been challenging platforms in order to get access to employment protections (Codagnone et al. 2016; Cherry 2016). The second reason of interest concerns the outcomes of this new business model. As a matter of fact, the workers involved here face a very high risk of economic uncertainty. Recent studies have shown that many WsDA (e.g. 30% of Uber drivers), no matter how skilled they are, rely on low-skilled gigs provided by platforms as their main or even sole source of income (Berg 2016).

It is not our intention to focus on the debate about whether they are just seeking "pin money". We just want to stress that economic uncertainty is a very likely condition in the work-on-demand as well as in the crowdworking model: workers are considered independent contractors and they have no bargaining power since competition "in the crowd" is tough and unionisation is very unlikely (De Stefano 2016b, p. 479; Prassl and Risak 2016, p. 626).

Workers are probably the losers of what is supposed to fall under the header of "sharing economy" (Arthurs 2017). They do not usually have any guaranteed amount of work or the rights and entitlements typically accorded to employees, such as the minimum wage or social security benefits. Labour costs and costs of "empty moment" are so obviously minimised[1] (Prassl and Risak 2016, p. 7), making this model convenient and very profitable for platforms and their final users.

Granting WsDA basic social protection, the minimum wage above all, might bring a reasonable minimum protection to workers engaged in the gig economy. It might also represent a way of sharing profits between platforms and its workers in a more equitable manner. It would also lead to a fairer competition between gig economy firms and more "conventional" ones.

The purpose of this article is to explore whether and how WsDA can be granted a minimum wage. It will explore the possibility of giving them access to the right to a minimum wage, from the main door—i.e. the recognition of the subordinate employment status—or from a secondary entrance—through intermediate categories, wherever existing. It will also consider solutions from a *de iure condendo* perspective—in particular, a proposal towards a new redistribution of employment protections, aimed at reworking the rigidity of the dichotomy of employment (full rights)/ self-employment (no rights), and its problematic implications concerning antitrust law prescriptions and, as far as the European Union is concerned, the freedom to provide services within the single market.

Are Workers on-Demand via App "Employees"?

The right to a minimum wage is—in almost every country, apart from the notable case of the UK—recognised only for employees. It follows that workers operating in the gig economy, being generally considered independent contractors, are normally deprived of this right.

More in detail, the "formal reality" emerging from customary contractual terms and conditions provided by platforms is normally the following:

(a) Platforms are not comparable either to temporary work agencies or to employers; they just offer independent contractors, who are not employees, workers or agents, a technology platform as a referral tool for a service and facilitate payments and other operational details.

(b) Workers are almost free from direction in the performance of their services. Platforms might just set certain quality standards. Platforms do not directly monitor workers. However, final users rate and review the performance of workers at the end of any gig.

(c) Workers are not obliged to grant a minimum availability, and the platforms do not have to grant a minimum amount of work. Workers often have the opportunity to review jobs and select those that meet the preferred specifications regarding time frame, date, neighbourhood or geographic location.

(d) Platforms manage payments. They usually pay fees to their workers periodically while retaining their share. The workers must meet all expenses associated with running their business and carry the related risks.

70   E. Menegatti

With regard to the relationship between workers and final users:

(a) The final user is often an individual; sometimes, it can be a business undertaking.
(b) Often, platforms set terms and conditions of gigs and mediate by apps matching users' needs and workers' availability. There is normally no negotiation between workers and final users.
(c) The final user should share a rating of a worker's performance with platforms and other users.
(d) The final user is not normally the owner of working tools and equipment.

Besides this approximate description, it should be considered that work-on-demand is a nuanced phenomenon, in which a rough distinction can be drawn between two main business models: that of platforms just matching workers to final users and managing payments and other operational details and that of "vertically integrated" platforms (Codagnone et al. 2016, pp. 47–48), which tend to maximise control over the "affiliated" independent contractors in order to ensure coordination, speed, reliability, and good quality of the service provided. The latter platforms—e.g. Uber, Uber Eats, Fodoora and Deliveroo—very often go as far as to impose working tools or equipment specifications, routes, strict timing for the gig, and almost mandatory fees; the whole thing is enforced through a kind of disciplinary power which may involve the "deactivation" of the worker.

No matter which model of business they are following, platforms are always really keen on excluding any employment relationship from the triangulation platform–worker–final user. However, this is a controversial statement and it has been often challenged in courts, especially with regard to "vertically integrated" platforms.

Claims have not normally been about the relationship between the worker and the final user of the service. Final users often are individuals, getting in contact with the on-demand workers for just one gig. It is thus worth looking at the way the relationship between the platform and the worker is carried out, notwithstanding the description given by the parties, as courts usually do (so-called primacy of facts principle). It is also necessary to consider the relationship through the lens of employment tests and indicia provided by judiciaries. They have been in charge of shaping the definition of subordinate employment all over the world since national legislations traditionally have not really been helpful in classifying work relations, rarely providing definitions of "employee" or "employment contract" (Casale 2011, pp. 17–29).

"Legal subordination"—i.e. the employee's subjection to the employer's unilateral direction and supervision—used to be the main line of enquiry for most civil law countries (Countouris 2011, p. 57). Nonetheless, things have changed in the post-industrial era. The employer, especially for high-skilled or very-low-skilled jobs, often is not interested in the control over the manner of work and is more interested in the result of work (Supiot 2000, p. 146). Other indicators of subordination apart from direction and supervision, based on the time-to-time prevailing social models of employees, have been put forward by judiciaries.

For example, French judicial authorities use mainly two tests to identify *le lien de subordination juridique* (Supiot 2000, p. 140; Perulli 2011, pp. 150–154; Countouris 2011, p. 55). The first one refers to the *integration* into an organised service (*service organisé*), meaning that the employer controls the execution of the work (i.e. gives technical direction and establishes the place of work and the working time). The second one considers the participation within one employer's business (i.e. *dependency* on the employer's organisation) from a negative perspective: the worker does not employ anyone, he or she does not have his or her own clientele and he or she does not have to cover the business risk. In German law, the distinction between subordinate employment and self-employment lies in the degree of *personal dependence* (*Persönliche Abhängigkeit*), identified by courts through a wide set of indicators, according to a classic typological method (Weiss 2000, p. 251; Nogler 2009, p. 43). The most important refers to the *integration* into the employer's organisation (*Organisatorische Abhangigkeit*): workers offer their work in the frame of an organisation determined and directed by another (Weiss 2000, p. 254; Perulli 2011, p. 258; Däubler 1999); besides the fact that they do not have their own clientele, they do not employee anyone, they do not make investments, and they are not free to determine the price of products or services, etc. In

Italy, according to Article 2094 of the civil code, an 'employee' is under *technical subordination* (control), *functional* for the organisation of the employer's business.[2] *Integration* (often referred to as *hetero-organisation*) into the employer's organisation[3] and *continuity*[4] of the employee's obligation to cooperate are other common indicators of subordination (Perulli 2011, pp. 144–149; Nogler 2009, pp. 88–99). The employee's duty to comply with a set working time, a fixed amount of remuneration, the absence of risk of loss, and the "label" attached by the parties to the contract are other subsidiary "indicia" (Spagnuolo Vigorita 1969). Italian case law tends not to consider *dependency* on the employer's business, despite the emphasis placed on it by the constitutional court.[5]

As far as the UK and other common law countries are concerned, the "control test" was at the beginning the only test, according to which employment is a relationship of control, where the employer gives orders, plans out jobs in minute detail and monitors the employees' work.[6] Other tests have been developed by English courts: the integration test,[7] the economic reality test[8] and the mutuality of obligation test.[9] Integration corresponds exactly to the considered namesake indicator developed by civil law courts. Even the economic reality test, aimed at assessing whether the individual is not working for his or her own account, does not differ much from the negative tests used in civil law countries. Mutuality of obligation, looking for a promise by both parties to provide and accept future work, is known in other countries as continuity of obligation and has had a strong and controversial impact (Supiot 2000, p. 141). Currently, UK courts tend to use the so-called "multiple" test, taking into consideration the above-mentioned test and all aspects of the relationship, no single feature being in itself decisive (Countouris 2011, pp. 51–52). Eventually, courts still consider control and mutuality of obligation the "irreducible minimum criteria" for the establishment of a contract of employment[10] (Deakin 2007, p. 79).

The "control" test is also at the core of the common law test in the US (Dau-Schmidt et al. 2011, pp. 31–45; Davidov et al. 2015, p. 125). According to the Supreme Court, it applies for defining an "employee" under statutes not providing their own definition. It does not concern the Fair Labor Standards Act (FLSA)—providing a wide range of employment rights, including the minimum wage—which has introduced a broader definition of employment in comparison with that based on the common law "control" test. In that way, the FLSA definition of "employ" includes "suffer or permit to work" (Section 203 (g)), i.e. the work that the employer directs or allows to take place. On the basis of the "suffer or permit" concept, the Supreme Court and Circuit Courts of Appeal have developed the multi-factorial "economic realities" test: workers who are dependent on the business of the employer are considered employees. This shall be determined from several factors, none alone determinative, including that related to an employer's control.[11]

Despite the different labels, employment indicators and tests look remarkably similar across the above-considered countries. To sum up, judiciaries normally start their investigation from *legal subordination* or in common law jurisdiction from the very similar *control* test. Whenever these have little relevance or no relevance at all in assessing the employment status, they tend to resort to a set of indicators/tests that, again, do not substantially differ from country to country: *integration* into the organisational framework created by the employer, *dependency/economic reality test*, and *legal continuity/mutuality of obligations*.

If we are able to classify gig economy workers as employees, they need to pass the just-mentioned tests since it is not realistic to think that they could change because of these (apparently) new schemes of work. The prevailing social model of employee, on which employment indicators are carved, is very far from being embodied by gig workers, who still represent a very small fraction of total employment in the US (Katz and Krueger 2016) as well as in Europe (Huws and Joyce 2016a, b).

Starting from the *control* test (direction and supervision), it should be remembered that the degree of control varies widely depending on the model of business on which the platform is based: some platforms just match workers and final users, others have a strict control over the workers. As far as the latter are concerned, it is interesting to quote the North California District Court in *O'Connor*,[12] acknowledging that "Uber does not simply sell software; it sells rides" by harnessing its drivers' performance. According to the court, Uber has managerial and disciplinary powers over the drivers, enforced by threating deactivation; drivers, in turn, retain very little freedom to determine their working conditions since ride fees are not negotiable and they have to comply with a detailed performance protocol; the customers are "virtual supervisors" and this gives the company a "tremendous amount of control over the manner and means of its drivers' performance". The same court put forward similar findings with regard to the drivers working for Uber's main competitor, Lyft.[13] Notwithstanding the above, the final impression, which appears to be shared even by the quoted California court, is that the platform's control over the workers' performance does not have the same extent as that of a "traditional" employer. Even in Uber, Lyft and similar models, platforms normally have little power to decide the place and time of work of their affiliates. Workers retain the freedom to set up their own work schedule, deciding when, for how long and where they wish to work time after time. This does not seem to match up with *control test* requirements (Rogers 2016; K. Cunningham-Paemeter 2016) and it is also significant not to complete *integration* of WsDA into the organisation set up by platforms.

As far as the *economic reality* of the relationship is involved, the degree of dependency of the worker on the platform seems not to reach the same extent as that of an employee. Let us again consider the example of Uber drivers. On the one hand, they seem to work *for* Uber, which decides the market strategies, deals with the clients, and coordinates the result of workers' performances; on the other hand, the driver does not get a fixed remuneration, and he or she owns the car, which is the relevant asset for the service at stake; all related expenses are for him or her, and if something goes wrong, he or she can even run a loss.

Up to here, the employment tests and indicia seem to suggest that WsDA are more similar to self-employed than employees. However, the decisive pointer towards the exclusion of the subordinate employment comes from the lack of one last "basic ingredients": the *mutuality of obligations*. WsDA do not have any obligation to turn up for work if they do not want to; in turn, platforms do not have any obligation to provide gigs to the workers.

Some authors argued that, in some cases, platform rating systems take into account the times of inactivity and that this can result in lower opportunities to work. Moreover workers tend normally to be as available as possible since for many of them this is the main source of income (Prassl and Risak 2016 p. 631; Aloisi 2016, p. 662). In other terms, a situation of economic dependence which replaces the lack of a legal obligation to accept future work, placing the employee in an effective subjection to the employer control.[14] This argument cannot be shared since it confuses the possible socio-economic reality with the legal one. The employment contract provides legal subordination in order to let the employer organise his or her business. The worker's obligation to show up for work is essential to this end and the employer clearly relies on it when organising his or her business undertaking. Therefore, if this obligation is not provided by one given work contract, it seems difficult to recognise it as an employment contract. Moreover, the argument does not consider that even many genuine and "traditional" self-employed (not working via app) are forced to accept jobs because they need to make a living as well. And that does not automatically turn them into "employees".

Do Workers On-Demand via App Fit into Existing "Intermediate Categories" of Workers?

If we want to grant a fair degree of economic certainty to WsDA, we need to consider the extension of the minimum wage beyond subordinate employment. In this respect, workers operating within "vertically integrated" platforms (i.e. Uber drivers or Foodora riders) present the same degree of control, integration and dependency of quasi-subordinate workers. This similarity might lead to the recognition of some rights to WsDA in countries providing "intermediate categories" of workers.

The selective extension of some employment protections and, especially, of social security rights to certain workers took place, for example, in Germany for "employee-like persons" (*Arbeitnehmerähnliche Personen*), who work mainly for just one client and do not employ anyone (Perulli 2011, p. 170), as well as for "dependent contractors" in Canada (Davidov and Langille 1999). In Italy, economic dependence is implicit in the definition of "*collaboratori coordinati e continuativi*" (coordinated and continuous cooperation relationship) provided by Article 409 of the code of civil procedure and is based on three elements: continuity (as opposed to merely occasional performance) of the relationship, coordination with the client's business, and the personal nature of the work (Pallini 2013). In 2007, Spain introduced "*trabajo autónomo económicamente dependiente*", which shares the characteristics of continuity and the personal relationship of the employment, adding dependence on the principal client for at least 75% of the worker's income (Cherry and Aloisi 2017, p. 667).

As far as the right to a minimum wage is concerned, few countries (none of those mentioned above) apply the minimum wage to workers located in the grey area between employment and self-employment. The UK is one that does. Its law provides a system of protection laid out in concentric circles (Davidov 2005): in the inner circle are located the "employees"; then, moving outward, the "workers", the "professionals" (self-employed) and finally the "dependent entrepreneurs" (micro-entrepreneurs working for a single client). Employment rights fully apply only to "employees"; other categories are recognised as having some rights to a decreasing extent the more one moves away from the inner circle. The minimum wage is granted to employees and also to workers. The qualification as "workers" under the Employment Rights Act 1996 section 230(3)(b) and identically by the National Minimum Wage act of 1998 section 54(3) and the Working Time Regulation of 1998 section 36(1) relies on the personal performance of "*any work or services for another party to the contract whose status is not by virtue of the contract that of a client or customer of any profession or business undertaking carried on by the individual*". According to UK doctrine, the distinction between employees and workers lies just in the degree of control of the employer/client (Deakin 2003, p. 441).

This qualification, with the express purpose of obtaining the right to the minimum wage, has been successfully claimed by some Uber drivers before the Employment Tribunal sitting in Central London,[15] whose conclusions have recently been confirmed by the Employment Appeals Tribunal.[16] The London Tribunal recognised that Uber does not simply sell software but "runs a transportation business", so "it is not real to regard Uber as working 'for' the drivers... the relationship is the other way around". In this respect, the platform shows a certain control over the drivers: wherever the drivers are forced to accept trips (without knowing destinations) or are bound to a default route, fares, and other requirements such as the kind of vehicle they should use and wherever Uber imposes penalties for shortcomings. A degree of control which is sufficient to conclude that Uber drivers shall be considered employed under a "worker" contract when (a) they have the App switched on, (b) they are within the territory in which they are authorised to work, and (c) they are able and willing to accept assignments.

The outcome of the Uber case in the UK confirms that when an "intermediate" category is given by the legislation, it probably represents the relevant category for platform workers. However, this might be true for "vertically integrated" platforms. Many other platforms grant the worker a great deal of flexibility and independence just doing what a platform is supposed to do: business-to-business service, behaving like brokers that simply connect workers to customers.

Anyway, even assuming that WsDA should be regarded as quasi-subordinate, only a few countries recognise "intermediate" categories and even fewer (probably just the UK) extend the scope of the minimum wage to these categories. So, in the end, if legislation is to grant to WsDA the right to the minimum wage, we should move to a *de iure condendo* perspective.

A New Category for Workers On-Demand Via App?

From the standpoint of the US, where the classification of workers is still based on the binary division of employment/self-employment, some authors have recently advocated for the creation of a new intermediate category (Harris and Krueger 2015; Hagiu and Wright 2015): a category based on the concept of *economic dependence*, which accurately describes the situation of WsDA providing a personal service mainly for one platform. According to these proposals, the main client of these "dependent contactors" should be considered responsible for some employment protections.

It is a very evocative possibility. Nevertheless, it reveals considerable problems in practice. First of all, as the attempts made by some legal systems testify (De Stefano 2016b, pp. 494–499; Cherry and Aloisi 2017), it is really difficult to find a suitable definition for this category, a definition able to identify the "weak" contractors. Thus, rather than providing a secure solution to issues affecting WsDA, a new category would probably lead to more uncertainty and litigation. The empirical analysis of existing intermediate categories raises a second major counter-argument. As a matter of fact, they have often created a good opportunity for a misclassification of workers hitherto considered "employees" into a category of atypical and under-protected workers (Countouris 2007, p. 8).[17]

At the end of the day, the creation of new intermediate categories appears to be a lose-lose solution, not able to solve the problems for workers of the gig economy and possibly creating new ones for "regular" employees.

Thinking Bigger: A Fair Wage for "Personal Work Relations"

Still from a *de iure condendo* perspective, there is another way to extend the minimum wage, as well as other suitable employment protections, to WsDA. It is based on the assumption that work through application is not "paradigm shifting" (Davidov 2017, p. 2) and does not bring anything really new since some of its features can be traced back to the earliest days of capitalism (Finkin 2016; Valenduc and Vendramin 2016). However, the new schemes of digital work are reinforcing an important message: it is high time to think about a new distribution of rights between employment and self-employment.

More precisely, it is not in question the employment contract as main gateway to employment protections. What probably no longer makes sense, as the work in the gig economy seems to show, is the fact that employment rights are still targeted only to subordinate employment. The idea prevailing for a large part of the twentieth century—

of providing protections only for those who, in order to make a living, had to accept subordinate employment and ignoring those who, for the same purpose, had invested in their self-organisation—had already become outdated during the '80s (Mengoni 2002, Supiot 2000, Bronstein 2009, pp. 11 ss.). Many self-employed, especially those employed through emerging atypical work arrangements, now including WsDA, are in a weaker position compared with employees (Weil 2015; Garofalo D. 2017, p. 91). This is reflected by the fact that the average earnings of independent contractors have, in many countries, fallen below those of employees (ISTAT 2016). Self-employment has clearly become a survival strategy for those who are not able to get a "regular" job through an employment contract, typically those belonging to the weakest segments of the labour market (migrants, young workers, disable, etc.). Gig economy workers are just the latest example of low-income persons being particularly attracted by self-employment (Gapper 2015, p. 29).

In order to decide which employment protections could be extended beyond the employment contract, it is possible to make use of a purposive approach,[18] applying it to possible future legislation. Therefore, with specific regard to the right to a minimum wage, it is necessary to understand whether, according to its justifications and purposes, the right can be provided with a scope broader than just 'employees' so as to include WsDA. Since goals of the minimum wage are commonly intended to be a reduction of in-work poverty and respect for human dignity, there is merit in extending the right to the minimum wage to all personal work relations. These goals are clearly appropriate for everyone who personally performs any work or service for another party, no matter whether he is an employee under the employer's control and integrated to his/her business or an independent contractor self-organizing his/her work. Many independent contractors as well as employees get their livelihood by means of their personal work, selling their energies, often to just one client. Therefore, they might have dignity only if their work receives fair compensation. Otherwise, they might fall into in-work poverty and not be able to participate in society.

The idea of equipping with some "core rights" all of the workers performing work personally, whether employees or not, is not far from that

80 E. Menegatti

on which the "Statuto dei lavori" ("Jobs Statute") proposed by Marco Biagi almost 20 years ago was based (Biagi and Tiraboshi 1999) or from the "personal employment contract" construction proposed by Mark Freedland (Freedland 2003; Freedland and Countouris 2011). It is also close to the doctrinal construction of the work "sans phrase", which refers to any work contract providing the integration of someone's performance into someone else's business (D'Antona 1996).

Challenges: (I) Competition Law

As for the means, there are obviously two possible ways of extending the minimum wage beyond the employment contract: collective bargaining and statutory law. They both involve some issues.

First of all, competition law normally considers mandatory fees for the self-employed set out by collective agreements to be an illicit restraint on trade to the detriment of businesses and consumers. In the US, for example, the Sherman Antitrust Act provides that "every contract, combination [...] or conspiracy, in restraint of trade or commerce among the several States, or with foreign nations, is declared to be illegal". An exception to that principle (the so-called labour exception) was provided under the Clayton Antitrust Act, making it possible for trade unions to engage in collective bargaining so as to promote legitimate labour interests related to employment relationships. But in *Columbia River Packers Assn., Inc. v. Hinton*,[19] the US Supreme Court ruled that the exception does not apply to associations of independent contractors or representing independent contractors.

A similar restriction is provided by the EU law. More precisely, Article 101 of the Treaty on the Functioning of the European Union (TFEU) prohibits "agreements between undertakings, decisions by associations of undertakings and concerted practices which may affect trade between Member States and which have as their object or effect the prevention, restriction or distortion of competition within the internal market". As in the US, an exception has been worked out by the European Court of Justice (ECJ) for collective negotiation aimed at "the improvement of conditions of work and employment".[20] However, collective agreements setting minimum fees for self-employed service providers are ruled out. In the *FNV Kunsten Informatie en Media* case,[21] the ECJ pointed out that service providers, even performing activities similar to those performed by employees, are in principle "undertakings" within the meaning of EU law[22]; therefore, an organisation carrying out negotiations in their name or on their behalf does not act as a trade union but as an association of undertakings, falling under the scope of Article 101 (1) TFEU. The labour exception applies only in case service providers turn out to be "false self-employed", according to the definition of "employee" provided by the ECJ itself. A definition which is very similar to that spread across EU national case laws—based on "integration into" and "dependency on" the employer's business[23]—which is not normally inclusive of WsDA as well as many other self-employed having the freedom to choose the time and place of their work. Therefore, a reinterpretation or amendment of antitrust laws would be essential if self-employed performing personal work are to have access to collectively bargained minimum wages.

The limitations imposed by antitrust law are not such as to affect the inclusion of self-employed under the scope of statutory minimum wages. Actually, in the opinion of the jurisprudence of the ECJ, even national legislations shall respect the antitrust provisions posed by Articles 101 and 102 TFEU. According to the principle of sincere cooperation set forth in Article 4 (3), member states are required not to introduce or maintain in force measures, even of a legislative or regulatory nature, which may render ineffective the competition rules applicable to undertakings.[24] Therefore, a violation of EU rules on competition is at stake whenever a member state delegates responsibility to private economic operators or bodies for making decisions affecting trade.[25] On the contrary, statutory minimum fees do not breach EU law whenever they are established first-hand by governments and public authorities or when public bodies have at least the last word on them. Normally, that is the way the various national minimum wage setting machineries work. Apart from countries where the minimum wage is established by collective agreements, just a minority reserve the minimum wage setting to a specific body (often tripartite). Probably none is entirely not under government control.

Challenges: (II) Free Movement of Services Within the EU Single Market

Still in the EU, the provision of statutory minimum fees for the self-employed at the national level will face even more complicated challenges regarding the freedom to provide services within the single market. In particular, Article 56 TFEU precludes the application of any national rules which could have the effect of making the provision of services between member states more difficult than the provision of services solely within a given member state, even if this applies without distinction to national providers of services and to those of other member states.[26]

A significant application of Article 56 by the ECJ can be found in the *Cipolla* case,[27] concerning mandatory minimum fees for lawyers provided by the Italian legislation. The court sentenced that such a provision is liable to render access to the national market more difficult for service providers established in another member state. It deprives them of the possibility of competing more effectively by requesting lower fees with service providers established in the state concerned, so the latter have greater opportunities for winning clients because of their better knowledge of the national market. The same conclusions would certainly apply to mandatory minimum fees recognised for all personal work relations.

However, there is a way out from restrictions posed by Article 56, drafted by the ECJ itself. National measures liable to hinder or make less attractive the exercise of fundamental freedoms guaranteed by the treaties, such as the freedom to provide services in another member state, are lawful if they fulfil four conditions (the so-called "Gebhard formula")[28]:

(1) *They must be applied in a non-discriminatory manner, referring to objective needs, and* (2) *they must be justified by imperative requirements in the general interest prevailing over the freedom of movement.*

Discrimination is not at stake since minimum fees would apply to all of the self-employed performing their work personally, whether they were national or foreign. It is also out of the question that the recognition of a mandatory minimum wage for employees corresponds to the general interest that might prevail over the free movement of services. Recently, this was expressly recognised by the ECJ in the RegioPost case[29]: "the imposition, under national legislation, of a minimum wage on tenderers and their subcontractors ... may, in principle, be justified by the objective of protecting workers". As I already explained, the same objectives of general interest supporting the imposition of a minimum wage for employees might support a similar measure for independent contractors, especially those getting their livelihood from work performed personally.

Moreover, if one looks at recent national legislation[30] and documents of supra-national institutions,[31] the need for protection of self-employed seems to have become a matter of "public interest". There is a clear trend towards a framework of new guarantees for the self-employed. The EU itself shares this process. A recent example is the initiative of the European Commission "Establishing a European Pillar of Social Rights Social", including among various proposals that of granting to self-employed full access to social protection, covering both social assistance and social security, under conditions comparable to those of employees (European Commission 2017). This goal, together with that of alleviating in-work poverty, appears to be fully included in the EU social policy general aims provided by Article 9 TFEU: "guarantee of adequate social protection" and "fight against social exclusion". EU institutions have been clear in considering that those targets referred to people and workers in general, regardless of their employment status (Commission of the European Communities 2006; European Parliament's Committee for Employment and Social Affairs 2011; European Economic and Social Committee 2013).

(3) *They must be suitable for securing the attainment of the objective which they pursue, and (4) they must not go beyond what is necessary in order to attain it (principle of proportionality).*

The extension of a minimum wage to "personal" self-employment is obviously, as argued above, a suitable solution for securing human dignity and preventing in-work poverty by redistributing resources to low-income workers.

The respect of proportionality depends on the (relative) level of minimum fees compared with the threshold of poverty in a given country. If minimum fees turn out to be excessive, they would certainly be considered an unacceptable restriction on the freedom to provide a service. This would not be the case if the level of minimum fees were the same as the minimum wage provided to employees. Since the imposition of host-country statutory minimum wage on posted workers is expressly recognised by Article 3 of Directive 96/71/EC as an acceptable restriction to free movement of services, it should also be considered tolerable to impose the same minimum wage on independent service providers. As repeatedly stressed above, independent contractors present a need of protection of their income similar to that concerning employees.

Conclusions

For some of the workers engaged in the gig economy, economic uncertainty is of major concern. The guarantee of a minimum wage could give them some relief. One very obvious way to achieve this target is to consider them employees. However, this does not seem feasible according to current employment tests and indicia. When platforms operate through a keen control over workers' performance, the work relationship involved could fit into an intermediate category between employment and self-employment (e.g. quasi-subordinate, employee-like persons and dependent contractors). Nonetheless, few countries—probably just the UK—extend the right to a minimum wage to these categories.

The answer to the problem of economic uncertainty affecting WsDA can then be found by changing current rules. We proposed a solution not just referring to WsDA but considering the whole category of self-employed performing "personal" work. At the end of the day, workers involved in the gig economy represent just the tip of the iceberg of alternative work arrangements departing from the traditional employment model which urge protection. However, the extension of the scope of the minimum wage to personal work relations by collective agreements would be impeded by current antitrust law. Even the extension via statutory law is not free from obstacles, especially for EU countries.

Statutory minimum fees for self-employed might represent an illicit restriction to the free movement of services on the ground of Article 56 TFEU. Nonetheless, there are good reasons to believe that the ECJ, through the lens of the so-called "Gebhard formula", would accept this restriction.

Notes

1. It has been estimated by Hagiu and Wright (2015) that an independent contractor is about 25/30% cheaper than an employee if the costs related to employment protections and social security rights are taken into consideration.
2. See, for example, Corte di Cassazione 20 Feb. 1995, no. 1827, Il Foro Italiano, 1995, I, p. 1152 and the recent Corte di Cassazione 22 Jan. 2015 no. 1178, Rivista Italiana di Diritto del Lavoro, 2015, II, p. 684.
3. See Corte di Cassazione 13 May 2004, no. 9151, Il Lavoro nella Giurisprudenza, 2004, p. 1163; Corte Costituzionale 5 Feb. 1996, no. 30, available at https://www.cortecostituzionale.it/actionGiurisprudenza.do.
4. See Corte di Cassazione 4 Feb. 1986, no. 708, Lavoro e Previdenza Oggi, 1986, p. 1122.
5. *Dependency* from the employer's business has been identified as a reliable indicator of subordination by a famous Italian Constitutional Court sentence—5 Feb. 1996, no. 30, Giustizia Civile, 1996, I, p. 915—referring to a condition of "double alienations" of the employee: "alienation (in the sense of exclusive destination for the benefit of others) from the result of the work activity, and alienation from the productive organisation of which the work performance is part". However, this approach has been rarely followed by subsequent case law.
6. *Ready Mixed Concrete (South East) Ltd v Minister of Pensions and National Insurance* [1968] 2 QB 497.
7. *Stevenson, Jordan and Harrison Ltd v Macdonald and Evans* [1952] 1 TLR 101.
8. *Market Investigations Ltd v Minister for Social Security* [1969] 2 QB 173
9. Carmichael and Leese v National Power plc (1999) UKHL 47.
10. *Montgomery v Johnson Underwood Ltd* [2001] IRLR 269; *Mingeley v Pinnock* [2004] IRLR 373.

11. More precisely (DOL 2015), the test is based on six factors: (a) the extent to which the work performed is an integral part of the employer's business, (b) the worker's opportunity for profit or loss depending on his or her managerial skill, (c) the extent of the relative investments of the employer and the worker, (d) whether the work performed requires special skills and initiative, (e) the permanency of the relationship, and (f) the degree of control exercised or retained by the employer.

12. United States District Court Northern District of California Case No. C-13-3826 EMC, *O'Connor v. Uber Technologies, Inc. et al.*, available at http://www.cand.uscourts.gov/home.

13. United States District Court Northern District of California, Case No. 13-cv-04065-VC, *Cotter et al. v. Lyft Inc.*, available at http://www.cand.uscourts.gov/home.

14. Interestingly, a rather similar argument was proposed by an Italian Court—in particular by Pretore di Milano, 20 June 1986, Rivista Italiana di Diritto del Lavoro, 1987, II, p. 76—at the end of the '80s to recognise the subordination of so-called Pony Express. However, the argument was rejected by the subsequent judgement of appeal (Trib. Milano 10 Oct. 1987, Foro Italiano, 1989, I, p. 2632), and then by the Supreme Court (Cass. 10 July 1991, no. 7608, Rivista Italiana di Diritto del Lavoro, 1992, II, p. 370).

15. *Aslam and Farrar vs. Uber B.V, Uber London Ltd. and Uber Brittania Ltd*, Case No. 2202550/2015, available at https://www.judiciary.gov.uk. For a comment of the sentence and its implication, see Freedland and Countouris 2017.

16. Employment Appeals Tribunal, Appeal No. UKEAT/0056/17/ DA, available at https://assets.publishing.service.gov.uk/media/5a046 b06e5274a0ee5a1f171/Uber_B.V._and_Others_v_Mr_Y_Aslam_and_ Others_UKEAT_0056_17_DA.pdf (accessed on 4 Dec. 2017).

17. Criticisms against intermediate category based on the Italian and Spanish experience have been put forward by many scholars: Garofalo M.G. 2003; Freedland 2007; J. Cruz Villalon 2013.

18. Recently relaunched by Davidov (2017), also with regard to Uber drivers.

19. *Columbia River Packers Assn., Inc. v. Hinton*, 315 U.S. 143 (1942), accessible at https://supreme.justia.com.

20. See the leading case C-67/96 *Albany International BV v Stichting Bedrijfspensioenfonds Textielindustrie*, ECLI:EU:C:1999:430, available at https://curia.europa.eu.

A Fair Wage for Workers On-demand via App 87

21. Case C-413/13, *FNV Kunsten Informatie en Media v Staat der Nederlanden*, ECLI:EU:C:2014:2411, available at https://curia.europa.eu.
22. More in detail, they are undertakings because (a) they offer their services for remuneration on a given market and (b) they perform their activities as independent economic operators in relation to their principal.
23. The ECJ in *FNV Kunsten Informatie en Media* (quoted above at 23) refers expressly to a person who "acts under the direction of his employer as regards, in particular, his freedom to choose the time, place and content of his work, does not share in the employer's commercial risks, and, for the duration of that relationship, forms an integral part of that employer's undertaking, so forming an economic unit with that undertaking".
24. Case C-35/99 *Criminal proceedings against Manuele Arduino, third parties: Diego Dessi, Giovanni Bertolotto and Compagnia Assicuratrice RAS SpA.*, ECLI:EU:C:2002:97; C-250/03 *G.E. Mauri v Ministero della Giustizia and Commissione per gli esami di avvocato presso la Corte d'appello di Milano*, ECLI:EU:C:2005:96 both available at https://curia.europa.eu.
25. Case 267/86, *Pascal Van Eycke v ASPA NV*, ECLI:EU:C:1988:427; Case C-185/91 *Bundesanstalt für den Güterfernverkehr v Gebrüder Reiff GmbH & Co. KG.*, ECLI:EU:C:1993:886; C-96/94, *Centro Servizi Spediporto Srl v Spedizioni Marittima del Golfo Srl*, ECLI:EU:C:1995:308, available at https://curia.europa.eu.
26. C-17/00, *François De Coster v Collège des bourgmestre et échevins de Watermael-Boitsfort*, ECLI:EU:C:2001:651; Joined cases C-544/03 and C-545/03, *Mobistar SA v Commune de Fléron and Belgacom Mobile SA v Commune de Schaerbeek*, ECLI:EU:C:2005:518, available at https://curia.europa.eu.
27. Joined cases C-94/04 and C-202/04, *Federico Cipolla v Rosaria Fazari, née Portolese and Stefano Macrino and Claudia Capoparte v Roberto Meloni*, ECLI:EU:C:2006:758, available at https://curia.europa.eu.
28. Case C-55/94, *Reinhard Gebhard v Consiglio dell'Ordine degli Avvocati e Procuratori di Milano*, ECLI:EU:C:1995:411, available at https://curia.europa.eu.
29. Case C-115/14, *RegioPost GmbH & Co. KG v Stadt Landau in der Pfalz*, ECLI:EU:C:2015:760.
30. For example, the Italian legislator has just passed the "self-employment statute" (*legge* no. 81/2017), recognising some rights, such as maternity and parental leave, a sort of sick leave and tax credit for vocational training.

88   E. Menegatti

31. A report of the ILO (ILO 2002) stressed that many ILO standards refer to "worker" and not just to "employee"; following report (ILO 2003) added that many work arrangements fall outside the employment relationship and therefore the full range of employment and social security protections is enjoyed by only a minority of the global workforce.

References

Aloisi, Antonio. 2016. Commoditized Workers: Case Study Research on Labor Law Issues Arising from a Set of "On-Demand/Gig Economy" Platforms. *Comparative Labor Law and Policy Journal* 37 (3): 653–690.

Arthurs, Harry W. 2017. *The False Promise of the Sharing Economy.* Paper Presented at the 3rd LLRN Conference, Toronto, Canada, June 25–27.

Berg, Janine. 2016. Income Security in the On-demand Economy: Findings and Policy Lessons from a Survey of Crowdworkers. *Comparative Labor Law and Policy Journal* 37 (3): 543–576.

Biagi, Marco, and Michele Tiraboshi. 1999. Le proposte legislative in materia di lavoro parasubordinato: tipizzazione di un tertium genus o codificazione di uno «statuto dei lavori»? *Lavoro e Diritto* 13 (4): 571–592.

Bronstein, Arturo. 2009. *International and Comparative Labour Law: Current Challenges.* Basingstoke: Palgrave Macmillan.

Casale, Giuseppe. 2011. *The Employment Relationship. A Comparative Overview.* Oxford: Hart Publishing.

Cherry, Miriam A. 2011. A Taxonomy of Virtual Work. *Georgia Law Review* 45 (4): 951–1013.

———. 2016. Beyond Misclassification: The Digital Transformation of Work. *Comparative Labour Law and Policy Journal* 37 (3): 577–602.

Cherry, Miriam A., and Antonio Aloisi. 2017. Dependent Contractors' in the Gig Economy: A Comparative Approach. *American University Law Review* 66 (3): 637–689.

Codagnone, Cristiano, Fabienne Abadie, and Federico Biagi. 2016. *The Future of Work in the 'Sharing Economy'. Market Efficiency and Equitable Opportunities or Unfair Precarisation?.* Institute for Prospective Technological Studies, JRC Science for Policy Report. https://ec.europa.eu/jrc/en/publication/eur-scientific-and-technical-research-reports/future-work-sharing-economy-market-efficiency-and-equitable-opportunities-or-unfair. Accessed 10 Dec 2017.

A Fair Wage for Workers On-demand via App   89

Commission of the European Communities. 2006. *Green Paper – Modernising labour law to meet the challenges of the 21st century*. http://www.europarl. europa.eu/meetdocs/2004_2009/documents/com/com_com(2006)0708_/ com_com(2006)0708_en.pdf. Accessed 10 Dec 2017.

Countouris, Nicola. 2007. *The Changing Law of the Employment Relationship: Comparative Analyses in the European Context*. Hampshire: Ashgate Publishing.

———. 2011. The Employment Relationship: A Comparative Analysis of National Judicial Approaches. In *The Employment Relationship. A Comparative Overview*, ed. Giuseppe Casale, 35–68. Oxford: Hart Publishing.

Cunningham-Parmeter, Keith. 2016. From Amazon to Uber: Defining Employment in the Modern Economy. *Boston University Law Review* 96: 1673–1728.

D'Antona, Massimo. 1996. Ridefinizione della fattispecie di contratto di lavoro. Seconda proposta di legge. In *La disciplina del mercato del lavoro. Proposte per un testo unico*, ed. Giorgio Ghezzi, 195–210. Roma: Ediesse.

Däubler, Wolfgang. 1999. Working People in Germany. *Comparative Labor Law and Policy Journal* 21 (1): 77–98.

Davidov, Guy. 2005. Who Is a Worker. *Industrial Law Journal* 34 (1): 57–91.

———. 2017. The Status of Uber Drivers: A Purposive Approach. *Spanish Labour Law and Employment Relations Journal* 6 (1–2): 6–15.

Davidov, Guy, and Brian Langille. 1999. Beyond Employees and Independent Contractors: A View from Canada. *Comparative Labor Law and Policy Journal* 21 (1): 7–46.

Davidov, Guy, Freedland Mark, and Countouris Nicola. 2015. The Subject of Labor Law: 'Employees' and Other Workers. In *Research Handbook in Comparative Labor Law*, ed. Matthew W. Finkin and Guy Mundlack, 115–131. Cheltenham: Edward Elgar.

De Stefano, Valerio. 2016a. Introduction: Crowdsourcing, the Gig-Economy, and the Law. *Comparative Labor Law and Policy Journal*. 37: 461–470.

———. 2016b. The Rise of the 'Just-in-time Workforce': On-demand Work, Crowdwork and Labour Protection in the 'Gig-economy. *Comparative Labor Law and Policy Journal*. 37 (3): 471–503.

Deakin, Simon. 2003. *Interpreting Employment Contracts: Judges, Employers, Workers*. ESRC Centre for Business Research, University of Cambridge Working Paper No. 267.

———. 2007. Does the 'Personal Employment Contract' Provide a Basis for the Reunification of Employment Law? *Industrial Law Journal* 36 (1): 68–83.

Department of Labour (DOL) Administrator's Interpretation, no. 2015-1. 2015. *The Application of the Fair Labor Standards Act's 'Suffer or Permit' Standard in the Identification of Employees Who Are Misclassified as Independent Contractors*. https://www.dol.gov/WHD/opinion/adminIntrprtnFLSA.htm. Accessed 10 Dec 2017.

Eurofound. 2015. *New Forms of Employment*. Luxembourg: Publications Office of the European Union.

European Commission. 2017. *Commission Staff Working Document Accompanying the Document Communication from the Commission to the European Parliament, the Council, the European and Social Committee and the Committee of the Regions, establishing a European pillar of social rights*. http://eur-lex.europa.eu/legal-content/EN/TXT/?uri=COM:2017:250:FIN. Accessed 10 Dec 2017.

European Economic and Social Committee. 2013. *Opinion on 'Abuse of the status of self-employed'*. http://eur-lex.europa.eu/legal-content/EN/TXT/?uri=uriserv:OJ.C_.2013.161.01.0014.01.ENG&toc=OJ:C:2013:161:TOC. Accessed 10 Dec 2017.

European Parliament's Committee for Employment and Social Affairs. 2011. *Social Protection for All, Including Self-Employed Workers*. http://www.europarl.europa.eu/sides/getDoc.do?pubRef=-//EP//TEXT+REPORT+A7-2013-0459+0+DOC+XML+V0//EN. Accessed 10 Dec 2017.

Finkin, Matthew W. 2016. Beclouded Work in Historical Perspective. *Comparative Labor Law and Policy Journal* 37 (3): 603–618.

Freedland, Mark. 2003. *The Personal Employment Contract*. Oxford: Oxford University Press.

———. 2007. Application of Labour and Employment Law Beyond the Contract of Employment. *International Labour Review* 146 (1–2): 3–20.

Freedland, Mark, and Nicola Countouris. 2011. *The Legal Construction of Personal Work Relations*. Oxford: Oxford University Press.

———. 2017. Some Reflections on the 'Personal Scope' of Collective Labour Law. *Industrial Law Journal* 46 (1): 52–71.

Gapper, John. 2015. Gig-Economy Spells End to Lifetime Careers. *Financial Times*, August 5.

Garofalo, Mario Giovanni. 2003. La legge delega sul mercato del lavoro: prime osservazioni. *Rivista Giuridica del Lavoro* I (2): 359–382.

Garofalo, Domenico. 2017. "Lavoro, impresa e trasformazioni organizzative." Paper presented at the annual meeting for the *Associazione Italiana Diritto del Lavoro e della Sicurezza Sociale*, Cassino, Italy, May 18–19.

Hagiu, Andrei, and Julian Wright. 2015. Multi-Sided Platforms. *International Journal of Industrial Organization* 43: 162–174.

Harris, Seth D., and Alan B. Krueger. 2015. *A Proposal for Modernizing Labor Laws for Twenty-first Century Work: The 'Independent Worker'.* Brookings Institute, Washington DC. http://www.hamiltonproject.org/assets/files/modernizing_labor_laws_for_twenty_first_century_work_krueger_harris.pdf. Accessed 10 Dec. 2017.

Huws, Ursula and Simon Joyce. 2016a. *Crowd Working Survey: Size of the UK's "Gig Economy" Revealed for the First Time.* http://www.feps-europe.eu/assets/a82bcd12-fb97-43a6-9346-24242695a183/crowd-working-surveypdf.pdf. Accessed 10 Dec. 2017.

———. 2016b. *Size of Germany's 'Gig Economy' Revealed for the First Time.* http://www.uni-europa.org/wp-content/uploads/2016/11/crowd_working_sur- vey_Germany.pdf. Accessed 10 Dec. 2017.

International Labour Organization (ILO). 2002. *Report IV. Decent Work in the Informal Economy.* Geneva: ILO Publications. http://www.ilo.org/public/english/standards/relm/ilc/ilc90/pdf/rep-vi.pdf. Accessed 10 Dec. 2017.

———. 2003. *Report V. The Scope of Employment Relationship.* Geneva: ILO Publications. http://www.ilo.org/public/english/standards/relm/ilc/ilc91/pdf/rep-v.pdf. Accessed 10 Dec 2017.

ISTAT. 2016. *Condizioni di vita e reddito. Anno 2015.* https://www.istat.it/it/files/2016/12/Reddito-e-Condizioni-di-vita-Anno-2015.pdf?title=Condizioni+di+vita+e+reddito+-+06%2Fdic%2F2016+-+Testo+integrale+e+nota+metodologica.pdf. Accessed 10 Dec. 2017.

Katz, Lawrence F., and Alan B. Krueger. 2016. *The Rise and Nature of Alternative Work Arrangements in the United States, 1995–2015.* NBER Working Paper No. 22667. http://www.nber.org/papers/w22667. Accessed 10 Dec 2017.

Mengoni, Luigi. 2002. Il contratto di lavoro nel XX secolo. In *Il diritto del lavoro alla svolta del secolo,* 3–22. Milano: Giuffrè.

Nogler, Luca. 2009. *The Concept of «Subordination» in European and Comparative Law.* Trento: Quaderni del Dipartimento di Scienze Giuridiche.

Pallini, Massimo. 2013. *Il lavoro economicamente dipendente.* Padova: Cedam.

Perulli, Adalberto. 2011. Subordinate, Autonomous and Economically Dependent Work: A Comparative Analysis of Selected European Countries. In *The Employment Relationship. A Comparative Overview,* ed. Giuseppe Casale, 137–187. Oxford: Hart Publishing.

Prassl, Jeremias, and Martin Risak. 2016. Uber, Taskrabbit, & Co: Platforms as employers? Rethinking the Legal Analysis of Crowdwork. *Comparative Labor Law and Policy Journal* 37 (3): 619–651.

Rogers, Brishen. 2016. Employment Rights in the Platform Economy: Getting Back to Basics. *Harvard Law & Policy Review* 10: 479–520.

Spagnuolo Vigorita, Luciano. 1969. Impresa, rapporto di lavoro, continuità (riflessioni sulla giurispruenza). *Rivista di Diritto Civile* I:570–610.

Supiot, Alain. 2000. Les nouveaux visages de la subordination. *Droit Social* 2: 131–145.

Valenduc, Gérard, and Patricia Vendramin. 2016, *Work in the Digital Economy: Sorting the Old from the New.* European Trade Union Institute, Working Paper 2016.03. https://www.etui.org/Publications2/Working-Papers/Work-in-the-digital-economy-sorting-the-old-from-the-new. Accessed 10 Dec 2017.

Villalon, Cruz J. 2013. Il lavoro autonomo economicamente dipendente in Spagna. *Diritto Lavoro Mercati*: 287–312.

Weil, David. 2015. *The Fissured Workplace: Why Work Became So Bad for So Many and What Can Be Done to Improve It.* Cambridge: Harvard University Press.

Weiss, Manfred. 2000. Employment versus Self-Employment: the Search for a Demarcation Line in Germany. In *New Trends of Labour Law in the International Horizon—Liber Amicorum for Prof. Dr. Tadashi Hanami*, 251–270. Tokyo: Shinzansha.

6

Assessment by Feedback in the On-demand Era

Alessandra Ingrao

Introduction: What Is a Feedback System?

In the era of on-demand economy, information plays a key role. In particular, if you take into consideration "gig economy" platforms, which provide services and goods, the information related to their quality is especially important (Felstiner 2011; Prassl and Risak 2016; De Stefano 2016). To obtain the latter, they use many different types of mechanisms, exploiting information and communication technology. One of these, which is common to several platforms, is represented by the use of feedback systems (Dellarocas 2003; Ghose et al. 2009; Rosenblat and Stark 2016).

Economists report that feedback systems are supplanting traditional sources of consumer information, such as advertising (You and Sikora

---

A. Ingrao (✉)
Labour Law, Department of Civil Law and Legal History, University of Milan, Milan, Italy
e-mail: alessandra.ingrao@unimi.it

© The Author(s) 2018
E. Ales et al. (eds.), *Working in Digital and Smart Organizations*,
https://doi.org/10.1007/978-3-319-77329-2_6

93

2014, p. 418). The power to rate and review service is vested in the consumer, which plays a new responsibility role in the modern social market economy. Some scholars think that becoming the producer of former consumers ("prosumer") suggests a new economic model which is different from capitalism (Harvey 2007; Rifkin 2014; Ryan 2011).

On many websites, it is usual that consumers can rate and review goods and services: TripAdvisor, for instance, provides a forum where many people offer tips on hotels and restaurants. Surfing the web, you can bump into platforms that provide service reviews. Moreover, Yelp allows customers to comment on and rate businesses. However, we are now witnessing the frequent phenomenon of "gig economy" platforms that use information, collected by the consumer of service and elaborated with feedback systems, about the quality of performance of each worker (Lee et al. 2015).

This topic will be discussed in this paper.

Feedback systems are reputation mechanisms that build trust among strangers engaging in on-demand transactions. These systems provide histories of past behaviour of a contracting party, so it records and stores its reputation, thus increasing the opportunities of well-behaved partici-pants and decreasing those of poorly behaved ones (Thierer et al. 2015). In this way, trust is improved by rewarding cooperation.

In the literature (Thierer et al. 2015; Dellarocas 2003), it is common to distinguish between online reputational systems: centralized systems and peer-to-peer–based mechanisms.

Centralized or Third-Party Mechanisms

These mechanisms have nothing to do with the personal reputation of one of the contracting parties. They build trust in the centralized plat-forms, which act as a third party seeking to facilitate transactions. eBay, for instance, has a "money back guarantee" that refunds buyers if they do not receive their items. This mechanism does not increase the buy-er's trust in the seller, but it increases the level of security in online transactions.

Peer-to-Peer Mechanisms

Ratings and reviews are among the most popular peer-to-peer feedback systems. Peer-to-peer mechanisms are related directly to the reputation of one of the contracting parties. They build trust in a relationship between the two parties involved in an online transaction because one of them rates the other by using the rating system mechanism provided by the platform (Massa 2012, p. 15).

These mechanisms were born with the Internet and have existed since the rise of eBay and Amazon. But only with the birth of Web 2.0 services, they have been endorsed by a development change due to the fact that the public was allowed "to have a voice in commercial and non-commercial transactions".

Moreover, sharing-economy digital platforms have enabled even more direct and instantaneous interactions between those supplying and those demanding services. The sharing economy relies completely on rating and review systems: many companies, such as Uber, Lyft, TaskRabbit and Helpling, solicit their customers to provide feedback and reviews in order to find out something about the performance of the crowdworkers by using several tools, from simple stars or point systems to detailed reviews. Ride-sharing companies employ some of the most extensive rating systems, whereby both the rider and driver use a five-star system to rate each other after every ride.

Peer-to-Peer Mechanisms in Gig Economy Working Relation/Contract: The Difference Between Control of Result of Activity and Monitoring of the Way of Execution

Gig economy platforms use simple star systems or point systems to check reviews from customers. Rating and review systems allow platforms to measure the quality of the service offered by one worker. They collect a huge amount of personal data in order to assign workers a "professional score" as a result of algorithmic methods. In other words, platforms analyse ratings and reviews to measure the professional reputation of each worker in order to exercise the typical employer's power of control (Sachs 2015; Dzieza 2015; De Stefano 2016).

The reason why they use this kind of method is that such a method is mainly aimed at providing a solution to the problem of asymmetric information between the parties of a contract. The platform, indeed, selects an unknown party who will do the job or provide the service requested by a client.

Someone might object that this is a traditional method of recruitment. Nevertheless, it is not the case. The so-called "sharing economy companies" use platforms to select workers "*in the crowd*". Membership of the platform is open to everyone surfing the web and having the ability to use devices that allow one to access the portal and to register in it. Therefore, platforms need to get as much information as possible about the person who will provide the service.

Particularly, where the service requires the physical presence of workers (e.g. transport or cleaning), platforms have an interest in avoiding forms of liability, which may arise from unlawful conduct that employees can perform during the course of the work. Data recorded in the US, for instance, have demonstrated that there are conspicuous cases of sexual harassment committed against consumers by workers of the platforms.

Therefore, on the one hand, it is true that peer-to-peer feedback systems ensure that platforms are providing a good quality service by means of control of service results provided by each worker. Businesses need to offer high-quality and safe services, and the consequent control of the result of work is compatible with the self-employed nature of the relationship.

On the other hand, peer-to-peer feedback systems allow companies to evaluate performance of each crowdworker controlling their personal data. They do not evaluate the result of the activity, but sometimes platforms maintain the power to control the way of work performance (Sachs 2015).

In this respect, the well-known judicial cases of Lyft and Uber— spreading all over the world, from the US to Brazil, from Switzerland to the UK[1]—are emblematic. The case law clearly shows that the functioning of peer-to-peer feedback systems is closely related to the classification issues, i.e. *whether* these workers are employees or self-employed. The debate over the status of Uber drivers (Davidov 2017; Cherry and Aloisi 2017; Aloisi 2016), who are classified as "partners" (i.e. independent contractors) under the general terms and conditions, shows that the new technological forms of organizations can be an "excuse for evading law"— not only labour law but also competition law.

Uber allows customers to rate drivers by using a five-star scale feedback system, but customers cannot rate the result of the drivers' activities.[2] Uber asks customers to rate many different skills and features of the service: the cleanliness of the car, the type of music listened to in the car, where the driver picked the passenger up, whether the Uber driver helped with luggage, etc.

Also, Lyft requires drivers to "be the only non-passenger in the car", "keep car clean on the inside and outside", "go above and beyond good service such as helping passengers with luggage or holding an umbrella for passengers when it is raining", and "greet every passenger with a big smile and a fist bump". The ground of the judgement of the London Employment Tribunal clearly shows that Uber instructs their partners, giving them a "Welcome Packet" containing materials used in "onboarding" new drivers.[3]

After that, Uber uses the peer-to-peer feedback system as *a tool to enforcing specific work rules*, which are pre-defined by Uber, as an employer. Uber controls a lot of the ways that drivers behave while they work and then check whether they respect rules, looking at customers' feedback. This is a *new form* of monitoring employees, which comes from using technology: it has nothing to do with the technological remote monitoring, bounded in the Italian legal system with the meaning of Article 4 of Worker's Statute. In fact, the algorithmic analysis of reviews used by platforms has turned customers into "unwitting and sometimes unwittingly managers" (Dzieza 2015), sometimes more efficient than an individual boss.[4]

In the platform economy, the control power leads to the exercise of disciplinary power and is also put in place in a strange and innovative way (Rosenblat and Stark 2016). When a driver's average star rating falls below a certain level, established by Uber, the company deactivates the profile of this driver in the platform. Therefore, Uber and other companies like Lyft retain the power to automatically exclude a worker from the use of the platform if his or her performance does not meet the employer's expectation. US District Judge Chen[5] stated: "Uber may terminate any driver whose star ratings falls below the applicable minimum star-rating, and a significant amount of evidence in the record indicates that Uber does, in fact, terminate drivers whose star ratings fall below a certain threshold determined by Uber". In this case, deactivation of the platform account sounds like *an unjustified dismissal.* The power to withdraw from a contract is immediate, automatic and without apology.

Uber and Lyft systems highly motivate drivers to keep their scores up. This is reflected by the fact that companies sometimes send out e-mails with very specific advice about what drivers can do to earn positive ratings, such as offering snacks or not talking to customers about other business interests.

Therefore, it is clear that the digital work platforms use digital technologies to exercise a form of control that is not compatible with the autonomous nature of the contract stated in their general terms and conditions. For this reason, the settings of feedback systems could be an element that the judge has to analyse in order to declare that an employment relationship exists between the platform and the crowdworker.

It is not fitting and efficient for gig economy platforms to hire workers as employees. First, "and most obviously, a fleet of employee drivers would be more expensive than a fleet of independent contractor drivers" (Sachs 2015a); second, if gig workers were employed, platforms would have to ensure labour law legislation, the application of which would make them lose flexibility in managing the workforce. For this reason, it is important to point out that platforms, after several court rulings that recognize the employee status of drivers, will be inclined to rapidly change the settings of feedback systems to cut the chance of that happening in the future. Presumably, they will refrain to exercising power of control as an employer and they will develop a data performance tracking method that is opaque and more refined. So it is becoming relevant for labour law scholars to study new ways to protect human dignity against algorithmic and automated decision, irrespectively of the classification of the contract.

Rating and Review Systems Under Competition Law: The Issue of Classification of Uber's Economic Activities: Is It a Mere Intermediary or a Transportation Company?

The way in which platforms use feedback systems is relevant not only under labour law but also under competition law.

In Europe, many different national courts[6] are wondering whether Uber is a mere intermediary between supply and demand of a digital service, as Uber argued, or a transportation company. Qualification of Uber's economic activities is crucial in the states where competition law imposes stricter regulation for taxi services since the provision of this type of service is subject to governmental licences and authorizations, which Uber does not have. For this reason, the Juzgado de lo Mercantil n° 3 de Barcelona ruled to refer the question concerning the classification of Uber activity to the European Court of Justice[7] in order to assess it in light of European competition law. In particular, it must be determined whether the service offered by Uber benefits from the principle of the freedom to provide services, as "information society services" under the provision of Directive on electronic commerce 2000/31/EC of the European Parliament and of the Council of 8 June 2000, or whether its services fall within the field of transport which is regulated by the law of the member states. In the first case, licences and authorizations required by a member state may be incompatible with the principle of the freedom to provide services.

The European Court of Justice will decide, presumably, in line with the opinion of Advocate General Maciej Szpunar. According to Szpunar, the service offered by Uber does not fall within the concept of "information society service" under Directive 2000/31/EC.

The opinion that Uber is a company providing a transportation service is based on the quantity of algorithmic control that Uber exercises over drivers. The Advocate General observes that drivers who work via the Uber platform "do not pursue an autonomous activity that is independent of the platform". On the contrary, that activity exists solely because of the platform, without which drivers could not work. The Advocate General also points out that Uber controls the economically important aspects of the urban transport service offered through its platform. Indeed, Uber imposes conditions which drivers must fulfil in order to take up and pursue their activity; financially rewards drivers who accumulate a large number of trips, and informs them of where and when they can rely on a high volume of trips or advantageous fares or both; exerts control over the quality of drivers' work, which may even result in the exclusion of drivers from the platform; and effectively determines the price of the service.

European Protection of Personal Data and Ratings and Reviews: The Question of Reliability of Reputational Feedback Systems

Based on the analysis of the platform feedback system, it is possible for us to deal with the second major problem arising from the use of rating and reviews: the reliability of the evaluation and reputation system (Dellarocas 2003; You and Sikora 2014; Strahilevitz 2007; Schor 2016).

The evaluation system is based on an algorithm which collects and analyses third-party evaluations of the professionalism of each worker. There is no doubt that this kind of evaluation is a form of personal data "processing" under both the Italian and European Personal Data Protection Law. And it gets really interesting when you think about those ratings and reviews coming from consumers to become personal data on workers' performance collected and "stocked" by gig economy platforms. Consequently, they fall within the scope of Directive 95/46/CE.[8] The Directive applies to personal information that is subject to "processing". For the purposes of the Directive, the term "processing" applies to a comprehensive range of activities: it includes the initial obtaining of personal information, the retention and use of it, and access and disclosure. All of these operations under the privacy regulation must be clear and transparent for data subjects (workers or independent contractors) to enable them to exercise their right to object, in whole or in part, on legitimate grounds, to the processing of personal data concerning them.

Sharing-economy rating systems, in this context, might not be the best way to predict the quality of a contractual service or to evaluate the performance of each worker. These reviews often include more subjective judgements that are not taken into account by potential buyers.[9] For this reason, feedback systems increase the risk to create inaccurate, inexact and incorrect reputational profiles, which do not provide a real representation of the evaluated subject. The risk of unreliability depends on the absence of mechanisms that ensure objectivity in evaluating performances. For instance, the kind of person who writes a review is not necessarily a good representative of all the people using the service, or review writers are likely to be people who have had either a very positive or a very negative response to a service, and often only few people rate a service.

Owing to the impact of the system on labour contractual relationships, the potential negative repercussions and damages that workers may suffer in the gig economy are especially relevant. Crowdworkers passively undergo a negative evaluation, which may have harmful consequences both on the salaries (TaskRabbit) and, in extreme cases (Uber), on the existence of their employment relationship. The gig workers, furthermore, are exposed to the risk of discriminatory decisions by users, and the dynamics of rating systems do not guarantee transparency in users' evaluation or the possibility for the evaluated party to reply (Hannak et al. 2017).

Particularly relevant in this regard is a decision of the Italian Data Protection Authority, the first Italian measure that ruled on the question of legitimacy of web-based platforms that collect, analyse and store personal data in order to create a "reputational profile".[10] The Authority declared illegal an algorithmic system which assigns to each registered user (professional) alphanumeric indicators in order to permit continuous assessment of economic and professional capacity. It was stated to be illegal on the grounds that such an activity is an affront to human dignity. By imposing a prohibition on any present and future operation of data processing, the Data Protection Authority considered that the system involves significant privacy issues because of the delicate nature of the information that it uses, the pervasive impact on the data subject, and the ways in which the company intends to put the evaluation in place. Although, in principle, it is legitimate to provide services that can help make the socio-economic relations more efficient, transparent and secure, the system under consideration of the Authority presupposes a massive collection (also online) of information which is likely to have a significant impact on the economic and social representation of a large audience (clients, candidates, entrepreneurs, freelancers and citizens). The elaborated "reputational rating" could affect the lives of "catalogued" people influencing others' choices and conditioning the evaluated subjects' facility to enjoy the admission to benefits, services or performances (Masum and Tovey 2012). As for the alleged objectivity of professional evaluation, the company was unable to demonstrate the reliability of the algorithm that would govern the determination of the rating system. Furthermore, the Data Protection Authority ruled against a kind of feedback system which does not foresee any possibility of contestation and opposition of the screened subjects. In general, the Authority doesn't want to allow an automated system to decide on such delicate and complex aspects as those related to reputation, because, in these situations, there is a high risk of creating inaccurate profiles and not responding to the social identity of people screened.

The mechanism examined by the Italian Data Protection Authority is very similar (but not identical) to the one which the platform of gig economy relies on, because it collects personal information concerning reputation and uses data to affect professional, business and worker life of the evaluated subject who passively suffered the rating evaluation.

European General Data Protection Regulation on "Automated Individual Decision Making": A New Measure for Gig Economy Workers Against Algorithmic Decision

The importance of finding legal measures which protect human dignity against algorithmic decision brings us to consider the "Copernican Revolution" in data protection law. In April 2016, for the first time in over two decades, European Parliament adopted new regulations for the collection, procession and use of personal information. The General Data Protection Regulation (GDPR) EU/2016/679 will replace the Directive 95/46/CE from 25 May 2018 in order to provide identical provisions applicable in all EU countries. The scope of the GDPR, which does not require an enabling legislation to take effect, is strengthening the protection of natural persons' information.

In this respect, the GDPR contains Article 22, which regulates "Automated individual decision-making, including profiling", which potentially prohibits a wide forms of algorithms used by the gig platform (Goodman and Flaxman 2016). Article 22 states, as a general principle, that the data subject has the right not to be subject to a decision based exclusively on automated processes which produce legal effects concerning him or her. "Profiling" aimed at "analysing or predicting aspects concerning natural person's performance" (see definitions provided by Article 4, paragraph 4) falls within the scope of Article 22.

The reasoning behind the legal provision deals with the right of a gig worker to receive a human explanation for an algorithmic decision in order to "contextualize" the platform's decision.

This has been confirmed by the exception provided in the second and third paragraphs: a total ban of automatic decisions disappears if the latter is "necessary for entering into, or performance of a contract between the data subject and a data controller"; however, even in the case of exceptions, data controllers (the platform) must provide "suitable to safeguard the data subject rights and freedoms", most notably first "the right to obtain human intervention on the part of the controller", second "to express his or her point of view" and third (and most important) "the right to contest the decision".

In view of the above, described safeguards do not solve all problems connected with the qualification issue but do have the effect to oblige all gig platforms to justify and contextualize every decision which may interfere with working lives in order to guarantee the right of defence of each worker.

The Right of Crowdworkers to Move from One Platform to Another and the Right of Data Portability

This section will discuss whether, regardless of the qualification of the contract, crowdworkers have the right to access and view the feedback score obtained from clients and whether they are entitled to transfer the ratings data from one platform to another.

As for the first question, there is no doubt that crowdworkers are aware of their professional score from the platforms. Uber drivers, for instance, have the right to see and access their current rating in the ratings tab of the platform application. Pursuant to privacy regulations, data subjects can still use their right "to obtain from controller confirmation as to whether or not personal data concerning him or her are being processed and access to the personal data".

The answer to the second question is more complicated. There is no doubt that once a person worked for a certain period of time for an employer, the employee has built up a background of knowledge, which will take with him or her if he or she changes job. It is also possible that his or her former employer will get in touch with the new one in order to give references on the worker. This can also happen to crowdworkers. It has been said that their professional skills are measured by the platform algorithms based on the customer feedback. Therefore, the problem is whether it is possible to assign to each crowdworker the right to transfer the feedback obtained from one platform to another. This is very important within a market as highly competitive as the gig economy, in which one worker can perform his duty to several platforms.

Article 20 of GDPR 2016/679 introduced a new right to "data portability" laid down in Article 20 of GDPR. It states: "The data subject shall have the right to receive the personal data concerning him or her, which he or she has provided to a controller, in a structured, commonly used and machine- readable format and have the right to transmit those data to another controller without hindrance from the controller to which the data have been provided (...)". The purpose of the right to data portability is, on the one hand, to empower the "data subject", giving him or her more control over the processing of his or her personal data by one "data controller" and, on the other hand, to support the free flow of personal data in the European market with a view to promote competition between service providers and, in general, "data controllers".[11]

Right to data portability allows the direct transmission of personal data from one data controller to another in a structured, commonly used and machine-readable format. This kind of right might be helpful to gig economy workers because it will help them switch between different competitive platforms. For instance, an Uber driver who can move to Lyft, taking his professional rating score with him, is not discouraged from leaving Uber, because he does not have to start over to build his personal rating score when moving to a new platform. By providing gig working empowerment by preventing lock-in, the right to data portability is expected to foster opportunities to share rating scores between different platforms in a safe and secure manner.

In regard to the requirements of Article 20 GDPR, only personal data "*provided*" to a data controller by an individual are included in the scope of the right to data portability. Moreover, Article 20, paragraph 4, GDPR states that compliance with this right shall not adversely affect the rights and freedoms of third parties. In our case, third parties are the consumers-users who, under the heading of freedom of expression, expressed their evaluation on the service.

The first condition does not raise any significant problem: Article 20 GDPR states that only personal data fall within the scope of the right to data portability. This means that any anonymous data will not fall within such scope. In addition, Article 29 (Working party) states that when personal data, processed by a controller (the platform), include information on personal data of several data subjects, "data controllers must not take an overly restrictive interpretation" to the requirement of Article 20.[12] In regard to the second condition, the requirement of data provided by the subject constitutes a major obstacle in the recognition of the right to data portability of crowdworkers. In fact, in the opinion of Article 29—which is soft law and therefore not legally binding—"provided by" means that only data totally generated by data subjects fall within the scope of the right to data portability. Data created by the platform algorithm via ratings and reviews of customers are "inferred" and "derived", even though such data may be part of the worker profile stored by the platform.[13]

In light of the above, the denial of the right to data portability can be a source of economic damages for gig workers; for this reason, in the context of a sharing economy, a broad interpretation, which includes inferred and derived personal data about professional reputations in the concept of data "provided" by data subjects, must be adopted.

Notes

1. The first judicial cases were American. Many administrative bodies have concluded for the existence of form of employment, using the right to control test and the economic reality test: US Labor Commissioner of the State of California, O'Connor v. Uber Technologies Inc., n. C-13-3826, EMC, 2015; Id., Berwick v. Uber Technologies, Inc., C-11-46,739 EK, 2015; Bureau of Labour and Industries of Oregon, Advisory Opinion, 14 Oct. 2015; the Department of Labour and Workforce Development, Alaska, 3 Sept. 2015, with which Uber is obliged to pay employee contributions to the State; United States District Court for the District of Columbia, Erik Search v. Uber Technologies Inc., Defendants Civil Action n. 15–257 (JEB), in a case of civil liability. After that, two Brazilian courts reached the conclusion that Uber drivers are employees because they receive by Uber detailed instruction and are subjected to algorithmic control: Tribunal Regional do Trabalho da 03ª Região, 33ª Vara do Trabalho de Belo Horizonte, Brazil, 13 Feb. 2017, n. 2534b89 and Tribunal Regional do Trabalho da 2ª Região, 13a Vara do Trabalho de São Paulo, 20 April 2017, n. e852624; *contra* Tribunal Regional do

Trabalho da 03ª Região, 09ª Turma, Minas Gerais, Brazil, 23 May 2017, n.75181a9. After that, in Switzerland, the National Institute of Social Security, Suva (http://www.cdt.ch/svizzera/cronaca/169480/uber-deve-pagare-i-contributi-sociali, 5 Jan. 2017) stated that Uber drivers are employees because the platform is not a simple tool that connects customers seeking driving services, but it acts like an employer. Finally, it is crucial to mention the decision of the London Employment Tribunal, 28 Oct. 2016, Aslam, Farrar e a. v Uber, c. 2,202,551, *Dir. rel. Ind.*, 2017, 2, commented by D. Cabrelli. The judge stated that Uber riders *are* "workers" and not employees, and so they have right to minimum wage and working time, because they aren't under any obligation to switch on the Application or, even if logged on, to accept any driving assignment that may be offered to them and stated that "these freedoms" are incompatible with the existence of an employment relationship.

2. General condition of Uber contract stated: "Star Ratings. After every trip, drivers and riders rate each other on a five-star scale and give feedback on how the trip went. This two-way system holds everyone accountable for their own behaviour. Accountability helps create a respectful, safe environment for riders and drivers. Drivers can see their current rating in the Ratings tab of the Uber Partner app.

How is my rating as a driver calculated? Your rating is based on an average of the number of post-trip stars riders gave you (from 1 to 5 stars). In the Partner app, you'll see your rating as an average of the last 500 rated trips, or the total number of rated trips you've taken if less than 500.

The easiest way to keep your average rating high is to provide good service on every trip. Drivers on the Uber platform provide excellent service, so most trips run smoothly. But we know that sometimes a trip doesn't go well, which is why we only ever consider an average of many ratings when calculating your rating instead of individual trips.

What leads to deactivation? There is a minimum average rating in each city. This is because there are cultural differences in the way people in different cities rate each other. We will alert you by email and text message if your rating is approaching this limit.

We check your rating after every 50 rated trips, so that we can let you know as early as possible if you are approaching this limit and provide you with any support you might need to improve your rating, like tips from our top-rated partner-drivers.

108 A. Ingrao

If you are a new driver and your rating falls below the minimum in your first 50 trips, we will invite you to participate in a quality session for further support, either online or in person at the Uber office.

If your average rating still falls below the minimum after multiple notifications after a 50 trip period, your account will be reviewed and may in some cases be deactivated".

3. *London Employment Tribunal*, 28 Oct. 2016, cit. The judge makes a very detailed analysis of the operation of feedback system in the chapter called "Instruction, management and control or preserving the integrity of the platform?". He describes the way in which Uber instructs drivers to ensure a satisfactory "rider experience" to the customers. Uber gives a "Welcome packet" to each driver containing material, including "5 Star tips" that explain "What riders like" and "What Uber Looks For". Then Uber uses the rating system as a tool to exercise control over drivers and their behaviour.

4. Tribunal Regional do Trabalho da 03ª Região, 33ª Vara do Trabalho de Belo Horizonte, in which Judge Filipe de Souza Sickert explains that technological power of the gig economy platform has been dramatically exaggerated.

5. O'Connor v. Uber Technologies, Inc. et al., C13–3826 EMC.

6. Compare, *College van Berop voor het bedrijfsleven* (Paesi Bassi), 8 Dec. 2014, AWB 14/726, ECLI:NL:CBB:2014:450; Trib. Milano, 2 July 2015, n. 35,445 e 36,491, *Riv. it. dir. Lav.*, 2016, II, commented by A. Donini; *London Employment Tribunal*, 28 Oct. 2016, cit.; *Audiencia Provincial de Madrid*, 23 Jan. 2017, n. 15, Trib. Torino, sez. I civ., 24 March 2017 n. 1553, Trib. Roma, sez. IX, 7 April 2017, n. 76,465; *Juzgado de lo Mercantil* di Barcellona, 7 Aug. 2015 n. 3;

7. ECJ, c-434/2015, Asociación Profesional Elite Taxi/Uber Systems Spain.

8. Working Party ex art. 29, opinion no. 4/2007;

9. It's very interesting the Italian case law about the civil liability of intermediaries like TripAdvisor that comes from fake reviews: Trib. Rimini, 7 May 2013, *Dir. informazione e informatica*, 3, 2013, 382–389. See also decision of Authority for Communications Guarantees, 22 Dec. 2014, proc. PS9345 "TripAdvisor—false recensioni online", with which the Authority impose a fine of 500,000 euros to the Platform because it hasn't an appropriate control system against "fake reviews". The sanction has been cancelled by the Administrative Court, Tar Lazio, sez. I, 13 July

Assessment by Feedback in the On-demand Era **109**

2015 no. 9355, because TripAdvisor cannot be held responsible for a misleading business practice because the deceit is not relevant enough.

10. Italian Data Protection Authority, decision no. 488 del, 24 Nov. 2016, [doc. Web n. 5,796,783], "Piattaforma web per l'elaborazione di profili reputazionali". Compare also Italian Data Protection Authority, Newsletter no. 423 del, 28 Dec. 2016, "No all'algoritmo della reputazione, viola la dignità della persona".

11. Compare, Article 29 Data Protection Working Party, *Guideline on the right to data portability*, adopted on 13 Dec. 2016.

12. Article 29 Data Protection Working Party, *Guideline*, cit. 7. They provide the example of telephone records which may include details of other people, especially parties involved in incoming and outgoing calls. In this case pursuant to Opinion of Article 29, the data subject has the right to transmit data from one controller to another one.

13. Compare Article 29 Data Protection Working Party, *Guideline*, cit. 8, which states "For example a credit score or the outcome of an assessment regarding the health of a user is a typical example of inferred data".

References

Aloisi, Antonio. 2016. Case Study Research on Labour Law Issues Arising from a Set of "On-demand/Gig Economy Platforms". *Comparative Labor Law & Policy Journal* 37 (3): 653–690.

Cherry, Miriam A., and Antonio Aloisi. 2017. "Dependent Contractors" in the Gig Economy: A Comparative Approach. *American University Law Review* 66 (3): Article 1.

Davidov, Guy. 2017. The Status of Uber Drivers: A Purposive Approach. *Spanish Labour Law and Employment Relation Journal* 6 (1/2): 6–15.

De Stefano, Valerio. 2016. The Rise of the "Just-in-Time Workforce": On-demand Work, Crowdwork and Labor Protection in the "Gig-Economy". *Comparative Labor Law & Policy Journal* 37 (3): 471–504.

Dellarocas, Chrysanthos. 2003. The Digitalisations of Word of Mouth: Promise and Challenges of Online Feedback Mechanisms. *Management Science* 49 (10): 1407–1424.

Dzieza, Josh. 2015. The Rating Game. How Uber and Its Peers Turned Us into Horrible Bosses. https://www.theverge.com/2015/10/28/9625968/rating-system-on-demand-economy-uber-olive-garden. Accessed 28 Oct 2017.

Felstiner, Alek. 2011. Working the Crowd: Employment and Labor Law in the Crowdsourcing Industry. *Berkeley Journal of Employment & Labor Law* 32 (1): 143–204.

Ghose, Anindya, Panagiotis G. Ipeirotis, and Arun Sundararajan. March 20, 2009. *The Dimensions of Reputation in Electronic Markets*. NYU Center for Digital Economy Research Working Paper No. CeDER-06-02. Available at SSRN: https://ssrn.com/abstract=885568 or https://doi.org/10.2139/ssrn.885568.

Goodman, Bryce, and Seth Flaxman. 2016. European Union Regulations on Algorithmic Decision-Making and a "Right to Explanation". Paper presented at annual ICML Workshop on Human Interpretability in Machine Learning, New York, June 23.

Hannak, Anikò, Claudia Wagner, David Garcia, Alan Misolve, Markus Strohmaier, and Christo Wilson. 2017. Bias in Online Freelance Marketplaces: Evidence from TaskRabbit and Fiverr. Paper presented in 20th ACM Conference on Computer-Supported Cooperative Work and Social Computing (CSCW 2017), Portland, February.

Harvey, David. 2007. Breve storia del neoliberalismo. Milano:Il Saggiatore p. 54 ss.

Lee, Min Kyung, et al. 2015. Working with Machines: The Impact of Algorithmic and Data-Driven Management on Human Workers. In *Proceedings of the 33rd Annual ACM Conference on Human Factors in Computing Systems, CHI'15*, 1603–1612. New York: ACM. https://doi.org/10.1145/2702123.2702548.

Massa, Paolo. 2012. Trust It Forward: Tyranny of the Majority or Echo Chambers? In *The Reputation Society: How Online Opinions Are Reshaping the Offline World*, ed. Hassan Masum and Mark Tovey. Cambridge: The MIT Press.

Masum, Hassan, and Mark Tovey, eds. 2012. *The Reputation Society: How Online Opinions Are Reshaping the Offline World*. Cambridge: The MIT Press.

Prassl, Jeremias, and Martin Risak. 2016. Uber, Taskrabbit and Co: Platforms as Employers? Rethinking the Legal Analysis of Crowdwork. *Comparative Labour Law & Policy Journal* 37 (3): 619–651.

Rifkin, Jeremy. 2014. La società a costo marginale zero. Milano:Giuffrè 352 ss. and 396 ss.

Rosenblat, Alex, and Luke Stark. 2016. Algorithmic Labor and Information Asymmetries: A Case Study of Uber's Drivers. *International Journal of Communication* 10: 3758–3784.

Ryan, Johnny. 2011. Storia di internet e il futuro digitale. Torino:Einaudi, 166 ss.

Sachs, Benjamin. 2015. Uber and Lyft: Customer Reviews and the Right-to-Control. Last modified 20 May www.onlabor.org.

———. 2015a. Uber: Employee Status and "Flexibility." Last modified 25 September www.onlabor.org.

Schor, Juliet. 2016. Debating the Sharing Economy. *Journal of Self-Governance and Management Economics* 3: 7–22.

Strahilevitz, Lior J. 2007. Wealth Without Markets? The Wealth of Networks: How Social Production Transforms Markets and Freedom. *The Yale Law Journal* 116: 1472–1516.

Thierer, Adam, Christopher Koopman, Anne Hobson, and Chris Kuiper. 2015. How the Internet, the Sharing Economy, and Reputational Feedback Mechanisms Solve the "Lemons Problem". Mercatus Center at George Mason University Working Paper, Arlington, May, 1–47.

You, Liangjun, and Riyaz Sikora. 2014. Performance of Online Reputation Mechanisms Under the Influence of Different Types of Biases. *Information Systems and e-Business Management* 3: 417–442.

7

The Classification of Crowdwork and Work by Platforms: Alternatives and Implications

Gionata Cavallini

Introduction: The Challenge of Platform Work

Nosedive, the first episode of the third season of the British series *Black Mirror*, released worldwide on Netflix in October 2016, depicts a dystopian reality where everyone can give a score to anyone else through a five-star system implemented on their smartphones, displaying everyone's name and current rating. As personal rating determines social status and access to the best jobs and housing, Lacie, the main character, spends most of her day frenetically handling her smartphone trying to improve her rating, until she goes through a sudden and unexpected rating decrease. Such a "nosedive" will drive her to madness while the spectator falls as well into increasing anxiety towards the sinister and yet believable reality she lives in. The episode witnesses quite precisely how "digitalisation" is not just the breakout of new organisational and productive

---

G. Cavallini (✉)
Labour Law, Department of Civil Law and Legal History, University of Milan, Milan, Italy
e-mail: gionata.cavallini@unimi.it

© The Author(s) 2018
E. Ales et al. (eds.), *Working in Digital and Smart Organizations*,
https://doi.org/10.1007/978-3-319-77329-2_7

schemes. It interferes with the very essence of human life, reshaping the invisible borders between work time and free time and between work place and home, as anyone who gets work mails on his or her smartphone, at any time of day or night, can confirm.

Lightening the risks of reputational systems, *Nosedive* makes a fine yet clear reference to Uber's five-star rating system, one of the core points of the organisational scheme of the famous American platform. Reputational systems constitute one of the *leitmotifs* of many of the platforms offering "digital work" services, including "crowdwork"[1] and "work by platform"[2] (or "work-on-demand-via-app"), the two main forms of work which emerged in the so-called "gig economy" (De Stefano 2016; Prassl and Risak 2016; Däubler and Klebe 2016; Dagnino 2015).

Notwithstanding the differences among the many platforms of the gig economy, in regard to the nature of their activities and to the functioning of their online applications (Aloisi 2016; Valenduc and Vendramin 2016), there are significant similarities with respect to the legal schemes they adopt to organise the workforce, which call for a unitary legal approach. In fact, the gig economy platforms claim that they operate under a legal scheme where there is no room for the application of statutory employment law. The terms and conditions set by the platforms contain specific "independent contractor clauses", which expressly underline that the worker is performing services as an independent contractor and not as an employee nor as a worker within the meaning of any statutory employment law provision.[3] The temporal and spatial flexibility enjoyed by the worker, who is in most cases theoretically free to decide *when* or *where* to work (or both), is an element of rupture with the traditional notion of employee. Platforms take advantage of this situation and seem to be capable of denying that they carry any employer's obligation, although they exercise significant control in many aspects of the transaction.

The organisational models adopted by the gig economy platforms question several legal disciplines, from contract law to competition law, but it is perhaps in the field of labour law that their challenge (Weiss 2016) undermines a truly founding idea: the idea, enshrined in the International Labour Organization's motto, that "labour is not a commodity".

From the perspective of undertaking the challenge of platform work and of the commodification of labour it entails (Bergvall-Kåreborn and Howcroft 2014; Aloisi 2016), this contribution aims to analyse the different paths pursued by case law and legal literature in order to prevent platform workers from falling into an "empty space of law". To this end, the contribution will examine the attempts to seek the reclassification of platform workers as subordinate employees in order to provide them with employment rights, and, in the second instance, it will try to verify whether it is useful and possible to search for protective provisions even outside the field of statutory employment law.

The Reclassification of the Platform Work Relationship

The classification of the labour relationship as one of employment or self-employment represents a crucial standpoint in almost every jurisdiction (Perulli 2003, p. 6) as well as in International Law (Creighton and McCrystal 2016). On the ground of their supposed higher bargaining power and economic independence, employees generally enjoy several statutory provisions (on wages, on working time, on leaves, on the discipline of dismissal, and on social security benefits) that independent contractors do not.

It is quite difficult to qualify digital workers univocally, either as employees or as independent contractors, as they find themselves in some sort of grey area between autonomy and subordination (Felstiner 2011, p. 168). The platform operates at the same time as a broker matching labour supply and demand, as a provider of goods and services and as an employer establishing the most important rules governing the transaction (Tullini 2015, p. 8), including its termination, which may consist of the deactivation of the worker's account.

As one of the first decisions from the US litigation on platform drivers pointed out very clearly, "*Lyft drivers don't seem much like employees* [...] *but Lyft drivers don't seem much like independent contractors either*".[4] In the US, the difficulties in reaching a clear consensus on the legal status of platform workers brought a significant litigation (Cherry 2016), which appeared to undermine the entrepreneurial model adopted by the platforms (Kessler 2015; DeAmicis 2015). Notwithstanding the worldwide debate it gave rise to, as many platforms agreed to negotiate millionaire settlements (Cherry 2016, p. 584) or even decided unilaterally to acknowledge the employee status of their workers (Alba 2015), the question is still open.

It is also hard to properly assimilate digital workers to the intermediate categories of "quasi-subordinate workers" or "dependent contractors", which have been developed in several legal systems and proposed as an instrument for the modernisation of labour law in the twenty-first century (Harris and Krueger 2015). In general, the notion of "economic dependency" postulates that the worker devotes the main part of his or her activity to a single client (Perulli 2015a, p. 16), whereas in the case of digital work there is often no stable counterparty to burden with duties and responsibilities (Forlivesi 2016, p. 666). Moreover, some platforms did qualify their workers as quasi-subordinate workers (e.g. the case of the "foodora" delivery platform in Italy), and yet the platform was able to pay fees far under the minimum wage, as workers would earn something like four gross euros per hour. The qualification in terms of quasi-subordinate work is not per se sufficient to guarantee further protection and should not be considered a sort of panacea (De Stefano 2016, p. 497; Cherry and Aloisi 2017, p. 688).

The judicial claim to obtain the reclassification of the relationship, with the consequent application of statutory employment law as a whole, does indeed appear to be the most direct and efficient strategy in order to provide the highest degree of protection to platform-mediated workers. This is the perspective of the first European decision on the *status* of Uber drivers[5] (Lloyd 2016; Davidov 2017), issued by London's Employment Tribunal and recently confirmed by the Employment Appeal Tribunal,[6] as well as of some Brazilian judgements.[7]

Emphasising a series of circumstances—from the fact that Uber interviews and recruits drivers to the fact that Uber subjects drivers to the rating system and reserves the power to unilaterally amend the terms and conditions of the contract—the British judge ruled that Uber drivers are not independent contractors but do fall within the notion of "worker", an intermediate category of workers who enjoy statutory employment law provisions on minimum wage and paid leave.

The anti-formalistic approach of the British judge reflects the efforts of the literature that suggested determining the scope of statutory employment law by adopting a functional approach to the concept of employer instead of by recurring to the "received" notion of employee (Prassl 2015), even with particular reference to platform work (Prassl and Risak 2016).

The Opportunity to Conceive Alternatives Paths: The Case of Italy

However, the strategy of reclassification may not always be adequate, correct or sufficient. Even the Employment Tribunal of London admitted that Uber "*could have devised a business model not involving [it] employing drivers*",[8] and the Advocate General of the EU, delivering his opinion in the Uber Case pending before the European Court of Justice, noticed that "*the company may very well provide its services through independent traders*".[9]

Moreover, platform work is a global phenomenon, which has to pass through the lenses of different legal systems, characterised by relevant differences with concern to the several criteria that employment judges use to classify the relationship correctly.

In some jurisdictions, judicial reclassification would be extremely difficult to reach, as judges would give crucial relevance to the circumstance that the worker is not technically bound to perform the assigned tasks in so far as he or she is free to decide *when* and *how much* to work.

In such jurisdictions, it seems necessary to make further reflections on the development—both at an interpretative and at a policy-making level—of protective schemes applicable to all human beings who work, regardless of the legal scheme under which they carry out their activities (Tullini 2015, p. 9).

This happens to be the case in Italy, where gig economy–related litigation was raised first on competition law issues (Rampazzo 2015), and licenced taxi drivers successfully prevented Uber from releasing the UberPop service, which would have allowed (unlicenced) private citizens to provide transportation services.[10] The Italian gig economy faced its first defiance from the labour side in October 2016, when the workers of the delivering platform foodora took collective action against the decision of the company to change their payment scheme from a gross hourly rate of 5.60 euros to a payment of three gross euros for each drop (Mosca 2016). The mobilisation of foodora riders brought the problem of platform work to the centre of the debate, reaching the cover of the prestigious magazine *Internazionale* (translating into Italian O'Connor 2016), and required the intervention of the Labour Department, after which the company increased the payment for each drop to four gross euros (Savelli 2016). During the protests, the platform deactivated some of the workers' accounts, and the judicial claim against the dismissal—which postulates the ascertainment of a subordinate employment relationship—is pending before the Tribunal of Turin.

Although in Italy the ascertainment of the employment status follows a path that is similar to the several employment tests developed in common law systems, to seek the reclassification of many digital workers under Italian law could be somewhat "gasping" (Tullini 2015, p. 11).

Italian labour law, like many other continental systems, provides for a unitary notion of employee, i.e. "*who engaged himself to cooperate for remuneration in an enterprise by working manually or intellectually under the direction of the entrepreneur*" (Treu 2007, p. 35). The identification of the characters of the employee's *subordination*—as opposite to the self-employed worker's *autonomy*—has always been an evergreen topic, accompanying the development of Italian labour law from its very beginning to the challenges brought by technological innovation (Razzolini 2014).

The reasoning made by case law and administrative authorities on the qualification of the *status* of pony expresses and of call centre workers represented an important step in the elaboration of the criteria used to identify employment relationships. Today, before the challenge of the platform economy, that reasoning looks like the most persuasive argument for whoever would have to sustain the self-employment *status* of platform workers.

The Status of "Workers On-Demand-via-App" in Light of Italian Case Law on Pony Express Workers

If you just change his old-fashioned walky-talky with a smartphone, a pony express worker from the roaring '80s would offer many similarities to the forms of work by platform related to present-day delivery services such as Deliveroo, foodora and JustEat, whose drivers one can easily spot in many Italian streets (Ichino 2016; Di Vico 2016).

Significant litigation accompanied the development of the pony express business model, together with an animated doctrinal debate (De Angelis 1988; Chiesi 1986). Several first-instance judges acknowledged the existence of employment relationships in labour proceedings promoted by the worker[11] or by the Social Security Authority[12] and in criminal trials.[13] Emphasising the economic dependency of the worker, his or her insertion into an entrepreneurial organisation, the control exercised by the company and the continuity of the performance, those decisions deemed as irrelevant the allegation that workers were free to refuse the single tasks assigned, rejecting the companies' main defence. Such decisions in fact represented the attempt to interpret the notion of "employee" as an open reference *"to the economic and social reality in its variety and historical dynamicity"*,[14] subverting the formalistic orientation followed by Italian case law based exclusively on the existence of a technical tie of subordination. The reasoning made more than 30 years ago that *"it is not realistic to sustain that messengers are free to accept or decline the single task. [...] once he chooses to work to gain money, the messenger is substantially bound to answer the call"*[15] indeed resembles some of the considerations made by the British judge in the Uber case, who noticed that Uber drivers *"are never under any obligation to switch on the App"*.[16]

Higher courts, however, did not embrace this interpretation and overruled the first-instance decisions. According to second-instance judges, the freedom to refuse tasks represented precisely the main element excluding the existence of a tie of subordination[17] and the material continuity of the activity was *per se* irrelevant. Some authors defended such an outcome, sustaining a legal-only notion of continuity, meant as the "*legitimate expectation of the creditor on the continuity of the performance according to a program agreed in advance*" (Ichino 1987, p. 80).

Since higher courts continue to uphold this orientation,[18] it seems difficult for those digital workers from the transportation or delivering sectors to achieve reclassification, except for the possibility of individuating elements of distinction with the pony express cases.

The Status of Crowdworkers in Light of Italian Decisions on Call Centre Workers

As they gave rise to the most massive concentration of allegedly self-employed workers in a particular economic sector, call centres were at the heart of the literature's reflections in the first decade of this century (Marazza 2007; Maresca and Carollo 2007) and became emblematic of the condition of precariousness of many Italian workers, deserving a role in popular culture and cinema.[19]

Some of the conclusions reached by legal literature, case law and public authorities on the issue of the classification of call centre workers should be taken into consideration when it comes to the classification of crowdworkers, who constitute a *global* and *virtual* workforce performing their tasks online (Dagnino 2015, p. 90).

In fact, there is not that much difference between some of the human intelligence tasks crowdsourced through Amazon Mechanical Turk and other crowdsourcing platforms and the tasks performed in call centres. In both cases, we are facing labour-intensive activities involving the execution of monotonous and repetitive "microtasks".

Also owing to the political relevance of the problem of repressing misguided employment relationships, the Italian Ministry of Labour repeatedly issued interpretative criteria to determine the conditions under which it was possible to work in call centres under the scheme of self-employment.

A 2006 circular addressed to labour inspectors[20] clarified that only call centre workers who perform *in-bound* activities—i.e. who undertake to answer to incoming calls—shall always be deemed employees. With reference to *out-bound* workers—i.e. those who undertake a campaigning project consisting of performing a certain number of calls—the circular stated that it is possible to qualify the relationship as a self-employed one insofar as the worker is free *"a) to decide whether to perform the activity and when; b) to schedule the daily working time; c) to suspend the execution of the performance"*. The circular also had a significant impact on case law, and some decisions deeming out-bound workers as self-employed,[21] but other judgements emphasised the non-binding nature of the document,[22] highlighted also by some scholars (Roccella 2008, p. 27).

A second circular[23] narrowed the scope of self-employed work in call centres, individuating a series of factors which would entail reclassification of *out-bound* workers (*in primis* the lack of the specific determination of the promotional campaign assigned to the worker), but the successive centre-right government immediately overruled such indications.[24]

Even adopting the broadest approach, however, the subjection to the direction of the employer also with regard to the definition of the working time still represents an element that is necessary in order to claim the existence of an employment status.

As crowdworkers do not share any spatial relationship with the platform, it would be even more difficult to classify them as employees. Not only are they—like the *out-bound* call centre workers—free to determine their working schedule but also they retain *"the freedom to choose when and where to work, how long to spend, and what work to perform"* (Felstiner 2011, p. 154).

Self-Employed Workers, in Many Cases

The considerations set forth on platform workers' legal *status* under Italian law suggest that even though the language used in platform terms and conditions indeed deserves a degree of scepticism, the claim that platforms cannot be properly considered employers is not that easy to undermine. Even outside of Italian law and its narrow notion of employee, the classification in terms of self-employment laid down in the platform terms and conditions appeared convincing at least *de iure condito*, except for pathological cases (Bergvall-Kåreborn and Howcroft 2014, p. 218; Dagnino 2015, p. 91; Däubler and Klebe 2016, p. 474; De Stefano 2016, p. 478), notwithstanding the attempts to sustain the thesis of reclassification (Prassl and Risak 2016).

The conclusion that the examined platform workers can be self-employed contractors does not derive from an overvaluation of the contractual label (*nomen iuris*), which is always irrelevant for labour law, but from the consideration that as long as they truly retain the freedom to choose *when* and *where* to work, they are not actually bound to any directive power.

Such a conclusion is also coherent with European law, as the European Court of Justice individuated a narrow notion of subordination, meant as the subjection of the worker to "*the direction of his employer as regards, in particular, his freedom to choose the time, the place and the object of his work*".[25]

Not Just an Intermediary

Although we have seen that the qualification in terms of self-employment laid down by the platforms may appear convincing, the claim that they are mere intermediaries between the workers and the clients seems to be more artificial, almost absurd (Weiss 2016, p. 656; Donini 2016, p. 166). About Uber's activity, labour judges pointed out that "*Uber does not simply sell software; it sells rides*"[26] and that it is "*unreal to deny that Uber is in business as a supplier of transportation services. Simple common sense argues to the contrary*".[27] Even competition law judges held the platform responsible for conducting a transportation service,[28] and a Barcelona judge requested a preliminary ruling from the European Court of Justice,[29] asking whether Uber runs a transportation service or is just a technological company.

The platform indeed acts as a "cumbersome middleman" (Donini 2015, p. 59; Moatti 2015), and the intermediation contracts are both deeply connected with the self-employment contract. In fact, the intermediation contract sets the frame within which several self-employment contracts are stipulated by the worker and a plurality of clients.

The following paragraphs will try to analyse more in depth the relationships involved in such a scheme, in order to verify whether—when reclassification may not be accorded—the rules governing the transaction may prevent digital workers from falling into an "empty space of law".

As platforms do intermediate, they will respond to the obligations deriving from the intermediation contracts they subscribe with the users and, most important, with the workers. However, as they also set the rules governing the self-employment relationship, they do become a party to that relationship or, at the very least, they may still be held responsible for those breaches of the self-employment contract in which they participated, even when the input comes from the user.

A good example of the effects of the contractual integration between the self-employment relationship and the frame intermediation contract comes from Chinese case law regarding the platform Didi Chuxing, which acquired Uber's Chinese operations in August 2016. Although Chinese courts were reluctant to accord the reclassification of the drivers' relationship, they have imposed some degree of responsibility on the platforms in cases concerning liability for traffic accidents, brought forward by third parties seeking compensation for incidents (Zou 2017).

Therefore, from the functional perspective of contractual integration, the worker can enforce his or her rights related to the self-employment relationship also against the platform. But which rights are we talking about?

Private Law Remedies for Digital Workers: In Particular, the Protection Against "Unfair Deactivation"

In most jurisdictions, the discipline of self-employed work contracts is quite gaunt (only seven articles in the Italian civil code, Articles 2222 to 2228) and it tends to construe the notion of "self-employed work" in the negative by stressing the lack of subordination of the worker. Labour lawyers, with some exceptions (Perulli 1996), have not often focused on such discipline, as they have limited the analysis to the primary problem of qualification (Carinci 2012, p. 176).

The challenge of platform work, however, could be an opportunity to develop new perspectives about the legal protection of self-employed personal work. In the last decades, European contract law has indeed developed a human dimension in regulating contracts characterised by the imbalance of the parties (Nogler and Reifner 2014) thanks to the legislative intervention in the field of consumer protection law and B2b contracts[30] (Gitti and Villa 2008). From this perspective, it has been underlined that nowadays contract law—perhaps even more than labour law itself—represents "*a fruitful field for the ethical evaluation of entrepreneurial behaviours*" (Perulli 2015b, p. 83).

In Italy, where the reclassification of platform worker would be difficult to reach, some important rules would still apply to platform work contracts: self-employment rules and standards; private law general principles, such as the principle of good faith and correctness, prohibiting those behaviours that result in the abusive exercise of the rights descending from the contract (Morello 2013, p. 685); and B2b contracts discipline, prohibiting the "abuse of economic dependency" of the worker on a main client.

The combination of these provisions may result in a discipline capable of providing protection against some of the critical issues raised by platform-mediated work.

For example, most platforms retain the power to exclude the worker from the use of the platform by deactivating his or her account. The relevance of the problem emerges when taking into account the circumstance that one of the conditions contained in the *Cotter v. Lyft* settlement proposal provided for the enforcement of a grievance process before account deactivation (Cherry 2016, p. 583).

If platform workers are reclassified as employees, such deactivation shall be considered a dismissal and therefore would require a justification under statutory employment provisions regarding the termination of the employment relationship, as provided for also at a supranational level by article 28 of the Charter of Nice and Article 30 of the European Social Charter. Self-employed workers, instead, do not enjoy the same warranties.

The Classification of Crowdwork and Work by Platforms... 125

On the other hand, if we consider deactivation not as the termination of the labour relationship but as the termination of the intermediation frame contract, we could try to recur to contract law general principles and B2b contract regulations to syndicate its legitimacy.

Two decisions from Southern Italy regarding the famous online auction and shopping website eBay may represent a good example. Both of the decisions ordered the company to re-activate the accounts of two sellers who had been deactivated because of negative feedbackl.

The first decision[31] deemed as unlawful the deactivation under the general rules on contract termination (Article 1454 and ff. of the civil code) given that the mere presence of low feedback ratings was not per se sufficient to demonstrate the existence of a serious breach of the contract. The judge qualified the clause allowing resolution due to negative feedbacks as a vexatious clause, which would have required double subscription (missing in the case) for its enforceability under Article 1341 (2) of the civil code. Some authors, however, pointed out that, even with the second subscription, such a clause allowing deactivation could still be void under Article 9 Law 192/1998, as it realises "an abusive imposition of unjustifiably vexatious conditions" (Cimino 2011, p. 132).

The second decision[32] seems to be more aware of the socio-economic dimension of the problem and considers the oligopolistic structure of eBay's online marketplace as well. The judge recognised the existence of the so-called *periculum in mora* (necessary to access to the urgency proceeding) because "*the exclusion from Ebay does not only produce the loss of some clients, but excludes a micro-business from the market*".[33]

What is extremely interesting about the two decisions is that—even moving within the field of general contract law—they are still able to grant the weak party of the relationship a *real* protection, a sort of reinstatement, thus recalling the traditional sanction against unjustified dismissal. It is a revolutionary outcome, as it goes even further than the—quite revolutionary—conclusions reached in the Renault case, where the ascertainment of an abusive termination of the contract entailed only compensatory remedies.[34]

Low ratings, therefore, can bring deactivation only when they derive from seriously neglectful conduct of the worker, and a minimal procedure shall be accorded in any case under the general clause of good faith.

The issue is strictly connected with the problem of the control that the platform is capable of exercising on the execution of the performance, even by delegating it to users by means of reputational systems (Rosenblat and Stark 2016; Prassl and Risak 2016, p. 626; Ingrao 2017). Such control, in fact, may be compatible with the self-employed nature of the relationship only as long as it remains a control on the *result* of the work—in order to guarantee minimum standards of quality and safety—and not on the *execution* of the worker's performance. Nonetheless, the border can indeed be quite evanescent.

Certainly, however, in keeping with the alleged self-employment status, personal ratings should not depend on the amount of time the worker devotes to work. Should the reputational system "punish" dormant workers, they could react by invoking their employment status since they would end up being at the disposal of an employer (as the Tribunal of London pointed out in the Uber case, quoting Milton, *"they also serve who only stand and wait"*[35]).

A similar approach could be adopted not only to ascertain the legitimacy of the clauses allowing the user to refuse the acceptance of a performed task without providing payment to the worker (AMT Participation Agreement, § 3) but also to question the legitimacy of the exclusivity clause that some platforms insert in their general conditions (De Stefano 2016, p. 488).

In the first case, special provisions on self-employed work regarding the right to receive due compensation may apply. In Italy, Article 2227 of the civil code provides the client with the right to terminate the self-employment relationship when the task has been partially executed, *"compensating the worker for the expenses, for the performed work and for his loss"*. Therefore, it seems that the clause allowing the client to refuse a fully completed task should be, *a fortiori*, not enforceable.

Even the exclusivity clauses may be deemed unlawful. As they result in "restrictions to the freedom to contract with third parties", they certainly require double subscription, and as they could determine an excessive imbalance of rights and duties, it could be appropriate to consider them vexatious and thus void.

Therefore, the recourse to civil law principles and regulations may address some crucial issues, but it is still far from being a satisfactory solution, as it leaves many critical points unresolved and also presents all the weaknesses of an interpretative-only solution.

The Perspective of Legislative Intervention on Self-Employed Work Discipline in General: The Italian "Jobs Act of Autonomous Work"

A first answer to the absence of an exhaustive discipline on pure self-employed work comes from recent Italian Law 81/2017 containing "protective provisions on non-entrepreneurial self-employed work".

As has been underlined, the legislator tried, for the first time, to construct a discipline of self-employed work based on the acknowledgement of its social value rather than on the prejudice that it just hides misguided employment relationships (Giubboni 2017; Perulli 2017).

The bill introduces several warranties for self-employed workers, ranging from the protection against payment delays (Article 2), to tax benefits (Articles 8 and 9), to the access to formation and collocation services (Article 10) and public procurement (Article 12), as well as to social security benefits such as maternity leave, sick leave and injury leave (Articles 7, 13 and 14).

From the perspective of digital self-employed work, one of the most important provisions is set up by Article 3 (4), which explicitly provides for the application to self-employment relationships of Article 9 Law 192/1998, which prohibits the abuse of economic dependency in B2b relationships. In addition, Article 3 (1) specifies that the clauses granting the client the power to unilaterally modify the terms and conditions of the contract, as well as to terminate the relationship without notice, are vexatious and void.

It is not clear whether the invalidity of the vexatious clause could lead also to the application of real remedies (such as the re-constitution of the relationship or reinstatement), as the article provides expressly that the worker would be entitled to receive a reparation (Article 3 (3)). However, it seems possible to interpret such a provision as granting reparation for the damage and loss produced by the enforcement of the vexatious clause but without excluding the possibility of the restoration of the *status quo ante*.

The Perspective of Specific Legislative Intervention on Platform Work: The French *Loi Travail...*

Specific attempts to regulate the provision of personal services in the gig economy are represented by the French regulation on (self-employed) platform workers and indirectly by the Italian bill, the so-called Sharing Economy Act.

The 2016 French reform known as *Loi Travail* introduced in the Labour Code (*Code du Travail*) a new specific section dedicated to "workers who use intermediation online platforms" (Articles L. 7341-1 to L. 7342-6). Although those provisions apply only to self-employed workers (*travailleurs indépendants*) who use one or more platforms, the law does not take any position regarding the problem of the status of platform workers, as the new rules do not affect the possibility to sustain the reclassification of the labour relationship. However, it seems relevant that the law explicitly allows that the determination by the platform of the price of the service and of its main characteristics is compatible with a self-employment relationship. Besides the provisions regarding the matter of formation and occupational health and safety, particularly relevant are those provisions establishing some warranties that recall typical trade union rights in favour of "digital workers", who can organise their own trade unions (Article L. 7342-6) and take collective action, including strikes, without suffering negative consequences such as deactivation (Article L. 7342-5).

...and the Italian "Sharing Economy Act"

Italian Bill 3564, the so-called Sharing Economy Act,[36] has chosen a very different approach.

Although it is not actually a labour regulation—indeed, it does not even use the word "worker" in any provision—and it presents a promotional purpose (recalling Wosskow 2014) that somehow reflects the misunderstanding that the gig economy is an aspect of genuine sharing economy (Eckhardt and Bardhi 2015; Mansharamani 2016), the bill contains some provisions which may be extremely relevant for the purpose of granting fair treatment to platform workers.

Article 4 of the bill provides that the platform owners shall adopt a written policy, subject to the Competition Authority's approval, including the contractual terms and conditions between the platform and its users. The bill provides for a list of clauses penalising the "user-operator" (broad label under which, however, it seems possible to include platform workers), which are expressly sanctioned with invalidity. In particular, platform terms and conditions cannot "a) *burden the user-operator with any kind of exclusive obligation; b) allow the control on the execution of his performance, not even through hardware or software systems; c) determine compulsory fees for all users; d) allow the exclusion of the user-operator from the platform or penalise him in the presentation of his offer without serious reasons; […] h) forbid the user operator from criticising the owner of the platform*" (Article 4 (2)).

Notwithstanding the criticalities of the bill, such a provision should be welcomed as a consistent step forward in filling up that "empty space of law" where digital workers seemed to fall.

Conclusions

The frustrations arising from the difficulty met in applying statutory employment law to platform workers (Weiss 2016, p. 662) should not lead to the misunderstanding that no protection can be found outside that domain. The "lightness" of platform work remains "unbearable", but some attempts to make it heavier may be crowned with success. Through the valorisation of contract law, we may already be able to address some of the issues raised by platform-mediated self-employed work. The legislative perspective of implementing new sets of rules for self-employed workers and digital "users-operators" may also give further answers.

Some crucial points, however, remain unresolved. In the first place, there is the problem of low wages, which represents a constant of platform work, in which workers are paid much less than the minimum wages set by applicable legislation or collective agreements. *Rebus sic*

130   G. Cavallini

stantibus, it seems extremely difficult to address the issue of low wages without passing by the reclassification of the relationship since the constitutional principle of a "proportionate and adequate salary" (Article 36 Italian Constitution) has been repeatedly declared inapplicable to self-employed workers[37] and the only provision granting an "equivalent" wage to quasi-subordinate self-employed workers has been abrogated by the *Jobs Act* reform in 2015.

However, about the problem of low wages, two doctrinal proposals deserve attention, as they move from the awareness of the difficulties in reaching reclassification for platform workers. The first one is to extend the scope of the minimum wage provisions provided for by law and collective agreements to (at least some) self-employed workers by means of a specific legislative intervention (Menegatti 2017). The second proposal, on the other hand, suggests an interpretative extension to (self-employed) platform workers of the principles provided for by Directive 2008/104/EC on Agency Work and in particular of the equality principle enshrined in Article 5 (1) of the Directive (Ratti 2017).

Moreover, many other issues, such as the risks of self-exploitation and of the exploitation of child labour (De Stefano 2016, 500) and the difficulties in pursuing effective collective representation for an atomised working force (Forlivesi 2016)—notwithstanding the efforts to conceive new forms of mobilisation (Silberman and Irani 2016; Graceffa 2016)—cannot, as of today, find a satisfactory solution outside the field of statutory employment law.

Therefore, the challenge of platform work calls for a political reflection to be conducted both at a national and at a supranational level.

Notes

1. The term "crowdwork" has been used in literature both to indicate all the new forms of work in the gig economy (Prassl and Risak 2016; Däubler and Klebe 2016) and, in a narrower sense, to identify only the platform-mediated provision, by a global workforce, of human intelligence tasks executed online in favour of third parties (natural persons but also firms). The prototype is Amazon Mechanical Turk, launched by Amazon in 2005.

The Classification of Crowdwork and Work by Platforms... 131

2. The term indicates the platform-mediated provision of services to be performed in the real world (such as driving a car, in the case of Uber and Lyft, or delivering goods, in the case of Deliveroo or foodora), mostly in favour of final customers.

3. "*As a provider you are performing services for a Requester in your personal capacity as an independent contractor and not as an employee of the requester [...] this Agreement does not create an [...] employer/employee relationship between Providers and requesters, or Providers and AMT*" (AMT Participation Agreement, § 3.d, available at https://www.mturk.com/mturk/conditionsofuse. Accessed on 1 Dec. 2017); "*Uber does not provide transportation or logistics services or function as a transportation carrier and that all such transportation or logistics services are provided by independent third party contractors who are not employed by Uber or any of its affiliates*" (Uber B.V. Terms and Conditions, § 2, available at https://www.uber.com/en-CA/legal/terms/ca/. Accessed on 1 Dec. 2017); "*You are a self-employed supplier and therefore acknowledge that you are neither an employee of Deliveroo, nor a worker within the meaning of any employment rights legislation*" (Deliveroo Supplier Agreement, § 2.1. http://www.parliament.uk/documents/commons-committees/work-and-pensions/Written_Evidence/Deliveroo-scooter-contract.pdf. Accessed 1 Dec. 2017).

4. California Northern District Court 11 March 2015, *Cotter* et al. vs. *Lyft Inc.*, Case No. 13-cv-04065-VC, Order denying cross-motions for summary judgement, available at http://adapt.it/adapt-indice-a-z/wp-content/uploads/2015/06/Cotter_Lyft.pdf.

5. London Employment Tribunal 28 Oct. 2016, *Aslam, Farrar* et al. *v. Uber B.V.* et al., available at https://www.judiciary.gov.uk/wp-content/uploads/2016/10/aslam-and-farrar-v-uber-reasons-20161028.pdf. Accessed on 1 Dec. 2017.

6. London Employment Appeal Tribunal 10 November 2017, *Aslam, Farrar* et al. *v. Uber B.V.* et al., available at https://assets.publishing.service.gov.uk/media/5a046b06e5274a0ee5a1f171/Uber_B.V._and_Others_v_Mr_Y_Aslam_and_Others_UKEAT_0056_17_DA.pdf. Accessed on 1 Dec. 2017.

7. Employment Tribunal of Belo Horizonte 13 Feb. 2017, available at https://www.conjur.com.br/dl/juiz-reconhece-vinculo-emprego-uber.pdf. Accessed on 1 Dec. 2017; Employment Tribunal of Sao Paulo 20 April 2017, available at https://d2f17dr7ourrh3.cloudfront.net/wp-content/uploads/2017/04/Sentenc%CC%A7a-Uber.SP-V%C3%ADnculo.pdf. Accessed on 1 Dec. 2017.

132   G. Cavallini

8. London Employment Tribunal 28 Oct. 2016 (note 5), n. 97.
9. Conclusions in the Case C-434/15, *Asociación Profesional Élite Taxi v Uber Systems Spain, S.L.*, ECLI:EU:C:2017:364.
10. Tribunal of Milan 25 May 2015 and Tribunal of Milan 2 July 2015, both in *Diritto dell'informazione e dell'informatica*, 2015, 6, p. 1053 and p. 1068 respectively.
11. Tribunal of Milan 20 June 1986, in *Rivista Italiana di Diritto del Lavoro*, 1987, II, p. 70.
12. Tribunal of Turin 12 Feb. 1996, in *Rivista Italiana di Diritto del Lavoro*, 1997, II, p. 290.
13. Tribunal of Milan 27 April 1987, in *Lavoro 80*, 1987, p. 258.
14. Tribunal of Milan 20 June 1986, in *Rivista Italiana di Diritto del Lavoro*, 1987, II, p. 71.
15. *Ivi*, p. 73.
16. London Employment Tribunal 28 Oct. 2016 (note 5), n. 85.
17. At first by second instance judges (Tribunal of Milan 10 Oct.1987, in *Il Foro Italiano*, 1989, I, c. 2632), and then by the Supreme Court (Court of Cassation 10 July 1991, n. 7608, in *Rivista Italiana di Diritto del Lavoro*, 1992, II, p. 370).
18. Court of Cassation 20 Jan. 2011, n. 1238, in *Giustizia Civile Massimario*, 2011, p. 85.
19. Some movies marked that turn-point, such as *Tutta la vita davanti* (2008).
20. Ministry of Labour Circular 14 June 2006, n. 17.
21. Tribunal of Rome 3 Dec. 2008, in *Diritto e Pratica del Lavoro*, 2009, p. 1887.
22. Tribunal of Milan 18 Jan. 2007, in *Diritto e Pratica del Lavoro*, 2007, p. 1264.
23. Ministry of Labour Circular 31 March 2008, n. 8.
24. Ministerial Note 3 Dec. 2008, n. 17,286.
25. European Court of Justice 2 Dec. 2014, C-413/13, *FNV Kunsten Informatie en Media v. Staat der Nederlanden*, ECLI:EU:C:2014:2411.
26. California Northern District Court 11 March 2015, *O'Connor et al. v. Uber Technologies Inc.* et al., available at http://digitalcommons.law.scu.edu/cgi/viewcontent.cgi?article=1935&context=historical. Accessed on 1 Dec. 2017.
27. London Employment Tribunal 28 Oct. 2016 (note 5), n. 89.
28. Tribunal of Milan 25 May 2015 and Tribunal of Milan 2 July 2015, both in *Diritto dell'informazione e dell'informatica*, 2015, 6, p. 1053 and p. 1068 respectively.

The Classification of Crowdwork and Work by Platforms... **133**

29. Request for a preliminary ruling C-434/15, *Asociación Profesional Élite Taxi v Uber Systems Spain, S.L.*
30. The expression "B2b contracts" (*Business to business contracts*) indicates those commercial contracts stipulated by a small firm (business with lower-case b) and a bigger business (business with upper-case B), under which the former provides the latter with goods or services on a continuative bases and in conditions of economic dependency.
31. Tribunal of Messina 7 July 2010, in *Diritto dell'informazione e dell'informatica*, 2011, 118.
32. Tribunal of Catanzaro 30 April 2012, in *Diritto dell'informazione e dell'informatica*, 2012, 1174.
33. *Ivi*, 1180.
34. Court of Cassation 18 Sept. 2009, n. 20,106, in *I contratti* 2010, 5, deemed abusive the sudden and unjustified termination of a retail relationship, granting reparation for damage and loss.
35. London Employment Tribunal 28 Oct. 2016 (note 5), n. 100.
36. Proposed on 27 Jan. 2016 and currently pending at the Chamber of Deputies.
37. Constitutional Court 7 July 1964, n. 75, in *Giurisprudenza Costituzionale*, 1964, 751. Recently, Court of Cassation 8 June 2007, n. 13,440, in *DeJure*.

References

Alba, Davey. 2015. Instacart Shoppers Can Now Choose to Be Real Employees. *Wired*, June 22. https://www.wired.com/2015/06/instacart-shoppers-can-now-choose-real-employees/. Accessed 1 Dec 2017.

Aloisi, Antonio. 2016. Commoditized Workers: Case Study Research on Labor Law Issues Arising from a Set of "On-Demand/Gig Economy" Platforms. *Comparative Labor Law & Policy Journal* 37 (3): 653–690.

Bergvall-Kåreborn, Birgitta, and Devra Howcroft. 2014. Amazon Mechanical Turk and the Commodification of Labour. *New Technology, Work and Employment* 29 (3): 213–223.

Carinci, Maria Teresa. 2012. Il contratto d'opera. In *I contratti per l'impresa*, ed. Gregorio Gitti, Marco Maugeri, and Mario Notari, 176–193. Bologna: Il Mulino.

Cherry, Miriam A. 2016. Beyond Misclassification: The Digital Transformation of Work. *Comparative Labor Law & Policy Journal* 37 (3): 577–602.

Cherry, Miriam A., and Antonio Aloisi. 2017. "Dependent Contractors" in the Gig Economy. A Comparative Approach. *American University Law Review* 66: 635–689.

Chiesi, Antonio M. 1986. *Il tempo del lavoro nel settore della consegna immediata.* Milano: Istituto di ricerche economiche e sociali della Lombardia.

Creighton, Breen, and Shae McCrystal. 2016. Who Is a "Worker" in International Law? *Comparative Labor Law & Policy Journal* 37 (3): 691–726.

Cimino, Iacopo P. 2011. Sospensione dell'account di vendita nel *marketplace* di *ebay*, tutela del contratto e della libertà di impresa nel commercio elettronico. *Diritto dell'informazione e dell'informatica*: 120–134.

Dagnino, Emanuele. 2015. Il lavoro nella *on-demand economy*: esigenze di tutela e prospettive regolatorie. *Labour & Law Issues* 1: 87–106.

Däubler, Wolfgang, and Thomas Klebe. 2016. *Crowdwork*: Datore di lavoro in fuga? *Giornale di diritto del lavoro e delle relazioni industriali* 151: 471–502.

Davidov, Guy. 2017. The Status of Uber Drivers: A Purposive Approach. *Spanish Labour Law and Employment Relations Journal* 6: 6–15.

De Angelis, Luigi. 1988. I *pony express* tra subordinazione e autonomia. In *Autonomia e subordinazione nelle nuove figure professionali del terziario*, ed. Giovanni Deodato and Ezio Siniscalchi, 57–65. Milano: Giuffrè.

De Stefano, Valerio. 2016. The Rise of the "Just-in-Time Workforce": On-Demand Work, Crowdwork, and Labor Protection in the "Gig-Economy". *Comparative Labor Law & Policy Journal* 37 (3): 471–504.

DeAmicis, Carmel. 2015. Homejoy Shuts Down After Battling Worker Classification Lawsuits. *Recode*, July 17. https://www.recode. net/2015/7/17/11614814/cleaning-services-startup-homejoy-shuts-down-after-battling-worker. Accessed 1 Dec 2017.

Di Vico, Dario. 2016. Foodora, Deliveroo e Just Eat: la vita da pony express hi-tech. *Corriere*, October 16. www.corriere.it/cronache/16_ottobre_16/vita-pony-express-hi-tech-592d131e-930e-11e6-aedf-4afd1bcdf31b.shtml. Accessed 1 Dec 2017.

Donini, Annamaria. 2015. Il lavoro digitale su piattaforma. *Labour & Law Issues* 1: 50–71.

———. 2016. Il lavoro su piattaforma digitale "prende forma" tra autonomia e subordinazione. Nuove regole per nuovi lavori? *Diritto delle relazioni industriali* 1: 164–177.

Eckhardt, Giana M., and Fleura Bardhi. 2015. The Sharing Economy Isn't About Sharing at All. *Harvard Business Review*, January 28. https://hbr.org/2015/01/the-sharing-economy-isnt-about-sharing-at-all. Accessed 1 Dec 2017.

Felstiner, Alek. 2011. Working the Crowd. Employment and Labor Law in the Crowdsourcing Industry. *Berkeley Journal of Employment and Labour Law* 32 (1): 143–204.

Forlivesi, Michele. 2016. La sfida della rappresentanza sindacale dei lavoratori 2.0. *Diritto delle Relazioni Industriali* 26 (3): 664–678.

Gitti, Gregorio, and Gianroberto Villa. 2008. *Il terzo contratto. L'abuso di potere contrattuale nei rapporti tra imprese.* Bologna: Il Mulino.

Giubboni, Stefano. 2017. Il Jobs act del lavoro autonomo: commento al capi I della legge n. 81/2017. *Giornale di diritto del lavoro e delle relazioni industriali* 155 (3): 471–495.

Graceffa, Sandrino. 2016. *Refaire le monde… du travail. Une alternative à l'ubérisation de l'économie.* Valence: Repas.

Harris, Seth D., and Alan B. Krueger. 2015. *A Proposal for Modernizing Labor Laws for Twenty-First-Century Work: The "Independent Worker".* Washington: Brookings.

Ichino, Pietro. 1987. Libertà formale e libertà materiale del lavoratore nella qualificazione della prestazione come autonoma o subordinata. *Rivista italiana di diritto del lavoro*: 76–85.

———. 2016. Sulla questione dei fattorini di Foodora. http://www.pietroichino.it/?p=42367. Accessed 1 Dec 2017.

Ingrao, Alessandra. 2017. La funzione dei sistemi di feedback nell'era della economia *on demand*: un problema di subordinazione? Paper presented at the 15th International Conference in Commemoration of Professor Marco Biagi, Digital and Smart Work, Modena, March 20–21.

Kessler, Sarah. 2015. The Gig Economy Won't Last Because It's Being Sued to Death. *Fastcompany*, February 17. https://www.fastcompany.com/3042248/the-gig-economy-wont-last-because-its-being-sued-to-death. Accessed 1 Dec 2017.

Lloyd, Ian. 2016. Uber Drivers in London: "To Be or Not to Be" an Employee? *Computer Law Review International* 17 (6): 161–165.

Mansharamani, Vikram. 2016. What Happens When the Sharing Economy Stops Sharing and Starts Owning? *Pbs*, February 4. http://www.pbs.org/newshour/making-sense/what-happens-when-the-sharing-economy-stops-sharing-and-starts-owning/. Accessed 1 Dec 2017.

Marazza, Marco. 2007. Il mercato del lavoro dopo il caso Atesia. Percorsi alternativi di rientro dalla precarietà. *Argomenti di diritto del lavoro*: 327–340.

Maresca, Arturo, and Lilli Carollo. 2007. Il contratto di collaborazione a progetto nel settore call center. *Diritto delle relazioni industriali* 3: 675–690.

Menegatti, Emanuele. 2017. A Fair Wage for Workers-on-Demand via App. Paper Presented at the 15th International Conference in Commemoration of Professor Marco Biagi, Digital and Smart Work, Modena, March 20–21.

Moatti, Sophie-Charlotte. 2015. The Sharing Economy's New Middlemen. *Harvard Business Review*, March 5. https://hbr.org/2015/03/the-sharing-economys-new-middlemen. Accessed 1 Dec 2017.

Morello, Umberto. 2013. Abuso del diritto: la difficile via della concretizzazione. In *Lezioni di diritto civile*, ed. Antonio Gambaro and Umberto Morello, 685–722. Milano: Giuffré.

Mosca, Giuditta. 2016. Lo sciopero contro Foodora è il sogno infranto della sharing economy. *Wired*, October 11. https://www.wired.it/economia/lavoro/2016/10/11/sciopero-contro-foodora-sogno-infranto-sharing-economy/. Accessed 1 Dec 2017.

Nogler, Luca, and Udo Reifner. 2014. *Life Time Contracts: Social Long-Term Contracts in Labour, Tenancy and Consumer Credit Law*. The Hahue: Eleven International Publishing.

O'Connor, Sarah. 2016. When Your Boss Is an Algorithm. *Financial Times*, September 8. https://www.ft.com/content/88fdc58e-754f-11e6-b60a-de4532d5ea35. Accessed 1 Dec 2017.

Perulli, Adalberto. 1996. *Il lavoro autonomo. Contratto d'opera e professioni intellettuali*. Milano: Giuffrè.

———. 2003. *Economically Dependent / Quasi-subordinate (Parasubordinate) Employment: Legal, Social and Economic Aspects*. Bruxelles: European Commission.

———. 2015a. Un Jobs Act per il lavoro autonomo: verso una nuova disciplina della dipendenza economica? *WP C.S.D.L.E. "Massimo D'Antona". IT—235/2015*.

———. 2015b. Il controllo giudiziale dei poteri dell'imprenditore tra evoluzione legislativa e diritto vivente. *Rivista italiana di diritto del lavoro* 1: 83–126.

———. 2017. Il "Jobs Act" degli autonomi: nuove (e vecchie) tutele per il lavoro autonomo imprenditoriale. *Rivista italiana di diritto del lavoro* 2: 173–201.

Prassl, Jeremias. 2015. *The Concept of the Employer*. Oxford: Oxford University Press.

Prassl, Jeremias, and Martin Risak. 2016. Uber, Taskrabbit, and Co.: Platforms as Employers? Rethinking the Legal Analysis of Crowdwork. *Comparative Labor Law & Policy Journal* 37 (3): 619–652.

Rampazzo, Natale. 2015. Rifkin e Uber. Dall'età dell'accesso all'economia dell'eccesso. *Diritto dell'informazione e dell'Informatica* 6: 957–984.

Ratti, Luca. 2017. Online Platforms and Crowdwork in Europe: A Two-Step Approach to Expanding Agency Work Provisions? *Comparative Labor Law & Policy Journal* 38 (3): 477–511.

Razzolini, Orsola. 2014. La nozione di subordinazione alla prova delle nuove tecnologie. *Diritto delle relazioni industriali* 4: 974–998.

Roccella, Massimo. Lavoro subordinato e lavoro autonomo, oggi. *WP C.S.D.L.E. "Massimo D'Antona". IT*—65/2008.

Rosenblat, Alex, and Luke Stark. 2016. Algorithmic Labor and Information Asymmetries: A Case Study of Uber's Drivers. *International Journal of Communication* 10: 3758–3784.

Savelli, Fabio. 2016. Quattro euro a consegna, contributi e assicurazione infortuni: vi spieghiamo perché paghiamo così. *Corriere della Sera*, November 4. http://www.corriere.it/economia/16_novembre_04/quattro-euro-consegna-contributi-assicurazione-infortuni-vi-spieghiamo-perche-paghiamo-cosi-5c81fbb4-a2b4-11e6-9bbc-76e0a0d7325e.shtml. Accessed 1 Dec 2017.

Silberman, Michael S., and Lilly Irani. 2016. Operating an Employer Reputation System: Lessons from Turkopticon, 2008–2015. *Comparative Labor Law & Policy Journal* 37 (3): 505–542.

Treu, Tiziano. 2007. *Labour Law and Industrial Relations in Italy*. Alphen aan den Rijn: Kluwer International.

Tullini, Patrizia. 2015. C'è lavoro sul *web*? *Labour & Law Issues* 1 (1): 1–20.

Valenduc, Gérard, and Patricia Vendramin. 2016. *Work in the Digital Economy: Sorting the Old from the New*, WP ETUI, 2016.03. Bruxelles: ETUI.

Weiss, Manfred. 2016. Digitalizzazione: sfide e prospettive per il diritto del lavoro. *Diritto delle relazioni industriali* 3: 651–663.

Wosskow, Debbie. 2014. *Unlocking the Sharing Economy. An Independent Review*. London: Department for Business, Innovation & Skills. https://www.gov.uk/government/uploads/system/uploads/attachment_data/file/378291/bis-14-1227-unlocking-the-sharing-economy-an-independent-review.pdf. Accessed 1 Dec 2017.

Zou, Mimi. 2017. 'Uberization' and the Digital Workforce in China: Regulating the Status of Ride-Hailing Drivers. Paper Presented at the 15th International Conference in Commemoration of Professor Marco Biagi, Digital and Smart Work, Modena, March 20–21.

Part III

Industrial Relations Strategies in Industry 4.0

8

Organizing and Collective Bargaining in the Digitized "Tertiary Factories" of Amazon: A Comparison Between Germany and Italy

Bruno Cattero and Marta D'Onofrio

Introduction

The widespread diffusion of terms and expressions such as "digitalization" and "Industry 4.0" is a clue for approaching one of the main themes of discussion within work organization studies. As in the past—when the focus of attention was on the consequences, both positive and negative, of automation—the argumentations lead to a techno-centric and

---

This chapter is the result of two papers which originally debated the cases of German (Bruno Cattero) and Italian (Marta D'Onofrio) trade unions separately, both presented at the international conference on "Digital and Smart Work" (Marco Biagi Foundation, on 20–21 March 2017).

B. Cattero
Economics Sociology and Labour, University of Eastern Piedmont,
Vercelli, Italy
e-mail: bruno.cattero@uniupo.it

M. D'Onofrio (✉)
University of Eastern Piedmont, Vercelli, Italy
e-mail: marta.donofrio@uniupo.it

© The Author(s) 2018   **141**
E. Ales et al. (eds.), *Working in Digital and Smart Organizations*,
https://doi.org/10.1007/978-3-319-77329-2_8

optimistic interpretation which shows its limits (GTAI 2014; Hirsch-Kreinsen et al. 2015; Kärcher 2014; Salento 2016).

Thus, the concrete result of technological innovation is not and will not be determined by technology itself but instead by the interaction between technical features (both constraints and purposefully planning decisions), organizational choices—or no choices—and intervening rationalities during all the phases of the decision-making process, from planning to implementation (Butera 1983, 1984; Ciborra and Lanzara 1984).

The balanced coexistence of technological choices, the pluralistic interaction between different rationalities—rather than the control exerted by a monocratic rationality—and the involvement of workers implies contextual conditions and institutional frames that do not emerge from the discussion about digitalization and Industry 4.0 and that were seldom debated in regard to Industry 3.0, 2.0 and even 1.0.

The case study of Amazon, the leading company in the e-commerce sector, allows one to emphasize, on the one hand, the important innovations fostered by technologies and, on the other hand, the negative impact that the workers experienced because of the same technologies. At the same time, this case study could be useful to add new insight to the topics of work organizations and employee involvement at the workplace.

The dark side of Amazon has already been displayed on many occasions, thanks mainly to journalistic inquiries, which showed the harsh working conditions within the company's fulfillment centers (ARD 2013; BBC 2013; Malet 2013; O'Connor 2013; Kantor and Streitfeld 2015; Osborne 2016). This dark side is the downside of the "bright" and successful history of the multinational, which has made it a powerful player in the global context, both economic and political. The economic growth experienced by Amazon allows it to invest substantial resources in research and development, on big data collecting and on buyouts of minor competitors. These factors contribute to the company's inclusion among those giant corporations which condition and weaken state *and* market (Crouch 2011).

An overall analysis of Amazon could be preferable because of the important insights for the sociological and organizational theories that may be extracted. Yet the purpose of this chapter has to be delimited and will focus on the "digital work" inside of the Amazon fulfillment centers and on the related union activism aimed at regulating the relationship between employees and employers.

The following analysis is divided into two parts: in the first one, we focus on the specific combination of old and new organization of work in the Amazon fulfillment centers, and in the second one, we compare the attempts at collective regulations in Germany and Italy. The case study of Germany could be interesting if compared with the Italian one. Amazon has been there for a long time (almost 20 years), has opened the largest number of distribution centers (12) and for the first time in its history has been confronted with a trade union dispute, started in 2013, characterized by intense conflict and the obstinate denial by the company to enter into negotiations with the union. The presence of Amazon in Italy is much more recent but is expanding (the opening of two new warehouses is imminent). How do company and trade unions act? What role do the different institutional contexts play? What are the prospects for collective bargaining in Amazon's digitized tertiary factories?

Work Processes and Work Organization at Amazon Fulfillment Centers

Inside the Amazon fulfillment centers, the logistics work processes are characterized, on the one hand, by an extensive digitization and, on the other hand, by minimal automation, which makes human labor still required.[1] At the same time, no significant differences have been observed in regard to how the work processes are organized in German and Italian warehouses, meaning that Amazon decided to apply a highly standardized model that can easily adapt to different contexts.

When looking at Amazon fulfillment centers, one can notice how digital technologies represent the most important feature in helping with the management of work processes. Every product that enters the warehouse is meticulously classified with respect to its physical characteristics (weight, size, material, etc.) so that the subsequent storing, picking and packing operations can be carried out quickly and with minimal mistakes. The stages of the work process are linked together in a continuous flow managed by the information and communication technology (ICT)-based system and this helps workers to carry out the required operations. The work processes are divided into two phases: the inbound phase and the outbound phase. All those activities related to the inspection and storage of incoming goods belong to the first phase. This stage must be carried out accurately and on time in order to prevent any errors during the outbond operations. To the latter belong all operations ranging from picking activities (in which the products are collected from shelves) and packing activities to the planning of shipments (whose related management is entrusted to external couriers). To understand the importance of digital technologies in the fulfillment of these processes, we can take into consideration the example of picking and packing operations. In the first case, the computer system is aware of the position of each stored product, and the tasks are simplified for workers thanks to the barcode scanner that points out the fastest way to collect the products. Similarly, in the case of packing operations, each workstation is equipped with a screen that indicates the high-priority orders and the relative products that have to be packaged as soon as possible. We also find cardboard models to be used for bundling, recommended to the workers by the ICT system on the basis of the shape and size of the object or objects, which have been accurately measured in physical characteristics beforehand, during inbound operations.

From these few examples, the importance of digital technologies within the fulfillment centers can be understood, yet automation is limited: human work still plays a crucial role. For this reason, it is useful to focus our attention on the model of work organization that we observe inside Amazon warehouses.

Inside the fulfillment centers, the work is organized in teams of about 20 people, each headed by a single supervisor. Before the beginning of the shift,[2] all of the workers of each team have to meet with their managers, who communicate the daily objectives, which will depend on the sales trend. Each employee, then, will carry out their activities individually and they will continue to execute the same job for the duration of the shift.[3] It can also happen that the same worker performs the same activity for several weeks, although normally employees are allowed to carry out different tasks. This is possible because of the nature of the various tasks included in inbound and outbound operations, namely very simple and low-skilled jobs, which require an extremely short—short enough to be almost nonexistent—period of training.[4]

Organizing and Collective Bargaining in the Digitized "Tertiary... 145

Employees are constantly monitored by the supervisors. This is possible thanks to the use of digital technologies since each worker is equipped with a badge that is associated with a working tool or a workstation with respect to the job to accomplish. In this way, through the use of Wi-Fi technology, managers can learn about all the details of the activities of each employee ("productivity", location, task carried out, etc.). Each Amazon fulfillment center, because of the use of these monitoring technologies, is characterized as an *"electronic panopticon"* (Sewell and Wilkinson 1992). Control over work is predominantly "technical" (Edwards 1979), performed in a depersonalized way by the technology used and its mode of operation. In the case of picking operations, for example, supervision over the workers is facilitated by barcode scanners, which can indicate the fastest way to reach the product to be collected. A similar situation, though with different technology, can be observed during the phase of packing, where thanks to the conveyor belt the pace of work can be determined and control can be exercised over the job performance while the technology directs the products to be packed toward the workers. Some features of the work organization in fulfillment centers (the division of labor into simple and repetitive tasks, separation between conception and execution of jobs and "technical control") recall the principles that were defined with Scientific Management, so that some have begun to use the expression Digital Taylorism (Parenti 2001). The only difference lies in the type of technology used: the assembly line in the past, the ICT systems in the present.

Another factor has to be taken into account: the work organization is also strongly influenced by sales. Sales are managed by the company with a large degree of flexibility in the workforce to prevent deficiencies and excesses. In general, the sales trend is a widely foreseeable variable, given that orders placed by consumers remain constant except for some peaks, which correspond to annual festivities (such as Christmastime) and at the beginning of the school year. Owing to special agreements with the employment agencies, Amazon can have wide availability of workforce when it is necessary; using mostly temporary work contracts, the company is able to quickly get rid of the workforce that become redundant in the periods that follow or precede the peaks in sales. Ultimately, Amazon is accustomed to making extensive use of what is called "numerical flexibility", which concerns "the degree of freedom with which a company can adjust the volume and professional characteristics of the employment to the trend in production" (Reyneri 2005, p. 76).

However, the work processes and the work organization as described above cause some issues concerning the working condition, which have been repeatedly highlighted by investigative journalists and the testimonies of workers. A pace of work described as unsustainable, pressing controls in the performance of work, permanent requests to do overtime work on overtime hours, and lack of transparency in the management of human resources are some of the accusations made by workers against the company.

Some similarities between the work organization within Amazon fulfillment centers and Scientific Management have been underlined above. The tasks performed, some more than others, leave the workers with extremely low margins of autonomy and discretion, making them mere executors of orders or appendages of the working tools. This results in the aforementioned separation between conception and execution of the job, where the first phase is entrusted exclusively to management and IT specialists and the latter to workers, who cannot have any say in what concerns the execution of the tasks. This model of work organization contributes to labor impoverishment, as has already been shown (Braverman 1978).

In the same way, the control over the job performances is an uncomfortable issue for employees. The "electronic panopticon", as its name suggests, implies that the supervision becomes pervasive: it is absolutely impossible for the individual worker to escape "production" tracking. Once the badge is linked to the workstation or to the work tool, controls are total and incessant. Managers and IT specialists who collaborate with the management are constantly informed about the level of "productivity" of employees, and if someone does not respect the standards required for achieving the target set, he or she will be exhorted to improve his or her performance. The working atmosphere, as is easily noticed, becomes really stressful for some workers, given the pressure exerted by controls. Every employee is, from one side, aware of the control to which he or she is subject but, on the other, tends to accept it as normality. Because the "electronic panopticon" is a highly depersonalized

Organizing and Collective Bargaining in the Digitized "Tertiary... 147

device, the consequence is that workers start to assume that their working tools are not used for monitoring operations but rather to indicate the most efficient way to carry out the tasks. Thus, the element of conflict inherent in labor relations moves to the background (Fiocco 2001), especially with respect to the relationship between the supervisor and the supervised. In workers' minds, the ICT system and the managers do not control the job performances; they simply show how to better carry out the tasks in order to accomplish, as quickly as possible, the requests that come from customers, who are considered directly responsible for the intensive work pace inside the warehouses.

At the same time, we must not forget the presence of social controls, triggered by an organizational culture oriented to publicly reward the best workers and to turn on the competitiveness among employees in order to align their interests with those of the company. The notice boards which indicate the names of the employees-of-the-month or report the least productive groups help in fueling a rather hostile and competitive work environment. The outcome that the company hoped for, and that is in fact realized, is the emergence of spontaneous forms of social control, which have already been studied in the past within companies similar to Amazon (Kunda 1992).

The pressing and pervasive controls, together with the "productivity" targets required, contribute to force employees to keep a very tight pace of work. During shifts, we found the so-called cut-offs, i.e. the time when the orders must be ready for shipments. In the imminence of a cut-off,[5] the pace of work is even more intense, and in the case of some tasks, it becomes so intense as to be perceived as unbearable:

> The daily productive goal is always the same: at 5pm all the orders have to be ready for the delivery. If the leader and his team do not reach the goal he receives penalties. As a consequence, the leader conveys all the pressure on his team: pickers and packers receive from the leader green or yellow cards. Green card is a praise, while the yellow one is a warning. Three yellow cards are enough to risk the layoff. (Leisegang 2015, p. 148)

Many testimonies of workers assigned to picking operations tell us about employees' inability to handle, day after day, the demanding pretentions for pursuing the goals set for every team. In many cases, pickers have to cover in length and breadth the vast area of the fulfillment center in order to reach the countless shelves in which the ordered goods are situated, and it is quite common to hear about workers who have to walk, on a daily basis, for distances ranging from 15 to 20 kilometers.

A significant problem, connected to the intensity of the pace of work, concerns the way employees who are unable to maintain or increase their productivity levels in the long run are treated. Both from what is testified to by the workers and from what we learned from members of trade unions, it seems that within Amazon fulfillment center the laws of "natural selection" are applied, so the ones who succeed at keeping their jobs are the most willing to meet the demands of the management. In this way, no specific attention is paid to issues raised by workers, who often cannot benefit from the advantages of permanent employment because of productivity loss caused by chronic diseases or work-related injuries or simply because they have been assigned to tasks which are not suitable for them. What we want to emphasize is the lack of interest for workers and their demands: in case of unfavorable events, which can unexpectedly happen to employees, working performance could be compromised in a situation where workers have few safeguards.

Digitalization, through tools like the barcode scanner, actualizes the work organization and the control on workers but does not make them necessary. What ultimately determines this kind of work organization model are the decisions made by the management. Moreover, digital technologies are far more adjustable, and lower in cost, than the assembly line during Taylor-fordism. Nevertheless, it seems unlikely that owners and managers of Amazon will convince themselves about the goodness of labor narratives regarding the "Fourth Industrial Revolution" and will rearrange the work processes in a labor-oriented perspective. In the future, if anything can go in that direction, it could happen through collective bargaining with workers' representatives. Without a doubt, within Amazon "trade union is necessary" (Armaroli 2015), but according to the aforementioned reports, it would be necessary in order to guarantee labor rights that are considered the bare minimum. Two examples among others: the work organization of Taylor-fordist factories provided for the "jolly" figure, which substituted for those workers who temporarily left their workstation. Inside of Amazon fulfillment centers this position does not exist. At the same time, lunch breaks—which last 30 minutes—are managed with little interest for workers' needs: since the warehouses are so extended, the position of the worker when the lunch break starts could cause a notable waste of the available time.

Amazon in Germany: The Struggle for the Collective Agreement

Amazon has been present in Germany since 1999, when it settled with a fulfillment center in Bad Hersfeld, near Frankfurt. In Germany, as in all other countries where Amazon is located, the warehouses of the company reflect two localization standards: (a) proximity to freeways with favorable links to an international airport and (b) presence in structurally weak regions with a local labor market characterized by high unemployment rates, particularly among the weakest segments of the workforce.

During the first 12 years, within Amazon we could not find any sort of union presence: at the sites of Bad Hersfeld and Leipzig, there are no delegates (Vertrauensleute, literally "trade union trustees") and no union structures. Amazon did not join the employers' association of trade and commerce and does not apply the sectoral collective agreement. The organizing campaign in Bad Hersfeld reached the goal of forming a first substantial group of members (from 79 members before the campaign to almost 1000 after it) that was able to set up, for the first time, a union structure at Amazon (Boewe and Schulten 2015; Bock 2016).

The activity of proselytism and the debate with the local and national structures of *ver.di* finally led to the establishment of a "bargaining commission", a trade union body responsible for initiating and handling a negotiating dispute with the managerial counterpart. The commission prepared and submitted to the management, during the autumn of 2012, a platform of claims with the main request to the company of joining the commerce sector collective agreement (*Einzel- und Versandhandel*). The indifference of the management of the Bad Hersfeld warehouse with respect to the request about opening the negotiations led to the first strike

(9 April 2013), which drew the participation of about 1,100 employees between the first and second round, for a total of 3,400.

As far as the content of trade union claims is concerned, the topic with which Amazon responds to *ver.di*—through press releases and media interviews—has not changed since the spring of 2013: Amazon is not a trade business but rather a logistics one and as such it has always adjusted its wages to the highest slot of the collective bargaining agreement of that sector without adhering to and applying it. This argument, compared with the transformation of work in the trade and service sector in terms of de-qualification that existed before Amazon but has been sharpened by its organizational model, is an argument that might also appear to be well grounded. But with respect to the sectoral belonging, it is clearly specious. Amazon does not just distribute goods but buys and sells them, as any other retailer does. Moreover, shipping is not managed by Amazon but by other logistic companies. Similarly, the spuriousness of Amazon's argument is quite evident if one takes into account that, in the US, where the wage entry in the logistics sector is higher than that of trade, the enterprise defines itself for what it is: a trade company (Jamieson 2014).

On the one hand, the collective agreement, in addition to making the pay and its trend discretionary, would allow at least some of the working conditions to be adjusted, from breaks to shifts, and would strengthen the role and action of works councils, which are called to check the correct application of the collective agreement. On the other hand, Amazon's refusal to negotiate with trade unions on issues that are related to employment relationship, hence of exclusive managerial competence, and to hold discussions with the works council has transformed the conflict from distributive to a *conflict of recognition* (Honneth 2011). The distributive conflict allows and can produce, except for pathologies, positive sum games for counterparties and as such socially legitimizes contractual autonomy and industrial relations in terms of *Konfliktpartnerschaft* (Müller-Jentsch 1999). A conflict of recognition is the exact opposite because the recognition concerns not only the position of the counterpart but also the whole institution of "collective autonomy", which sets the gound rules of the conflict itself. Once the conflict has been triggered, there is no space for mediations: those who give up first have lost. Recalling Scharpf (2000), in the spiral of reciprocal hostility, the costs incurred to win become irrelevant if they are judged inferior to the loss suffered by the counterpart. All of this explains the tenacity with which *ver.di* and Amazon continue in a conflict that has lasted for four years now. However, given the options and the available resources for two contractors, there is an enormous disparity.

Both in the reports and in the analysis of the conflict, but even in the interviews conducted, the metaphor of "David against Goliath" is often used. If we abstract from the fact that in the Bible the challenger is Goliath and not David, the metaphor is effective.

In the Biblical story, the Jewish people are in a critical moment in the war with the Philistines, the same critical moment in which *ver.di* currently is towards Amazon within the private service sector. Amazon-Goliath is not an exception but rather the most significant and problematic case in a sector that has always been complicated for trade unions but that has become even more arduous in the last 15 years. Out of the current 3 million Germans employed in the service sector, 62.1% have part-time contracts that are precarious or insufficient to guarantee an income for living with dignity; collective bargaining agreement coverage, which was close to 100% over the turn of the century, rapidly collapsed to 40% (25% of firms); the number of "co-determined" companies has fallen steadily over the past 12 years, from 765 in 2003 to 635 in 2015, and the fall is not so much a consequence of mergers and acquisitions but the result of strategies to exploit any legal gap to escape the law of 1976.[6] Lastly, from 2001 to 2015, *ver.di* recorded a nearly 800,000 decrease in subscription (from 2,806 to 2,039 million).

Goliath, for its part, cannot lose for ideological reasons. Behind the assertion that *ver.di* is a "stranger third party" (Oberhuber 2015), with whom, by definition, there is no reason or need to sit down to discuss, stands the neoliberal conception of the firm, which Amazon fully embodies: on the one hand, the enterprise is conceived as a *nexus of contracts*; on the other hand, the principle of direct relationship with employees, without any intermediation, has been spread in the managerial literature on human resource management since the 1980s. If trade unions are not involved in human resource management, there is no reason to recognize it as an "interlocutor", let alone negotiate with them unless one is forced to. But forcing Goliath, for David, seems extremely difficult.

The first barrier to trade union action is determined by corporate legal structure. Each distribution center is an autonomous GmbH (the equivalent to an Italian s.r.l.) with its own executive chiefs, which is part of a Luxembourg-based holding company (Amazon Europe). This legal construction—in addition to allowing Amazon to evade taxation in Germany, as elsewhere in Europe, by paying derisory amounts in the face of billionaire incomes—significantly hampers trade union actions and co-determination. First, since each fulfillment center is an autonomous enterprise, there are only individual plant-level works councils, but there is no firm-level works council (*Gesamtbetriebsrat*) and therefore no information flows and coordination that this would facilitate. Second, the same rule is applied to the supervisory board provided by the co-determination law: it can be established only at the plant level, and the plant must exceed the threshold of 2,000 employees.

In these conditions, it becomes very easy for Amazon to keep the number of employees under that threshold, if necessary by integrating it with seasonal workers who do not enter the calculation. Moreover, the supervisory board, where it exists,[7] has competencies and information rights that do not cross over the borders of the plant, and all relevant information and strategic choices are in the Luxembourg headquarters. Third, the presence and capacity of union mobilization must be built in every single plant individually; weaknesses in a single plant cannot be balanced by the results achieved elsewhere.

Keeping the attention on the institutional side, it is important to take into account the relationship with the Betriebsräte. The institutional architecture of the industrial relations system in Germany rests on the pair union/works councils and on the related functional separation between regulation levels: at the first level (industry or firm), the bargaining of the collective rules between the union (which has the monopoly of the strike) and employers' associations; at the second level, the negotiation of agreements between works councils and management. Here, the councils can rely on the co-determination rights they have recognized by law but they cannot renegotiate collective rules unless this is permitted by specific clauses in the collective agreement. The works councils, more-

Organizing and Collective Bargaining in the Digitized "Tertiary... 153

over, are formally independent from the union as far as the law requires them to monitor that the company correctly applies the collective rules. Not only that, the interpretation and application of the same co-determination rights in the company, their content, are closely interwoven with the content of the collective agreement. The existing linkages between wages, incentives, professional categories and so on constitute many "hinges" between the union's policy and the action of the works councils (Düll and Bechtle 1988). In the golden decades of the Rhine social compromise, this "contradictory unit" (Streeck 1981) was usually resolved in a substantial unit of action: in most cases, works councils had a union majority and information flows and resources were ensured, above all by the "double role" of the company actor. It usually was a trade union trustee and was elected as employee representative. But from the strategic point of view for the union, the second "jacket" was fundamental as it was the one that ensured the negotiating rights within the company.

However, if there is no collective agreement and the trade union is absent or too weak, as is the case with Amazon and with the increasingly widespread de-unionization of the private service sector (and industry sector), the situation turns around. The works council, if it is already constituted, is, from a trade union point of view, in the best possible way a sparked and unhelpful weapon: in a complicated corporation like Amazon, the works council member needs intense and continual training. It can be ensured only by a union and without it, it is unlikely that members will be able to effectively exercise their mandate. In the worst-case scenario, the works council becomes a problem because it can become easy prey for the management business strategies.

On this ground, though, Amazon has moved very well. With a very negative media exposure, resulting from the broadcasting of the ARD documentary on the status of temporary workers in Bad Hersfeld, the Amazon Deutschland CEO replied with an interview at the *Spiegel Online*, promptly relaunched by all press agencies, in which he explicitly praised the establishment of the *Betriebsrat* and invited his employees to set up work councils in all Amazon plants. With only one sentence in an interview, he achieved two results: on the one hand, the image of a company that, instead of trying to hinder the establishment of works councils, a growing practice in recent years in Germany (Behrens and Dribbusch 2014), moves in the opposite direction: recognizes, accepts, and even promotes a national symbolic institution. On the other hand, it was guaranteed that, at least during their first years of existence, the works councils would be entirely, or almost entirely, de-unionized. Apart from the two existing ones in Bad Hersfeld and Leipzig, all the others, except Graben, were formed in the first two years since the opening of the plant, in one case in the following year.

In the first two years of the activity of an Amazon fulfillment center, it is impossible to achieve significant unionization rates because it acts as the deterrent of the temporary employment relationship at the time of recruitment, which can be renewed for up to two years. Manifesting your adherence to the "third party stranger" at this stage equates to "occupational suicide". In contrast, applying for a list that is promoted by management is certainly a rational strategy with respect to the goal of transforming the employment relationship from temporary to permanent. In fact, the management has reached the goal it had set for itself: at the moment, works councils with a stable majority are the exception (Bad Hersfeld, Reihnberg); all others are pro-company or divided within them (Boewe and Schulten 2015). In Brieselang, where the "third party stranger" list has unexpectedly won the majority of seats, management has solved the problem in a short period of time: first, it began to lower the individual ratings of three works council members elected in the union list; then, when the contract expired, it relied on negative assessments in order not to renew the workers/members' contracts anymore. The three representatives have lost their jobs and the union list lost its majority (ibid.: 32–33). The story is symptomatic of Amazon's double strategy toward the "third party stranger": manifest disinterest outside, union-busting conduct inside.

Another obstacle to union action and mobilization, which is particularly difficult to overcome, is the strategic calculation inherent in Amazon's settlement choices. As already mentioned, Amazon systematically locates its plants in structurally weak regions with high unemployment rates. In such contexts, the implied promise is to offer permanent jobs to people (including foreigners and immigrants) with little or no qualifications, who are often long-term unemployed, or with precarious occupations, for which Amazon's employment offer is perceived as one of the best

Organizing and Collective Bargaining in the Digitized "Tertiary... 155

opportunities—even when it is not the best—that the territory can give. If you do not have the certainty of a permanent place yet, because you have been continually getting hired as a seasonal or temporary worker or because you are looking for a job, an opportunity given by Amazon can become a main goal to achieve. The digitalized "tertiary factory" has nothing to do with the rhetoric about digitalization and perhaps it is best understood with a bit more retro language: it relies on the "reserve army", squeezing it to the last drop but feeding it at the same time.

Finally, the last barrier for unions is closely linked to digitalization: digital technologies, coupled with the ultimate efficiency and standardization of the fulfillment centers, allows Amazon to temporarily relocate the organizational flows of orders and shipments to other warehouses, significantly reducing the effects of a potential strike or even nullifying any effectiveness. In itself it is a technic-organizational controversy that is far from being new since it was already found at the dawn of digitization at the "Asynchronous Engines Manufacturing" introduced in 1977 at Fiat Mirafiori. In that first case of flexible automation, the assembly line was replaced with fixed workstations supplied for the first time with automatic carriages; the carriages flowed on underground tracks, and the entire system was governed by the digitalized ICT system. The asynchronous production cycle released the work from the cadence of the assembly line but at the same time gave to the plant system a considerable margin of autonomy over workers' conflicts. In case of any abstention from work on a workstation or even in an entire area, the computer system reacted to it as to any other similar burst: it immediately redrew the flows by isolating the stations "in failure", and the whole process could continue for another 40 minutes. Someone inside the trade union in Turin called it "the time to rethink". In the case of Amazon, there is a qualitative leap: not a small department but an efficient network of fulfillment centers that are spatially distant. As for the "time to rethink", it is impossible to be estimated. In any case, Amazon has begun to stretch it by opening three new fulfillment centers in Poland in 2014—two in Wroclaw (one for large goods, the other for smaller and lighter ones) and the third in Paznań—as well as a recent one in the Czech Republic, near the Prague airport. The four sites are close to the eastern border with Germany and almost exclusively committed to the German market.

Recapturing the metaphor: the Biblical Goliath's armor weighed 40 pounds; Amazon's is intangible but is equally hard to damage with the traditional union weapons, thus allowing the management to ironize: "Strikes at Christmas? We care more about ice on the streets".

Amazon in Italy: The Way Toward the Unionization of Workers

According to what the Italian case shows, it could be said that within Amazon what is missing is the unionization of workers.

The Amazon case in Italy officially began at the end of 2010 with the investments made by the company in Castel S. Giovanni (PC). Since then, other auxiliary warehouses, though much less extended, have been opened in Milan Rogoredo, Milan Affori, Origgio (VA) and Avigliana (TO). With regard to the fulfillment center of Castel S. Giovanni, the number of workers has increased considerably over the years and currently there are 1,595 permanent employees, when only in 2016 there were 1,088 of them. However, it should be pointed out that the number of employees significantly grows during peak sales periods, especially Christmastime. On such occasions, the company assumes, exclusively by means of employment agencies, a real "army" of temporary (or contingent) workers, so that the total number of workers increases up to about 4,500. When the need for an additional workforce is over, almost all of the temporary workers are out, as the permanent employment contract remains a real option for few workers. In 2017, the number of employees in the company has increased due to the opening of two new fulfillment centers, in Passo Corese (RM) and Vercelli.

The path undertaken by Italian trade unions for the unionization of the company has been and still is characterized by many obstacles.

The main obstacle has always been the conduct of the management of the company, which, several times, has explicitly stated that it wants to manage the relationships with its employees without any kind of mediation. According to company mouthpieces, this decision has been made in order to favor a positive atmosphere between workers, team leaders and management. Nevertheless, what we are facing is a highly unbalanced and unilateral human resource management strategy, as the power is concentrated in the hands of one of the parties, which is, of course, the managerial one. In this way, remuneration, working time management, career advancements, workers' training, and everything that concerns human resource management are the exclusive prerogative of the company or, at the most, of the employment agencies with which Amazon has drawn up specific agreements. For a long time, the union could not even think about starting a dialogue around these issues since the attempts in approaching the company failed. At the same time, the exclusion of the trade unions did not allow the correctness of the application of collective bargaining agreements (where provided) to be verified. The case of the auxiliary warehouse near Varese offered a clear example of an incorrect application of collective agreement clauses. According to what an unionist from FILT-CGIL Lombardy has reported, managers "are accostumed to disproportionately rely on part-time and the working time coul arrive up to 15 hours" (Zorloni 2017), and workers involved were mainly the couriers of the companies with which Amazon has a partnership. The following union claims, together with the organization of a strike, have allowed the correction of such distortions by reaching a specific agreement at the plant level with CGIL (Italian General Confederation of Labour). This agreement, though signed with reference to an auxiliary plant, is an extremely important result since it is one of the first cases of collective agreement across Amazon's supply chain.

In the case of the Castel S. Giovanni plant, the situation is different despite the constant attempts slowly allowing trade unions to take a few steps forward. The first issue lies in the Amazon belonging sector, namely trade and private services sector, characterized by reduced unionization rates. On the one hand, this is due to the preference for certain type of employment relationship (temporary and seasonal jobs prevail, together with a widespread use of part-time jobs). On the other hand, it is due to the fact that a large part of the workers in this sector are women, young people and immigrants, whose unionization is usually more difficult (Crouch 2012; Carrieri 2012; Carrieri and Pirro 2016). Initially, unionization has proceeded slowly and with many obstacles, especially when considering the company's reactions in preventing employees from enrolling in the union associations. The testimonies, made by both trade unionists and workers themselves, show how joining a trade union by a worker contributed to making him or her a target for rather hostile attitudes. In any case, the company did not even need to put in place specific defense strategies against trade unions: the condition of temporary workers, who in most cases work to get a permanent employment contract, already works as an effective deterrent to enrollment in the unions. However, the growth of permanent workers on the one hand and union pressures on the other have contributed to the increase in the number of unionized employees, who, if we take into account the three main trade unions (CGIL, CISL and UIL), total 250 people.

At the same time, Italian trade unions moved to set up negotiation meetings with the company: it all started with negative responses from the company, then it continued with some institutional meetings, thanks to the intercession of local administrations, that were mostly inconclusive, until a meeting in March 2017, which was more promising. Moreover, it has been established that an RSA (*Rappresentanza Sindacale Unitaria*, namely the Italian representation bodies ad workplace) in the eyes of the union, could be a starting point for negotiating the drafting of a firm-level (second-level agreement) collective agreement.

However, the rather fluctuating events concerning the relationship between Italian trade unions and Amazon suggest that delegates and union officials face strong uncertainty in the future, for which it would be necessary to prepare. Other European contexts, especially the German one, have largely shown how Amazon does not give up easily under trade union pressures despite the start of (long) phases of conflict. Firm-level contracts, excluding those stipulated by the Solidarnosc syndicate in Poland and the FILT-CGIL trade union group, do not currently exist and those existing have content that, though very important, still does not substantially affect some of the most obvious Amazon's issues with regard to work organization and human resource management.

Conclusions

The case of Amazon, presented with its general features and analyzed from the industrial relations point of view in two different national contexts, makes it possible to draw some conclusions.

First of all, analysis of the organization of work through digitalization highlights the need to carry out further empirical research on the transformations of work in the digital era. Often, the contribution of ICT technologies in the workplace is read in a very optimistic way as if it were possible to achieve, through them, a kind of workers' paradise on Earth. However, the case of Amazon shows how the narratives about "Industry 4.0" need at least some other empirical evidence. If, in fact, the attention is focused on the worker, Amazon's working conditions show obvious limits, which have now been underlined by many, whether they are journalists, trade unionists or workers.

Second, Amazon represents an almost unique case of a company that shows high standardization regarding not only work processes but also the way it has approached industrial relations in different institutional contexts. The analysis of the two national cases shows this in several points. If the inevitable differences are set aside, it can be seen that the paths undertaken by the trade unions in the two national contexts are characterized by very similar trajectories. It all starts from the empirical evidence concerning the poor working conditions in the fulfillment centers, conditions that remain identical by changing the context of reference. Similarly, we find the management's response to the claims of workers and trade unionists: in both cases, Amazon puts up obstacles in the face of the attempts to unionize its warehouses. The trade unions' response is fast, which in this case diverges, precisely because, unlike Amazon, the German and Italian unions do not follow standardized action protocols. Whereas the German union *ver.di* has opted for the start of a conflictual phase—with several strikes—that has lasted since December 2013, Italian unions have preferred the path of dialogue through the use of the institutional channels of the bureaucratic trade union system and of the local governments. However, the results obtained are similar: Amazon grants very little and certainly not a collective bargaining agreement at the firm level, which would be the desired outcome.

The company seems to be indifferent concerning the institutional contexts: it applies the national collective agreement where this does not necessarily involve confronting with unions; it does not apply it in the opposite case. Whatever the choice, it has no significant consequences on work organization, human resource management and union (busting) politics, which remain the same everywhere. Institutions are too weak or too weakened to be able to influence the processes regarding these aspects. The same is true for trade unions. Even in Germany—where the institutional set-up seems to be more dense and the union a little more resilient than elsewhere—the deregulation of the last 20 years (also as a consequence of the EU policies on company law) has made it easy to get around institutions and neutralize union power. In particular, it is significant that the only concrete achievements so far by *ver.di* have been reached through judicial means; this is the case with the establishment of the supervisory board in Bad Hersfeld or the prohibition of holiday working hours, which the local administrations had initially authorized. From this point of view, the conflict between Amazon and *ver.di* confirms a trend that has been going on for some time (Rehder 2016), but the ever-greater role of judges and tribunals in settling conflicts calls into question the regulatory effectiveness of collective autonomy. In the case of Amazon, however, there is a specific factor, which is added to the structural obstacles already considered: Amazon is now a digital conglomerate whose sources of profit are not in e-commerce, which has never been profitable, but elsewhere, primarily in the "Amazon Web Services" cloud services to businesses and governments.[8] The e-commerce is used mainly to extend and retain customers and then to gradually offer new products and services to a proprietary eco-system in competition with those of Apple and Google, thus increasing the wealth of big data, another source of profits. If we add to this the enormous liquidity available to the company, the economic costs of the trade union conflict are probably irrelevant and in any case amply compensated. In a conflict for recognition like the one under way in Germany, this is the worst scenario for trade unions. This remains valid for the Italian case, where the "recognition" of trade unions appears purely formal.

Notes

1. Generally speaking, this is true for the European context. The situation is different in North America, where a stronger automation has been implemented, especially for managing the fulfillment of orders with large-sized goods.

Organizing and Collective Bargaining in the Digitized "Tertiary... 161

2. There are three shifts: morning shift, afternoon shift and night shift. Each one last for seven hours, plus meal breaks of 30 minutes. The night shift is not always available, only during periods when sales grow.
3. There are some cases in which job rotation is applied, but it is not used extensively for every worker.
4. The period of training lasts three days: the first two days are managed by work agencies, which inform workers about safety at work and contractual procedures. During the last day, workers are trained inside of Amazon fulfillment center and the main tasks are explained by workers who function as trainers.
5. There are three cut-offs, one per shift, at 1 a.m., 2 p.m. and 5 p.m.
6. These include the transformation into a European company (SE) before exceeding the threshold of 2,000 employees, the adoption of a foreign legal form (typically British or Dutch) or that of the headquarter (Aldi and Lidl), the corporate fragmentation in one multitude of minor businesses or the collage of formally independent operative units. Another strategy is not to comply with the law (this is the case of Rossmann, one of the three major German grocery chains, 29,000 employees): the strategy is effective because a possible legal procedure initiated by the trade union is basically useless for the possibility of the company to choose in the meantime one of the legal "escape routes" listed above.
7. Only in Bad Hersfeld, since 2014, and only after an application submitted by *ver.di.* to the provincial court of Frankfurt. The same union is part of it with two representatives. For Amazon, the paradoxical situation has thus arisen to deal with the supervisory board with that "third stranger" whom the company counterpart does not intend to recognize as an interlocutor.
8. Amazon's economic accounts are characterized by a continuous and exponential growth in turnover, which has been reflected in many loss-making in the past years. Profits that has been registered since 2015, in a percentage still little more than insignificant, are mainly attributable to Amazon Web Service (AWS), whose economic data were included, before that year, in the residual item "Other". Despite representing only about 10% of total income, the AWS segment stands out for the highest growth rates both in terms of sales volume (over 40% in 2016 and 2017) and, above all, in operating profit ($1.2 million in the third quarter of 2017). The last data is even more significant if compared with the rest of the Amazon conglomerate, which in the same period recorded a total of $ 824 million in loss. In summary, AWS is currently the division that allows Amazon not to get in debt and "to keep investing in the core business" (Kim 2017).

References

ARD—Erstes Deutsches Fernsehn. 2013. *Ausgeliefert!—Leiharbeiter bei Amazon.* https://www.youtube.com/watch?v=uRsMWIp4t28. Broadcasted on 13 Feb

Armaroli, Ilaria. 2015. Perché ad Amazon (e a tutti noi) serve il sindacato. Bollettino Adapt. http://www.bollettinoadapt.it/perche-ad-amazon-e-a-tutti-noi-serve-il-sindacato/. Accessed 7 Sept 2017.

BBC. 2013. *Amazon: The Truth Behind the Click.* https://www.youtube.com/watch?v=UQATFbLvIHk. Broadcasted on 29 Nov 2013.

Behrens, Martin, and Heiner Dribbusch. 2014. Arbeitgebermaßnahmen gegen Betriebsräte: Angriffe auf die betriebliche Mitbestimmung. *WSI-Mitteilungen* 2: 140–148.

Bock, Violetta. 2016. Ver.di@Amazon. Aufbau und Aktivierung eines gewerkschaftlichen Kerns. Brochure. Kassel: OKG.

Boewe, Jörn, and Johannes Schulten. 2015. *Der lange Kampf der Amazon-Beschäftigten.* Berlin: Rosa-Luxemburg-Stiftung.

Braverman, Harry. 1978. *Lavoro e capitale monopolistico: la degradazione del lavoro nel XX secolo.* Torino: Einaudi.

Butera, Federico, ed. 1983. *La progettazione organizzativa.* Milano: Franco Angeli.

———. 1984. *L'orologio e l'organismo.* Milano: Franco Angeli.

Carrieri, Mimmo. 2012. *I sindacati.* Bologna: Il Mulino.

Carrieri, Mimmo, and Fabrizio Pirro. 2016. *Relazioni industriali.* Milano: Egea.

Ciborra, Claudio, and Giovan Francesco Lanzara, eds. 1984. *Progettazione delle nuove tecnologie e qualità del lavoro.* Milano: Franco Angeli.

Crouch, Colin. 2011. *The Strange Non-death of Neoliberalism.* Cambridge: Polity Press.

———. 2012. Il declino delle relazioni industriali nell'odierno capitalismo. *Stato e Mercato* 1: 56–75.

Düll, Klaus, and Günter Bechtle. 1988. Die Krise des normierten Verhandlungssystems. Rationalisierungsstrategien und industrielle Beziehungen im Betrieb. In *Mensch, Arbeit und Betrieb,* ed. Karl M. Bolte, 215–244. Weinheim: Acta Humaniora.

Edwards, Richard. 1979. *Contested Terrain.* New York: Basic Books.

Fiocco, Laura. 2001. I dispositivi strutturali di potere in fabbrica. In *Melfi In Time. Produzione snella e disciplinamento della forza lavoro alla Fiat,* ed. Ada Cavazzani, Laura Fiocco, and Giordano Sivini, 47–84. Potenza: Consiglio Regionale della Basilicata.

Organizing and Collective Bargaining in the Digitized "Tertiary... 163

GTAI. 2014. Industrie 4.0: Smart Manufacturing for the Future. Brochure. Köln: Asmuth Druck & Crossmedia GmbH & Co. KG.

Hirsch-Kreinsen, Hartmut, Peter Ittermann, and Jonathan Niehaus, eds. 2015. *Digitalisierung industrieller Arbeit. Die Vision Industrie 4.0 und ihre sozialen Herausforderungen.* Baden-Baden: Nomos.

Honneth, Axel. 2011. *Verwilderungen des sozialen Konflikts: Anerkennungskämpfe zu Beginn des 21. Jahrhunderts*, Working Paper 11/4. Köln: Max-Planck-Institut für Gesellschaftsforschung.

Jamieson, Dave. 2014. Amazon Resorts to Wordplay to Keep Salaries Low. *Huffington Post*, September 23. https://www.huffingtonpost.com/entry/amazon-germany-strike_n_5868532.html. Accessed 18 May 2017.

Kantor, Jodi, and David Streitfeld. 2015. Inside Amazon: Wrestling Big Ideas in a Bruising Workplace. *The New York Times*, August 15. https://www.nytimes.com/2015/08/16/technology/inside-amazon-wrestling-big-ideas-in-a-bruising-workplace.html. Accessed 15 June 2017.

Kärcher, Bernd. 2014. Erfahrungen und Herausforderungen in der Industrie. Alternative Wege in die Industrie 4.0 – Möglichkeiten und Grenzen. In *Bundesministerium für Wirtschaft und Energie (BMWi) (Hg.)*, 19–25. Berlin: BMWi.

Kim, Eugene. 2017. Amazon Shares Spar After Massive Earning Beat. *Cnbc*, October 26. https://www.cnbc.com/2017/10/26/amazon-earnings-q3-2017.html. Accessed 18 Dec 2017.

Kunda, Gideon. 1992. *Engineering Culture. Control and Commitment in a High-Tech Corporation*. Philadelphia: Temple University.

Leisegang, Daniel. 2015. Der Fall Amazon: Arbeiten und Kaufen im Online-Versandhandel. In *Gute Arbeit und Digitalisierung. Prozessanalysen und Gestaltungsperspektive für eine humane digitale Welt*, ed. Ver.di—Bereich Innovation und Gute Arbeit, 146–155. Berlin: ver.di – Vereinte Dienstleistungsgewerkscahft.

Malet, Jean-Baptiste. 2013. *En Amazonie. Infiltré dans le «meilleur des mondes»*. Paris: Fayard.

Müller-Jentsch, Walther. 1999. *Konfliktpartnerschaft. Akteure und Institutionen der industriellen Beziehungen*. München: Mering.

O'Connor, Sarah. 2013. Amazon Unpacked. *Financial Times*, February 8. https://www.ft.com/content/ed6a985c-70bd-11e2-85d0-00144feab49a?mhq5j=e1. Accessed 13 June 2017.

Oberhuber, Nadine. 2015. Der Arbeitskrampf. *Die Zeit*, October 1. http://www.zeit.de/wirtschaft/2015-09/amazon-streik-tarifvertrag-kampf. Accessed 13 Nov 2017.

Osborne, Hilary. 2016. Amazon Accused of 'Intolerable Conditions' at Scottish Warehouse. *The Guardian*, December 12. https://www.theguardian.com/technology/2016/dec/11/amazon-accused-of-intolerable-conditions-at-scottish-warehouse. Accessed 15 June 2017.

Parenti, Christian. 2001. Big Brother's Corporate Cousin. *The Nation*, July 27. https://www.thenation.com/article/big-brothers-corporate-cousin/. Accessed 13 June 2017.

Rehder, Britta. 2016. Konflikt ohne Partnerschaft? Arbeitsbeziehungen im Dienstleistungssector. *Industrielle Beziehungen* 23 (3): 366–373.

Reyneri, Emilio. 2005. *Sociologia del mercato del lavoro*. Bologna: Il Mulino.

Salento, Angelo. 2016. Note sui problemi di ricerca su Industria 4.0 e sulle conseguenze per i lavoratori e le lavoratrici. *Inchiesta* 191: 44–49.

Scharpf, Fritz W. 2000. *Interaktionsformen. Akteurzentrierter Institutionalismus in der Politikforschung*. Wiesbaden: VS Verlag für Sozialwissenschaften.

Sewell, Graham, and Barry Wilkinson. 1992. 'Someone to Watch over Me': Surveillance, Discipline and the Just-in-Time Labour Process. *Sociology* 26: 271–289.

Streeck, Wolfgang. 1981. *Gewerkschaftliche Organisationsprobleme in der sozialstaatlichen Demokratie*, Königstein/Ts.: Athenäum.

Zorloni, Luca. 2017. Amazon scende a patti con i sindacati italiani. *WIRED*, May 30. https://www.wired.it/economia/lavoro/2017/05/30/amazon-sindacati-italiani/. Accessed 14 June 2017.

9

Evolution of Trade Unions in Industry 4.0: A German and Italian Debate

Matteo Avogaro

A New Concept of Manufacturing, a New Idea of Work

Manufacturing and the industrial sector are parts of the work contexts expected to be influenced by the process of digitization most. The process started two decades ago and nowadays seems to have reached its peak.

The prediction is supported by a wide series of elements. Recently, a new way of work—online or in outsourcing—has arisen (Valenduc and Vendramin 2016, pp. 19–20) and some productions have been digitized. The phenomenon has been inspired by the diffusion of smartphones, tablets, internet connections on mobile devices and geo-localization apps—currently used not only as means of amusement but also as instruments to improve productivity and efficiency on the job—and by the

---

M. Avogaro (✉)
Labour Law, Department of Civil Law and Legal History, University of Milan, Milan, Italy
e-mail: matteo.avogaro@unimi.it

© The Author(s) 2018
E. Ales et al. (eds.), *Working in Digital and Smart Organizations*,
https://doi.org/10.1007/978-3-319-77329-2_9

technological development that extended the possibility to use services such as cloud and big data (Valenduc and Vendramin 2016, p. 20; Lestavel 2015, pp. 70–73).

On the other hand, the most striking innovation giving rise to the process of digitization of manufacturing is represented by Cyber-Physical Systems (CPS): a new generation of robots that are able to assimilate experiences and to learn from the surrounding environment in a way to develop and to adjust their behaviour (Lee 2008). For this reason, there are some discouraging theories suggesting that this new kind of machinery will endanger some traditional and consolidated professions (Seghezzi and Tiraboschi 2016a, 8 ff.), causing increases in the unemployment rate.

The aforementioned scenario is indicated as Industry 4.0, entailing a new idea of production, founded on the integration between smart machinery, internet, robotics and remote work (Bentivogli 2016; Wetzel 2015) that, in recent years, has been moved to the top of the agenda of the most relevant economies in the world. Among them, the US, with the Manufacturing USA project, financed by government, public and private entities for an amount of about $0.5 billion (USD); France, which supports the programme *Industrie du future*, with an investment of 10 billion euros; Germany, where the federal government launched a plan of 1 billion euros to finance company projects, research centres and tax incentives; and Italy, which presented a plan of 13 billion euros of horizontal incentives for the years 2018–2024.

The technological improvement of manufacturing could entail a possible powerful relaunch of Western economies, but at the same time it could heavily affect the conditions of the workforce and create space for abuses and unemployment by 2025 (Cagol 2016; Dal Ponte et al. 2016).

In light of the above, other than bringing a new concept of company, Industry 4.0 seems to be intended to bring a new idea of work. Informatics and robots will deeply affect the workplace organization; the nature of work itself seems to be destined to change, moving towards Work 4.0 (Weiss 2016, 657 ff.; IG Metall 2015a).

In the new professional and economic context, the space for standardized products will be reasonably reduced while the efforts towards tailor-made production could increase. Therefore, new forms of continuous production will be experimented with in order to be able to promptly react to new market requests.

Employees' tasks will be modified as a consequence of the increasing role of CPS. The outcome seems to be a diminution of low-skilled employees, while more-qualified workers, such as technicians, will augment their relevance. The way of rendering the performance will increase its flexibility: workers will profit from the possibility to realize some maintenance or programme operations on machinery from long distances and therefore to work, at least partially, from their houses (Bentivogli 2015, 11 ff.).

In particular, two models have been developed (Kurtz 2014; Ganz 2014) to try to forecast the change brought by Work 4.0: the "automatization model" and the "specialization model".

The automatization model is a pessimistic prediction of the effects of Industry 4.0 on the labour market: CPS will acquire a leading role in factories, and human activities will be essentially directed and governed by them. It seems to lead to an organization of work based on robots assisted by a small number of highly specialized workers, charged with great responsibilities and whose continuous education will be realized mainly on the job. On the other hand, medium- and lower-skilled workers will be replaced by CPS (Seghezzi 2016, 188 ff.).

In contrast, the specialization model wagers on a virtuous cooperation between men and machinery. This theory conceives workers as the centre of the production systems, while robots and smart machinery will represent a new generation of technological tools designated to support them. This model entails a decrease of less trained workers, replaced by CPS, but an augmentation of the request of high- and medium-skilled employees, hired to cooperate and interact with advanced informatic systems. Tasks will become less repetitive, while cooperation will be enhanced, not only between men and machinery but also among workers. Knowledge requirements will increase, and employees will have the opportunity to improve their competences on the job (Seghezzi 2016, 188 ff.).

Neither of the above-mentioned two models is likely to be entirely applied. Perhaps, the outcome of Industry 4.0 will be a hybrid result, consisting of a medium point between the two theories, modulated on the basis of the automatization level, market requirements and characteristics of the commercial sector of the company (Hirsch-Kreinsen 2014).

In any case, both models indicate, as a further effect of Work 4.0, an increasing independence of employees. The new figure of worker—high-skilled and bearing the burden of augmented responsibilities deriving from managerial tasks and the possibility to interact with machinery from remote—will entail the introduction of new instruments to protect him or her in the workplace and during the labour relationship (Pero 2015, 24 ff.).

This seems to be, in particular, a two-sided problem.

The first issue concerns the classification of "employees 4.0" as autonomous workers, with a specific condition of dependency from their (in general, one) customers (Forlivesi 2016, 664 ff.), or as dependent workers, with the consequential need to introduce new criteria to enlarge the definition of dependent work. On this aspect, European scholars suggested different instruments to clarify the "grey zone" between the area of self-employment and the one of dependent work, such as the controversial institutes of the TRADE in Spain (Valdés dal Ré and Valdés Alonso 2010, 705 ff.; Villalón 2013, 287 ff.) and of *arbeitnehmerähnliche Person* in Germany (Grunsky 1980; Wank 1988). In relation to the extension of the legal definition of employee, it is worth analysing the debate concerning gig economy (Dagnino 2016, 137 ff.; Rogers 2015, 85 ff.) and also the new and recent Italian legal arrangement of heter-organized work (Ferraro 2016, 53 ff.; Santoro Passarelli 2015).

The second aspect is related to work–life balance in the age of BYOD (Bring Your Own Device) policies and company devices. The debate, developed mainly in France and Italy, concerning the right to disconnect, is expected to assume a key role in the future scenarios of Work 4.0.

To address the aforementioned issues, the main German and Italian trade unions promoted a wide debate in recent years. This research is aimed, in particular, at investigating the strategies proposed by these organizations to regulate the new digitized work environment, in order to protect employee's rights, and will be restricted to the main fields where

Industry 4.0 is developing: manufacturing and the metalworker and mechanical engineering industry. Hence, the point of departure will be the studies and the suggestions of the workers' organizations themselves, to be analysed in a critical way observing the degree of practical actualization of these ideas through collective bargaining. Attention will be mainly focused on the Italian workers' organizations FIM-CISL and the German IG-Metall, which privilege procedures of co-determination or cooperation between employers and employees. This should be done in order to underline the main characteristics of the approach of trade unions not refusing technological innovation or digitization but attempting to find new instruments to manage this transition in advance, protecting (also) workers' interests.

Trade Unions' Approach in Italy

In Italy, Industry 4.0 is at the top of the agenda of the government and of some social partners. In 2015, the Ministry of Economic Development launched a relevant financing plan to encourage manufacturing to embrace digitization and technological innovation. Among trade unions, FIM-CISL was the first attempting to promote a debate on the implications of Industry 4.0 on the Italian labour market and on the role of workers' organizations in defining the factory of tomorrow. Recently, this initiative has been followed by other Italian trade unions, such as CGIL, which launched the "Idea diffusa" project in May 2017 (CGIL 2017a).

From the practical side, collective bargaining also faced the technological change occurring in factories, providing for some solutions to be analysed to reconstruct the Italian debate.

Re-organize Workers' Rights in the Digitized Factory

The organization of work in the environment of Industry 4.0 is the main issue addressed by FIM-CISL, and by its leader Marco Bentivogli, to analyse the evolution of Italian workers' organizations.

In light of the above, attention is focused on lifelong learning, on the modification of tasks, on the redefinition of time and place to work and on the kind of labour law solutions that could best protect workers. FIM-CISL shares the specialization model: education and training are the key elements to prevent technological unemployment. Therefore, in order not to allow smart machinery to endanger human work, trade unions should anticipate the change (Bentivogli 2015, p. 6).

According to the said organization, professional levels of the era of Industry 4.0 will be reshaped, since tasks requesting relevant human labour and routine activities will be gradually replaced by high-skilled ones as planning, setting-up, maintenance, regulation and improvement of machinery and software. In this context, teamwork will play a central role: production lines and fixed and unskilled positions will decline as a consequence of the affirmation of robotics and informatics. At the same time, skilled workers are to become multitaskers such that each employee will not be appointed only one specific task or role in the production activity, but will have to reach different objectives together with the team (Pero 2015, pp. 26–27).

The "rotation of workers" and the so-called "strategy of suggestions" are effects directly descending from the adoption of the teamwork.

"Rotation" means that, in a team, workers will have to be interchangeable and cover different tasks in order to allow the crew to reach the assigned objectives. Through the experimentation of different positions, the workers will augment their opportunities to expand experience and improve their ability to find innovative solutions. At this stage, "strategy of suggestions" becomes relevant. Its philosophy is to collect the highest possible number of amelioration proposals advanced by workers appointed to a specific proceeding or machinery, in order to speed up production and work in a more efficient way. With reference to employees, this new form of work organization is characterized by pros and cons: working rhythms will intensify; in any case, the quality of work in general will be improved and as a result there will be a reduction in accidents and exertion. Finally, the aforementioned new development of work organization should increase employers' margin of income. Therefore, also workers will have the possibility to improve their salaries, in particular through the tool of collective bargaining (Pero 2015, pp. 28–29).

In this scenario, the central role is played by workers' training. A survey carried out in 2015 by Randstad indicated, at that point, that 44% of Italian workers interviewed are persuaded that their respective job will be automatized in the next 5–10 years. Among them, 30% is concerned not to have adequate knowledge to win the struggle of digitization, whereas the average European rate is 18% and the world rate is 22% (Minghetti 2016; Randstad Holding 2015). Accordingly, 66% of employees urges for more investments in on-the-job education. A new focus realized by Randstad at the beginning of 2016 confirmed the tendency (Randstad Holding 2016; Randstad Italia S.p.A. 2016): the skilled employees of Industry 4.0 will need continuous improvement in their knowledge during their working life.

A congruent reply to these issues, for FIM-CISL, is to widen the area covered by the workers' right of education, regulated, in Italy, through Article 6 of law 53 of 8 March 2000. The aforementioned provision, concerning leave of absence for continuous vocational training, after a premise in which it is stated that workers have the right to extend their educational period for all their life, at paragraph 2 delegates collective agreements to specify, *in concreto*, how workers can exercise this right. FIM-CISL suggests, at this point, that collective agreements of Industry 4.0 should renew the system of learning discharge, providing for an employee's individual right to stop working or to accede to a part-time regime irrespectively of the employer's opinion, for frequent periods, in order to take courses to improve its knowledge (Bentivogli 2015, 10 ff.). At this point, the first results were reached in November 2016 (see "The National Collective Agreement of the Metalworker and Mechanical Engineering Industry of 2016" section below).

With reference to the internal organization of factories, FIM-CISL is oriented towards a progressive abandonment of fixed professional levels set forth by collective agreements, in light of an exchange between more flexibility, remunerated with more services, and in particular more education (Navaretti 2015, pp. 31–33).

As indicated above, the new paradigm of Industry 4.0 will also modify the traditional concepts of time and place to work in manufacturing. The growing availability of tools that enable workers to interact with machinery at a distance, and the progressive relinquishing of manual production, will encourage employees to realize their performance, at least in some cases, from locations different from offices or factories. In addition, the foreshadowed emancipation from the traditional working place will impact temporal articulation, which will become less bound to office times and to the "classic" eight-hour working day. At this point, great attention is devoted by Italian trade unions to smart working (known as "lavoro agile" in Italy, Bentivogli 2015, 11 ff.) and to the respective bill passed in 2017 concerning the first attempt to regulate this phenomenon.

Although until 2015 the area of smart working was restricted to experimentations promoted, at the company level, by social partners, in 2016 the government, and at a subsequent time a group of members of Parliament, advanced two proposals about this matter, then reduced to one in the bill S. 2233-B, approved by the Parliament as Law 81 of 22 May 2017. In particular, smart working is regulated by Articles 18–24 of Law 81/2017. According to Article 18 of Law 81/2017, it is intended not as a new labour agreement but as a way of working applicable to wage labour. Smart working could also concern phases, cycles or objectives of the work relationship and request the utilization of technological devices. The performance could be realized partially in and partially outside the premises of the company, without a fixed working place, and within the maximum daily or weekly time limits set forth by law or collective bargaining. The agreement to accede to the regime of smart working must be written and, according to Article 19 of Law 81/2017, must regulate the activity that the worker could carry on outside the premises of the factory and, among other things, provide for technical and organizational measures to assure the worker of a right to disconnect from the technological devices. Finally, the law introduces other rights and guarantees for the smart worker, such as the ones concerning education (Article 20), limits to the power of control of the employer (Article 21), work health and safety (Article 22) and the extension of the mandatory assurance against injuries or professional illnesses to the activity performed outside the factory (Article 23). In a nutshell, Law 81/2017 provides for a general framework that will have to be completed by collective agreements or by the agreements reached directly between employer and employee.

The law concerning smart working was, in general, appreciated by the main social partners (Pogliotti 2015). Notwithstanding, both CISL and CGIL—in the respective communications presented during the auditions before the Labour Commission of the Senate in 2016 and of Chamber of Deputies in 2017, concerning the bill S. 2233-B—demanded that the regulation be improved but did not achieve the consent of Parliament.

With specific reference to the right to disconnect, CISL, being concerned with risks brought by an individual agreement setting the conditions of smart work, insisted on the introduction of a provision expressly recognizing at least the priority regulative role of collective agreements (CISL 2016). CGIL demanded, in addition, that the employer be prevented from using specific tools to survey workers when they are outside their offices (CGIL 2017b).

A further effect brought by the upcoming revolution of Industry 4.0, in this case criticized by the examined workers' organizations, deals with the individual bargaining between employer and employee. In the light of above, trade unions are concerned that the affirmation of just-in-time production and the increasing employee autonomy could move the most skilled and qualified workers to breach the front of standardized-dependent labour agreement, agreeing individual, most flexible and/or favourable conditions, with their company (Mandl et al. 2015, 72 ff.).

Finally, the debate is related to the structure and organization of trade unions of the age of Industry 4.0. At this point, the concept of "smart unions" was introduced. According to FIM-CISL, forthcoming worker's organizations could not be based only on traditional techniques of bargaining and representation of workers, but the upcoming period of change requires a new generation of officials, who are more competent, selected on the basis of their abilities and knowledge, and also able to suggest different and credible solutions to management. Therefore, education will become fundamental not only for the workers but also for their representatives. In addition, most of the services and information provided by unions should become available on the web in order to ease workers' access and to increase the appeal of these organizations among the new generation of employees. Some experts urged unions to become

174 M. Avogaro

more flexible, in line with the new generaion of employees: fundamentally, being the representative of a group of 1,000 "ordinary" metalworkers is different than representing 1,000 multitasking employees, and different interests and bargaining power are in evidence. Therefore, tailor-made production could lead also to a new form of tailor-made trade unions (Navaretti 2015, p. 33).

With reference to FIM-CISL's point of view, the described strategy will allow workers' organizations to maintain, and if possible to increase, their centrality in the age of Work 4.0. These proposals look to the future, but in workplaces some efforts to adapt the labour context to new scenarios have already been made by workers' organizations through collective agreements (Bentivogli 2015, 19 ff.; Pero 2015, pp. 26–27).

Practical Solutions to Improve Organization and Quality of Work: Collective Agreements

Through collective bargaining, Italian social partners recently attempted to develop the first solutions congenial to Industry 4.0.

In light of the above, reference is made, in particular, to two remarkable agreements:

– the company one executed between Fiat and FIM, UILM and FISMIC on 15 June 2010 to regulate the activity in the automobile factory of Pomigliano d'Arco (De Luca Tamajo 2011; Santoro Passarelli 2011) and
– the national collective agreement executed by the main metalworkers' and employers' organizations on 26 November 2016.

The Fiat Agreement of 15 June 2010

The Fiat agreement of 15 June 2010, called the "Pomigliano agreement", has been executed as a condition posed by Fiat to approve an investment of 700 million euros for the factory of Pomigliano d'Arco. This agreement provoked a relevant debate as a consequence of its impact on industrial relations (Carinci 2011, 11 ff.; Santoro Passarelli 2011, 161 ff.; Garofalo 2011, 499 ff.).

With reference to the matter of the current analysis, first of all, the Pomigliano agreement introduced, in its Article 5, a new organization of work that might represent a premise of Industry 4.0: the World Class Manufacturing ("WCM") system (Magnani 2011, 15 ff.).

WCM is a new management system of factories, developed in the US during the '90s and afterwards by Fiat during the first decade of the twenty-first century (for an analysis of principles and structure of WCM, see Mercadante and Spada 2015, 547 ff.; De Meyer et al. 1989, 135 ff.), aimed to improve the quality of production through a theory based on, among other things, principles of Lean Manufacturing (Liker and Attolico 2014; Womack et al. 1993). The principles also include the capability to promptly react to the modifications of the quantity and quality of products requested by clients. In this context, WCM seems to anticipate Industry 4.0, which, in the same way, is directed by means of intelligent products and machinery to expand the just-in-time production, and the final objective is to allow companies to reply immediately to new market tendencies.

In addition, the philosophy of WCM is focused on teamwork and on the participation of all the employees in improvements and successes of their company (Mercadante and Spada 2015, 551 ff.). This is another aspect shared with Industry 4.0, which tends to overcome the rigid boundaries between directors and workmen, privileging teamwork and the idea of a multitasking employee.

Finally, education is a key element of both WCM and Industry 4.0: on this point, the new organizational scheme introduced by the Pomigliano agreement supports the improvement of skills of the employees, and the aims were to increase the competitiveness of the company and to strengthen the security and safety of factories (Mercadante and Spada 2015, 558 ff.).

Beyond WCM, the Pomigliano agreement contains other innovations: the most relevant is set forth by Article 3 of the agreement, which introduced a new organizational scheme of tasks anticipating the reform of Article 2103 of the Italian Civil Code enacted some years later by the Jobs Act and, in general, the concept of the multi-role employee suggested by Industry 4.0 (see "A New Concept of Manufacturing, a New Idea of Work" section above) with the abandonment of the tayloristic production model (Brollo 2016, 308 ff.).

In light of the above, the Pomigliano agreement can be considered a step made by Italian industrial relations towards Industry 4.0 and to the new structure of factories that could be imposed by the diffusion of smart machinery.

The National Collective Agreement of the Metalworker and Mechanical Engineering Industry of 2016

Another important effort to pave the way for the upcoming innovation of Industry 4.0 is represented by the renewed national collective agreement of the metalworker and mechanical engineering industry, executed on 26 November 2016.

The agreement provides for a significant innovation in three specific areas: professional levels, workers' continuous education, and working time.

In regard to professional levels, the new collective agreement expressly recognizes the need to modify and overcome the old classificatory system, elaborated in 1973, and charges a Joint Committee to detail proposals to update it. In the same direction, it encourages companies to start experimental periods in which they will test new methods to organize workers' professional levels, under control of the aforementioned committee (Armaroli 2016, p. 3). The experimentation will cease in December 2018, and the results could be used by social partners to single out the more efficient way to improve work organization.

With reference to continuous education, section IV, title III, Article 7 of the national collective agreement recognizes, accepting a request of FIM-CISL (see "FIM-CISL: Re-organize Workers' Rights in the Digitized Factory" section above), an individual right of the employee to temporarily suspend work activity for educational purposes (Seghezzi and Tiraboschi 2016b, p. 3). In particular, a worker hired without term will benefit of 24 hours for each three-year period to be enrolled in projects organized by the company or at the territorial/sectorial level, aimed to enhance his education. In addition, workers not involved in the said education projects will have the right, in any case, to benefit of

Evolution of Trade Unions in Industry 4.0: A German...   177

a corresponding 24-hour period to be exploited in different activities to improve their competencies. In the latter case, two thirds of costs will have to be sustained by the employer. In relation to Article 7, the overall number of employees that, at the same time, will have the possibility to take part in education plans will be 3% of the total, but this number may be modified by collective agreements at the company level.

Finally, with reference to working time, the agreement, as provided by its section IV, title III, Article 5, encourages the workers' and employer's organizations to find, at the company level, solutions to promote the work–life balance. In addition, the same Article expressly mentions smart working, specifying that the parties will consider whether to integrate the collective agreement on the basis of Law 81/2017 (Armaroli 2016, pp. 3–4).

Work 4.0.: The German Recipe

Germany is the European country which, before the others, started reasoning about implications of Industry 4.0.

In 2013, the German government launched the *"Industrie 4.0"* platform (Scheremet 2015), which has been followed by different initiatives promoted by the Federal Ministry of Labour and Social Affairs (Bundesministerium für Arbeit und Soziales 2015) and by the Minister of Economic Affairs and Energy (Bundesministerium für Wirtschaft und Energie et al. 2015).

IG Metall—the main German trade union representing workers of manufacturing—has been strictly involved in the aforementioned processes.

Lifelong Learning and "New Normal" to Win the Digitization Struggle

In 2014, IG Metall launched a survey concerning the effects of digitization of the industrial sector (IG Metall 2016). The results underlined the key issues brought by the rising of Industry 4.0 and allowed the union to elaborate first solutions.

In general, IG Metall emphasizes that the increased role of robots and informatics in manufacturing will augment productivity, which will entail a significant growth in the capability of industries to obtain value from work and raw materials, maintaining the same workforce. Bitkom and the Fraunhofer Institute for Labor and Organization forecast a growth of the gross value of the German economy, as an effect of Industry 4.0 combined with other elements, between 2015 and 2025, of 78 billion euros, corresponding to an increase of 1.7% per year (Van Ackeren and Schröder 2016, pp. 22–23). This economic development will interest six sectors in particular: machinery and plant engineering, electrical engineering, automotive industry, chemical industry, agriculture, and information and communication technology (IG Metall 2016, p. 6).

Despite the optimistic economic predictions, IG Metall underlines that the effect of Industry 4.0 on German employment levels is open to discussion. The incumbent modification of the labour market will no doubt have an impact on the kind of jobs and on the skills demanded to workers, while risks concerning the increase of unemployment seem to be connected to the capability of workers to adapt to the new environment.

According to the survey of the German trade union, 42% of local employees are working in sectors that will be reasonably automatized in upcoming years. Therefore, the replacement risk rate corresponds to 45–46% for helpers and skilled employees, 33.4% for specialists, and 18.8% for experts with the highest levels of knowledge (IG Metall 2016, p. 10). The risk is strictly connected to the ability of workers, social partners and institutions to improve employees' education in order to allow them to be competitive in the new context. With reference to this aspect, by 2025, IG Metall shows an estimated diminution of employment rates in the areas of machine and plant control and maintenance (about −13%) and a lower diminution in metal construction, installation, assembly and electrical work (about −5%) and in other sectors involved in processing raw materials and repair (−3%). Meanwhile, the augmentation of the workers' request will be mainly in the areas of IT and natural science (+4%), law, management and economics (+3%) and media, arts and social sciences (+2%). Consequently, the need to arrange instruments for a possible shift of employees from the declining sectors to the rising ones urges the enactment of policies to provide them with fundamental knowledge concerning the new working fields. The company considers that the workers of the future will have to reply to two main requirements: high skills and the ability to relate with complexity (IG Metall 2016, pp. 10–11).

In light of the above, the first issue to be addressed concerns the national educational landscape, which IG Metall does not consider advanced enough for the requirements of digitization, soliciting its renovation.

New education opportunities, for people who already work, could be provided by collective bargaining. In this field, the workers' organization is requesting that the current collective agreements are updated with a list of key elements: (i) the arrangement of qualification plans based on the upcoming technical and organizational changes and (ii) the introduction of the right, for every employee, to a regular meeting with the employer in order to determine whether and which qualification is required and to reach a periodical agreement on the necessary qualification measures (see "The Training Model of Baden-Württemberg: From 2001 to 2015" section below).

Following the aforementioned plan, workplaces should be gradually transformed into learning places. As an example, digital devices, such as tablets, could acquire the double function of means to increase productivity and of new didactic tools. Furthermore, specific attention should be paid to small and medium enterprises in order not to exclude them from this process (on this point, see Bundesagentur für Arbeit 2016).

Meanwhile, for young trainees, notions of digital technology and practical lessons to apprehend how to adapt themselves to the working methods of tomorrow are considered to be fundamental in a work context where a good educational background is no longer sufficient.

Analysing the results of its survey, IG Metall highlights the positive and negative effects of digitization of manufacturing in employees' ordinary working life.

Industry 4.0 has the potential to remedy some critical traits generally characterizing work in the industrial sector: most stressful activities will be delegated to robots and hence reduced; ergonomic solutions could be introduced in the workplace, especially to alleviate the labour of older people; and new intellectual tasks will make several activities less routine.

On the other side of the fence, Industry 4.0 involves a series of critical aspects that could jeopardize the condition of workers, partially deriving from the new context and in some measure caused by an increase of the typical employer's power of control by mean of automatic and operating at a distance machinery. With reference to the above, IG Metall focuses attention on the ones concerning mobile working and the organization of work in smart factories.

Smart working is considered an opportunity to improve the quality of the work–life balance, implementing activities, such as maintenance services, directly from a place selected by the worker. Conversely, it could cause a worsening of the workers' condition: the inability to be totally disconnected from work could be the reason for stress, burnout or workaholism or, in any case, produce a substantial lengthening of the working time.

A limitless flexibility in work processes, fostered by new instruments brought by robotics and informatics, could lead to an augmented intensity of working cycles and an increase of workers' pressure and consequently an augmented risk to develop related diseases (Hofmann 2015, pp. 13–14).

The reply elaborated by IG Metall deals with a "new normal" working relationship, shaped in the digital environment. The key factors individuated by the German trade union are the following: to develop and reinforce new methods of employee participation in the decisions concerning the work environment, to extend to smart factories the co-determination rights already recognized in normal production plants, and to enact new and specific protection rights. A particularly critical issue, as in Italy, is referred to the regulation of remote work, in order to prevent it to augment the precariousness and jeopardize a correct work–life balance (IG Metall 2015b).

Finally, the evolution of work also concerns the structure of trade unions. The position of IG Metall is that digitization of work is compatible with workers' organized representation but requests a different approach. Innovation is not always unfavourable: therefore, the task of employee organizations will be to single out the opportunities, for workers, represented by technological progress and to use them to improve salaries or working conditions. The starting point is a positive approach: not only attempt to resist to change but join the challenge represented by Work 4.0.

Collective Bargaining: Work–Life Balance and an Improved Education System

With reference to Germany, the social partners revealed themselves to be very active in introducing to collective bargaining some relevant elements in light of Industry 4.0. The most important areas addressed by this process are work–life balance and instruments to improve workers' education.

The BMW Agreement of 2014: A Way to Combine Private Life and Working-Time Flexibility?

In relation to time conciliation, it is worth underlining that, in recent years, most companies, such as Volkswagen, Daimler and BMW, experimented with strategies to allow workers to reach a better work–life balance and to protect workers' health from illnesses, stress and other psychological diseases, strictly related to the abuse of technology.

While Volkswagen attempted to solve the problem switching off e-mail servers half an hour after the end of the working day and turning them on half an hour before the opening of offices the next morning (Oberwetter 2015, 1 ff.) and Daimler introduced a tool that permitted the automatic elimination of e-mails sent to the workers' addresses while they were out of office (Kaufmann 2014, 1 ff.), BMW tried to reach an ambitious agreement with trade unions to protect employees and increase productivity. Reference is made to the collective agreement executed in 2014, applied to about half of the 79,000 BMW employees in the German boundaries, which confers to workers the right to agree with their managers if the employee can be contacted or not by the employer outside the ordinary working time and in which part of the day these solicitations are potentially admitted. In addition, according to the agreement, the periods that the employee spends working at a distance are counted as

182   M. Avogaro

ordinary business hours in order to reduce the stay in the office the following days (IG Metall 2014; Grindt 2014). The results of the aforementioned agreement, analysed two years after its introduction, are therefore ambivalent. Workers and trade unions appreciated it as a flexible and planned way to organize the working time, one that also represented an important example of the increasing independence of employees in the age of Industry 4.0. Conversely, the described solution was criticised, because it seems not to discourage enough employees to continue their activity beyond the ordinary working time, increasing the risks for their healt.

The Training Model of Baden-Württemberg: From 2001 to 2015

As far as means to improve workers' lifelong vocational training are concerned, according to IG Metall, one of the main examples is the qualification system of employees of metal and electric industries, elaborated through several collective agreements in Baden-Württemberg, between 2001 and 2015 (Bahnmüller and Fischbach 2004, 182 ff.; Huber and Hofmann 2001, 464 ff.).

The core innovation of the agreement of 2001—the *Qualifizierungstarifvertrag*—was the introduction of an individual right to education for workers.

With reference to in-job education, each worker had been given the right to an interview with the company, to be held at least once a year, to single out training needs and the responding measures. The purpose was to make it easier for workers to pursue a lifelong education programme and to allow them to obtain the education needed to advance to higher professional levels.

In regard to the employee's right to personal education, the agreement also ensured, in any case, the possibility to abstain from work after five years from the date of hiring and the right to return to the workplace within three years.

The Hans Blöcker Foundation observed the positive impact of the *Qualifizierungstarifvertrag*. In 2003, the perception that tools provided to ensure continuous vocational training were insufficient dropped to about 50% among workers (69% in 1992) and to 12% in relation to managers' opinion (42% in 1992). At the same time, the system of identification of training needs, based on annual interviews, was promoted by 42% of employees and 71% of managers (Bahnmüller and Fischbach 2004, pp. 184–186).

In 2015, a further update of the *Qualifizierungstarifvertrag* agreement provided for relevant innovations (IG Metall 2017a): first of all, the social partners individuated part-time as the main tool to allow workers to profit from their education rights.

In particular, the aforementioned kind of part-time work, functional to training activities, allowed, in general, the employees to reduce his or her business hours for a maximum period of seven years for educational purposes, maintaining the right to return, afterwards, to his or her original workplace or in an equivalent position (IG Metall 2017b).

Furthermore, the 2015 agreement introduces means to sustain the wage of workers passed to part-time to increase their qualification: employees continue to perceive, in general, 50% of their original income and they can increase this rate until 70% by means of monetization of extra-time hours or other bonuses accumulated in a personal account (IG Metall 2017b).

Finally, the right to change to part-time for educational reasons is strengthened by the introduction, due to the agreement reached by social partners in 2015, of a joint committee composed of representatives of both parties. The committee is charged to smooth out conflicts between employer and employee when the part-time right is contested and attempt to solve the dispute where the clash is irreconcilable (IG Metall 2017b).

The introduction of the aforementioned tools could also yield reliable results in Italy, especially with reference to the new requests of continuous update in education that Industry 4.0 will entail. Therefore, the measures taken by the considered social partners to improve and correct the education system introduced in the mechanical engineering industry of Baden-Württemberg should also be considered in the Italian perspective, even to implement and ameliorate the education

184   M. Avogaro

rights initially provided by the collective agreement of the same industrial category executed in 2016.

Additional Best Practices and Prospective Solutions to Enhance Workers' Conditions

As indicated above, Industry 4.0 means for employees, according to its supporters, more independence in performing tasks, an augmented flexibility in organizing the working time, and a new centrality of the figures of the (qualified) workers in the organizational plans of the companies.

IG Metall underlines that all of the opportunities reported above should be concretized in workplaces and transformed in rights receivable by workers. Collective bargaining is the main way to reach these goals.

In addition, the above-mentioned trade union individuated a list of best practices that could enhance working conditions in the work environment of Industry 4.0.

Reference is made, firstly, to policies to train workers in handling technology—in particular, online devices. This matter is also important to prevent illnesses and diseases that could relate to Work 4.0. At this point, some German companies promoted policies of sensitization of employees in relation to risks hidden behind an excessive utilization of online devices to work remotely or during rest periods. In particular, E.on expressly invited its workforce not to send or reply to e-mails outside the ordinary business hours except for emergencies, and Bayer experimented with "days without e-mail" in the office to encourage people to enhance human relations with colleagues (Kaufmann 2014, 1 ff.).

The new concept of factory, analysed jointly with novel issues raised by the demographic changes that occurred in some developed countries in the two last decades, could also lead to the implementation of new instruments to support and protect ageing people who are not yet retired. On this point, a valid example is represented by ThyssenKrupp Rasselstein GmbH, which introduced among its premises a fitness studio, nutritional advice and a stress management structure, all financed by the company, to provide older workers with all of the functional services to protect their health and allow them to work in the best conditions (IG Metall 2015b).

Conclusions

Industry 4.0 seems to be the technical innovation that could concretely modify and possibly improve and relaunch manufacturing and consequently the economic growth in Italy and Germany.

The possibility—thanks to the development of robotics and informatics—to increase the productivity and bring back industrial sectors offshored in the preceding decades could be a remarkable opportunity for European weak labour markets.

As for industrial relations, the analysis of the Italian and German debate highlights some common positions.

In both countries, attention is focused mainly on the mutation of skills demanded of workers in the new scenario. Lifelong training is considered a key element to allow people to remain competitive in the labour market and to protect less-skilled workers from the concurrence of robots. On the other hand, flexibility on the job, the augmentation of opportunities to work remotely or with a non-standardized working time, and the different representation models requested by multitasking workers will be issues that trade unions of the future will have to address.

Whereas FIM-CISL seems, at the moment, more concentrated on forthcoming effects of Industry 4.0, and in particular on the modifications that it will provoke in the organization of work, concerning professional levels, time conciliation and the structure of labour agreements, IG Metall appears to be focused on the current protection of employed people and to reinforce education, considered the main instrument to defend workers from the concurrence of robots and intelligent machinery.

With reference to practice, the results of the debate highlight the role of collective bargaining as a fundamental instrument to conjugate technological evolution and the protection of workers' rights. Moreover, bargaining is seen as a tool that allows social partners to introduce relevant innovations in factories, such as the qualification system of the Baden-Württemberg agreements or the WCM production system of the Pomigliano agreement executed in 2010.

Therefore, collective agreements and dialogue between social partners remain, in the modified scenario, the main instruments to balance the workers' requests and the employers' need to innovation: this outcome, in any case, seems not to be destined to soothe the conflicting role of workers' organizations. Continuous vocational education, work–life balance and new rights and protections identified under the label of "new normal" are essential elements to ensure the protection of employees' conditions and employment rates in the future. Thus, trade unions seem to be ready to revitalize their conflicting role to obtain results in this domain if the way of dialogue fails. Consequently, it would be advisable that social partners would continue in the current positive effort to satisfy the new demands through "win-win" collective agreements, where technological improvement of production is paired with the increase of workers' condition, also to prevent the risk to have to find an equilibrium between opposite interests in the new digitized scenario through a period of conflicts.

References

Armaroli, Ilaria. 2016. Rinnovo metalmeccanica: i punti qualificanti. *Bollettino ADAPT Speciale* 12: 1–4.

Bahnmüller, Reinhard, and Reinhard Fischbach. 2004. Der Qualifizierungstarifvertrag für die Metall-und Elektroindustrie in Baden-Württemberg. *WSI-Mitteilungen* 4: 182–186.

Bentivogli, Marco. 2015. Sindacato futuro nell'era dei big data e Industry 4.0. In *#SindacatoFuturo in Industry 4.0*, ed. Marco Bentivogli, Dario Di Vico, Luciano Pero, Gianluigi Viscardi, Giorgio B. Navaretti, and Franco Mosconi, 3–21, ADAPT University Press.

———. 2016. *Abbiamo rovinato l'Italia? Perché non si può fare a meno del sindacato*. Roma: Castelvecchi Editore.

Brollo, Marina. 2016. La mobilità professionale dei lavoratori dopo il Jobs Act: spunti sul caso Fiat/FCA. *Rivista Italiana di Diritto del Lavoro* 3 (1): 307–320.

Bundesagentur für Arbeit. 2016. Program WeGebAU. http://www3.arbeitsagentur.de/web/content/DE/BuergerinnenUndBuerger/Weiterbildung/Foerdermoeglichkeiten/Beschaeftigtenfoerderung/index.htm. Accessed 15 Dec 2017.

Bundesministerium für Arbeit und Soziales. 2015. *Re-imagining Work. Green Paper Work 4.0*. Berlin: Federal Ministry of Labour and Social Affairs, Directorate-General for Basic Issues of the Social State, the Working World and the Social Market Economy.

Bundesministerium für Wirtschaft und Energie and Bundesverband der Deutschen Industrie and IG Metall et al. 2015. Bündnis Zukunft der Industrie. https://www.buendnis-fuer-industrie.de/fileadmin/mediathek/pdf/buendnis-zukunft-der-industrie-struktur-und-arbeitsweise.pdf. Accessed 15 Dec 2017.

Cagol, Paolo. 2016. A lezione di futuro: smart working e la trasformazione del lavoro. *Bollettino ADAPT Speciale* 17: 1–2.

Carinci, Franco. 2011. La cronaca si fa storia: da Pomigliano a Mirafiori. *Argomenti di Diritto del Lavoro* 1 (1): 11–38.

CGIL. 2017a. Cos'è la Piattaforma Idea Diffusa. http://www.cgil.it/cose-la-piattaforma-idea-diffusa/#. Accessed 15 Dec 2017.

———. 2017b. Audizione Cgil su ddl lavoro autonomo e lavoro agile. http://www.cgil.it/audizione-cgil-ddl-lavoro-autonomo/#. Accessed 15 Dec 2017.

CISL. 2016. Audizione della Cisl presso la Commissione lavoro, previdenza sociale del Senato della Repubblica. https://www.cisl.it/attachments/article/1963/Audiz%20Cisl%20presso%20Comm%20Lavoro%20Senato%20 8-3-2016%202.pdf. Accessed 15 Dec 2017.

Dagnino, Emanuele. 2016. Uber law: prospettive giuslavoristiche sulla sharing-demand economy. *Diritto delle Relazioni Industriali* 1: 137–163.

Dal Ponte, Guido, Dario Pandolfo, and Giulia Rosolen. 2016. The Future Is Agile. *Bollettino ADAPT* 20.

De Luca Tamajo, Raffaele. 2011. I Quattro accordi collettivi del gruppo Fiat: una prima ricognizione. *Rivista Italiana di Diritto del Lavoro* 1 (3): 113–125.

De Meyer, Arnoud, Jinichiro Nakane, and Jeffrey M. Miller. 1989. The Next Competitive Battle: The Manufacturing Future Survey. *Strategic Management Journal* 10: 135–144 ff.

Ferraro, Giuseppe. 2016. Collaborazioni organizzate dal committente. *Rivista Italiana di Diritto del Lavoro* 1 (1): 53–76.

Forlivesi, Michele. 2016. La sfida della rappresentanza sindacale dei lavoratori 2.0. *Diritto delle Relazioni Industriali* 3: 662–678.

Ganz, Walter. 2014. Welche Rolle spielen die Dienstleistungen in der Industrie 4.0?. Report presented at the Conference *FES-Fachgesprächs Industrie 4.0*, Berlin, October 8.

Garofalo, Domenico. 2011. Il contrasto all'assenteismo negli accordi fiat di Pomigliano d'Arco e di Mirafiori. *Argomenti di Diritto del Lavoro* 3 (1): 499–522.

Grindt, Cornelia. 2014. Mobile Arbeit Muss man im Betrieb regeln. http://www.boeckler.de/51506_51638.htm. Accessed 15 Dec 2017.

188 M. Avogaro

Grunsky, Wolfgang. 1980. *Arbeitsgerichtsgesetz Kommentar.* Munich: Verlag F. Vahlen.

Hirsch-Kreinsen, Hartmut. 2014. Welche Auswirkungen hat "Industrie 4.0" auf die Arbeitswelt? *WISO Direkt* 12: 1–4.

Hofmann, Jörg. 2015. Digitalisierung der Industriearbeit, 13–14. http://www.blog-zukunft-der-arbeit.de/wp-content/uploads/2015/03/IGM_Digitalisierung_ZdA.pdf. Accessed 15 Dec 2017.

Huber, Berthold, and Jörg Hofmann. 2001. Der Tarifvertrag zur Qualifizierung in der Metall- und Elektroindustrie Baden-Württembergs. *WSI-Mitteilungen* 7: 464–466.

IG Metall. 2014. Mobiles Arbeiten—fair geregelt. http://www.igmetall.de/betriebsraetepreis-2014-bmw-muenchen-14229.htm. Accessed 15 Dec 2017.

———. 2015a. Arbeiten im digitalen Zeitalter. http://www.igmetall.de/fortschrittsdialog-arbeiten-4-0-16097.htm. Accessed 15 Dec 2017.

———. 2015b. Eine Reise in die Zukunft der Arbeit. http://www.igmetall.de/detlef-wetzel-ueber-sein-buch-arbeit-4-0-16657.htm. Accessed 15 Dec 2017.

———. 2016. *Auswirkungen der Digitalisierung / Industrie 4.0 auf die Beschäftigung.* Frankfurt: IG Metall Vorstand.

———. 2017a. Zukunftsweisendes Ergebnis stabilisiert die Konjunktur. https://www.igmetall.de/tarifabschluss-fuer-die-metall-und-elektroindustrie-in-baden-15755.htm. Accessed 15 Dec 2017.

———. 2017b. Arbeitszeit ist Bildungszeit. https://www.igmetall.de/kampagne-mein-leben-meine-zeit-bildungsteilzeit-22696.htm. Accessed 15 Dec 2017.

Kaufmann, Matthias. 2014. Deutsche Konzerne Kämpfen gegen den Handy-Wahn. *Spiegel online. Karriere*, February 17.

Kurtz, Constanze. 2014. Mensch, Maschine und die Zukunft der Industriearbeit. Report Presented at the Conference *Maschinen entscheiden: von Cognitive Computing zu autonomen Systemen*, München, November 21.

Lee, Edward A. 2008. Cyber Physical Systems: Design, Challengers. In *Electrical Engineering and Computer Science. University of California at Berkeley*, Technical Report no. UCB/EECS-2008-8.

Lestavel, Thomas. 2015. Les promesses très commerciales du 'big data'. *Alternatives économiques* 350: 70–73.

Liker, Jeffrey K., and Luciano Attolico. 2014. *Toyota Way: 14 principi per la rinascita del sistema industriale italiano.* Milano: Hoepli.

Magnani, Mirella. 2011. Gli effetti dell'accordo di Pomigliano sulle relazioni industriali. *Iustitia* 1: 11–19.

Mandl, Irene, Maurizio Curtarelli, Sara Riso, et al. 2015. *New Forms of Employment*. Luxembourg: European Foundation for the Improvement of Living and Working Conditions.

Mercadante, Lucina, and Giuseppe Spada. 2015. Nuove soluzioni per la riduzione del fenomeno infortunistico aziendale: la *World Class Manufacturing* coniuga tutela e competitività. *Rivista degli Infortuni e delle Malattie Professionali* 3 (1): 547–568.

Minghetti, Marco. 2016. I lavoratori italiani chiedono maggiori competenze digitali. *Il Sole 24 Ore. Nòva*. January 26.

Navaretti, Giorgio B. 2015. Industria 4.0: le tecnologie, il lavoro, la creazione di valore. In *#SindacatoFuturo in Industry 4.0*, ed. Marco Bentivogli, Dario Di Vico, Luciano Pero, Gianluigi Viscardi, Giorgio B. Navaretti, and Franco Mosconi, 31–33. ADAPT University Press.

Oberwetter, Christian. 2015. Burnout. Brauchen wir ein AntiStressGesetz? *Zeitschrift für Rechtspolitik* 7: 204–205.

Pero, Luciano. 2015. Industry 4.0: tecnologie, organizzazioni e ruolo del sindacato. In *#SindacatoFuturo in Industry 4.0*, ed. Marco Bentivogli, Dario Di Vico, Luciano Pero, Gianluigi Viscardi, Giorgio B. Navaretti, and Franco Mosconi, 22–30. ADAPT University Press.

Pogliotti, Giorgio. 2015. Smart working: i metalmeccanici CISL aprono. *Il Sole 24 Ore*, December 1.

Randstad Holding. 2015. Global Report Randstad Workmonitor 4th Quarter 2015. Employee Outlook 2016. https://www.randstad.dk/om-os/presse/new-download-folder/workmonitor-2015-q4.pdf. Accessed 15 Dec 2017.

———. 2016. Global Report Randstad Workmonitor Wave 1, 2016. https://www.randstad.com.au/documents/randstad-workmonitor_global_report_march-2016.pdf. Accessed 15 Dec 2017.

Randstad Italia S.p.A. 2016. L'impatto delle nuove tecnologie sul mondo del lavoro: cosa ne pensano i dipendenti italiani. http://www.randstad.it/knowledge360/archives/limpatto-delle-nuove-tecnologie-sul-mondo-del-lavoro-cosa-ne-pensano-i-dipendenti-italiani_318/. Accessed 15 Dec 2017.

Rogers, Brishen. 2015. The Social Costs of Uber. *The University of Chicago Law Review—The Dialogue* 82: 85–102.

Santoro Passarelli, Giuseppe. 2011. I contratti collettivi della Fiat di Mirafiori e Pomigliano. *Rivista Italiana di Diritto del Lavoro* 2 (3): 161–167.

———. 2015. I rapporti di collaborazione organizzati dal committente e le collaborazioni continuative e coordinate ex Article 409 No. 3 c.p.c. *Working Papers Centre for the Study of European Labour Law "Massimo D'Antona"* 278: 1–25.

Scheremet, Wolfgang. 2015. Industrie 4.0: A German Perspective. http://www. omg.org/news/meetings/tc/berlin-15/special-events/mfg-presentations/ Scheremet.pdf. Accessed 15 Dec 2017.

Seghezzi, Francesco. 2016. Lavoro e relazioni industriali nell'Industry 4.0. *Rivista Italiana di Diritto del Lavoro* 1: 178–209.

Seghezzi, Francesco, and Michele Tiraboschi. 2016a. La fine del lavoro? No, un nuovo inizio. In *Verso il futuro del lavoro. Appunti e spunti su lavoro agile e lavoro autonomo*, ed. Emanuele Dagnino and Michele Tiraboschi, 8–10. ADAPT University Press.

———. 2016b. Metalmeccanici, un'intesa che apre la strada alla quarta rivoluzione industriale. *Bollettino ADAPT* 40: 1–3.

Valdés dal-Ré, Fernando, and Alberto Valdés Alonso. 2010. Lo Statuto del lavoro autonomo nella legislazione spagnola. *Diritto delle Relazioni Industriali* 3: 705–739.

Valenduc, Gérard, and Patricia Vendramin. 2016. *Work in the Digital Economy: Sorting the Old from the New*. Brussels: ETUI – European Trade Union Institute.

Van Ackeren, Janine, and Tim Schröder. 2016. *Trends in Industrie 4.0*. Munich: Fraunhofer-Gesellschaft.

Villalón, Jesus C. 2013. Il lavoro autonomo economicamente dipendente in Spagna. *Diritti Lavori Mercati* 2: 287–315.

Wank, Robert. 1988. *Arbeitnehmer und Selbständige*. Munich: C.H. Beck'sche Verlagsbuchhandlung.

Weiss, Manfred. 2016. Digitalizzazione: sfide e prospettive per il diritto del lavoro. *Diritto delle Relazioni Industriali* 3: 651–663.

Wetzel, Detlef. 2015. *Arbeit 4.0: Was Beschäftigte und Unternehmen verändern müssen*. Freiburg im Breisgau: Verlag Herder.

Womack, James P., Daniel T. Jones, and Daniel Roos. 1993. *La macchina che ha cambiato il mondo*. Bergamo: Rizzoli.

Part IV

The Impact of Digitalization on the Work Performance

10

Digitagile: The Office in a Mobile Device. Threats and Opportunities for Workers and Companies

Roberto Albano, Sonia Bertolini, Ylenia Curzi, Tommaso Fabbri, and Tania Parisi

Introduction

The new era of organized work related to digital technologies[1] is identified by many terms and neologisms, such as "smart working", "e-working", "ICT-based mobile working", and "agile work",[2] which are often ill defined and sometimes confused with each other. Generally, they are

---

This chapter is the result of the joint work of the authors. However, sections were authored as follows: "Introduction" by Tania Parisi; "Smart Working: A Statistical Portrait" by Roberto Albano and Tania Parisi; "Organizational Autonomy, Discretion and Control in the Organizational Regulation of Work" and related subsections by Ylenia Curzi; "Digitalization, Occupation and Productivity" by Tommaso Fabbri and Tania Parisi; "Reconciling Work with Private Life" by Sonia Bertolini and Tania Parisi; and "Conclusions" by Roberto Albano and Tania Parisi.

R. Albano • S. Bertolini • T. Parisi
Department of Cultures, Politics and Society, University of Turin, Turin, Italy
e-mail: roberto.albano@unito.it; sonia.bertolini@unito.it; tania.parisi@unito.it

Y. Curzi (✉) • T. Fabbri
Marco Biagi Department of Economics, University of Modena and Reggio Emilia, Modena, Italy
e-mail: ylenia.curzi@unimore.it; tommaso.fabbri@unimore.it

© The Author(s) 2018
E. Ales et al. (eds.), *Working in Digital and Smart Organizations*,
https://doi.org/10.1007/978-3-319-77329-2_10

193

194 R. Albano et al.

used to stress a radical change in labour relations, both by those who are enthusiastic about the change and by those who, in contrast, mostly anticipate negative consequences.

In the face of another dispute between "apocalyptic" and "integrated" intellectuals, we argue that even before setting forth any prediction, a critical and analytical perspective should be able to address some research questions that appear to be crucial, albeit not exhaustive, for interpreting the current changes.

Reflection upon some classic topics in the sociology of work and organizational theory seems to draw nourishment from the new forms of "smart" work, characterized by the intensive use of digital devices and increasing "disembedding" of the individual workstation from the standard working times and places of the formal organization. Our reflection particularly focuses on the following topics: (1) organizational autonomy and control in the regulation of agile work, (2) the potential consequences for individual and organizational effectiveness and productivity, and (3) the reconciliation of working time with time normally reserved for non-working life. The chapter starts with a review of the international literature on smart working, disambiguates the term, and provides some background data about the spread of the phenomenon in Italy and abroad. Later sections move on to apply some concepts drawn from sociological and organizational studies for a thoughtful analysis of the currently predominant rhetoric, both utopic and dystopic, and for a meta-analysis of results from qualitative and quantitative research.

Smart Working: A Statistical Portrait

Two decades ago, Davenport and Pearlson (1998) claimed that work was increasingly becoming something to do rather than a place to go. Similarly, Frances Cairncross foresaw epochal transformations about how and where people work: new information and communication technology (ICT) would have shortly realized the utopia of neoclassical economics, namely the "death of distance", and thus the end of a considerable portion of perfect market distortions. These analyses were not new. In the early 1980s, Alvin Toffler had already considered the "electronic cottage" in the small town as the typical workplace of the future. What these and further analyses seem to have overlooked, however, is that new technologies—like the old ones—do not grow up in a vacuum but are "embedded" in social structures, which are still strongly anchored in the space. The worker, with his or her own devices in the country cottage, cabin in the mountain, or on the beach—however far from large urban centres—does not yet seem to be a modal social category. According to the United Nations, in 2010, for the first time in history, more than 50% of the world's population was concentrated in large urban centres.[3] The Bureau of Labor Statistics recently published data on the use of time in the United States in 2015. This report shows that, currently, less than a quarter of workers carry out a considerable part of their work from outside the employer's premises.[4] Distance, therefore, is not still death. Even in Europe, labour is undergoing major transformations in this direction. The European Foundation for the Improvement of Living and Working Conditions (Eurofound) identified several new forms of employment, which include one of particular interest to us, namely "ICT-based mobile work", also called "eWork" or "mobile ICT-supported work", performed by "e-workers", "e-nomads" etc. (Eurofound 2015). The distinctive feature of this form is that the employee carries out his or her tasks outside the employer's office and uses computer technology to communicate with the organization.[5]

The overall impression is that the number of "remote" workers is constantly increasing, but available data on this phenomenon are scarce, outdated, and primarily derived from one-shot and scarcely comparable cross-sectional surveys.[6]

Providing a quantitative representation of the phenomenon first requires an operational definition. To that end, we refer to the European Commission (2010), who defines eWorkers as those who (1) use an Internet connection and (2) work at least 10 hours a week in locations other than the office or home.

The five-year European Working Conditions Survey (EWCS) (European Foundation for the Improvement of Living and Working Conditions 2017) collected data on both dimensions in 30 European countries, though not at the level of detail that would be necessary for the present analysis. The number of eWorkers can be estimated only with caution, counting employees in the sample who reported making intensive use of ICT for their work activities and simultaneously working for at least part of the week outside of the company.

Let's examine the first indicator (Table 10.1). In 2015, nearly half of employees in Northern European countries (e.g. France, Denmark and Great Britain) reported using a computer, laptop or smartphone for at least three quarters of their working day. Other countries (e.g. Italy and Spain) had minor—but still significant—percentages of workers making intensive use of ICT for their work.

In the selected countries, the percentage of employees using computer devices for at least three quarters of their working time nearly doubled in 10 years (20–36%) (Table 10.1); this was more the effect of a gradual process of computerization of jobs than of an increase in ICT-intensive occupational positions (Eurofound 2016).

Despite the increased use of mobile technologies, the main workplace for the majority of employees is still on the company's premises. However, in 2015, a significant percentage of employees declared that they frequently worked in different locations[7] (e.g. at customer sites, in the car, in open sites, or public spaces) (Table 10.2).[8]

By selecting workers who possessed both characteristics identified by the European Commission, we can now estimate the share of eWorkers in the total population of employees in 2015 (Table 10.3).

eWorkers represent a relatively small portion of the total population of employees, especially in Italy. Here, the absence of a systematic and

Table 10.1 Employees working with computers, laptops and smartphones for at least three quarters of their working time, by country

	2005 (%)	2010 (%)	2015 (%)	Percentage difference, 2005–2015
Italy	17	23	31	+82
Spain	22	31	37	+68
France	27	31	46	+70
Great Britain	28	37	53	+89
Denmark	33	34	54	+64

Source: Authors' own elaboration based on EWCS data (weighted by "W4")

Table 10.2 Employees working at least several times a week in locations other than the employer's premises, by country

	Client premises (%)	Car or other vehicle (%)	Outside site (%)	Public spaces such as coffee shops and airports (%)	At least one of the preceding locations (%)
Italy	10	8	10	7	23
Spain	17	10	13	8	32
France	18	20	14	6	32
Great Britain	18	17	12	6	28
Denmark	19	16	16	5	32

Source: Authors' own elaboration based on 2015 EWCS data (weighted by "W4")

Table 10.3 Estimated share of eWorkers in the total population of employees by country and 95% confidence intervals

	Estimate (%)	95% CI	
Italy	3	2	4
Spain	7	6	8
France	10	9	11
Great Britain	12	10	14
Denmark	13	11	15

Source: Authors' own elaboration based on 2015 EWCS data (weighted by "W4")

comprehensive national statistical survey connected with other data on the labour force hampers at present any effort to provide an accurate and reliable description of smart workers, their socio-demographic characteristics, and the organizations that apply specific policies in this field.

The only quantitative research on the phenomenon in Italy to date consists of a set of sample surveys carried out by the Smart Working Observatory of the Politecnico of Milan in collaboration with Doxa since 2012.[9] According to the 2016 research report (Smart Working Observatory 2016, p. 8), in Italy the overall number of large companies (with more than 250 employees) with formalized smart-working projects increased by about three quarters in one year, from 17% in 2015 to 30% in 2016. Moreover, in 2016, 11% of large companies reported having implemented smart-working practices without the official status of a project. The potential extension of corporate projects is high, given that in 2016 only 12% of large organizations in the sample reported not being interested in smart working or considered it inapplicable to their business.

With regard to the small and medium-sized enterprises (SMEs) (with 11–249 employees) of the sample,[10] in 2016 only 5% reported having implemented formalized initiatives (the same percentage as in 2015) whereas 13% reported having launched informal initiatives without structured projects (as compared with 9% in 2015). Thus, even in this case, the number of companies' projects grew significantly between 2015 and 2016. In 2017, smart-working projects further increased both in large companies (36% of companies introduced formalized projects and 7% of them adopted informal practices) and in SMEs (7% of organizations launched formalized projects and 15% of them implemented informal practices). The potential diffusion of the phenomenon appeared to be high in public administration as well: in 2017, 48% of the public administrations in the sample reported being interested in launching some initiatives in the near future (Smart Working Observatory 2017).

The Smart Working Observatory also estimated that the number of smart workers (i.e. employees characterized by remote working and discretion in their choice of spaces, time, and working tools)[11] was at least 250,000 in 2016 and 305,000 in 2017. These figures include both workers who had formalized such a labour relationship with their company and those without a specific company project. If we consider both public and private organizations with more than 10 employees, the estimated share of smart workers in the total population of employees who could potentially perform their job according to this way of working[12] grew from 5% in 2013 to 7% in 2016 and 8% in 2017.[13]

In 2016, most of the smart workers were male (70%) and concentrated in Northern and Central Italy (90%). The 2012 research report (Smart Working Observatory 2012, pp. 36–37) also gave estimates of remote workers, characterized by discretion in their choice of spaces (26%); flexible workers, characterized by discretion in their choice of working time (25%); and adaptive workers, characterized by discretion in their choice of working tools (37%)—i.e. groups of workers who in some sense were "on their way" to smart working. This information gives an idea of the potential development of smart working in Italy. The current potential seems to be high; in fact, the Observatory estimated that potential smart workers could total about five million—i.e. 23% of total employment.

Organizational Autonomy, Discretion and Control in the Organizational Regulation of Work

A key issue in the debate about smart working is whether it opens up new opportunities for workers to exercise their autonomy over the regulation of work or whether it strengthens managers' control (Brey 1999; Valenduc and Vendramin 2016). Another key issue concerns the main aspects of work over which smart workers are allowed to exercise their autonomy.

The answers to these questions may depend on, among other things, how we define organizational autonomy. To address the above-mentioned issues, we refer to studies that distinguish organizational autonomy from organizational discretion (Maggi 2003/2016). Autonomy refers to the capability of producing one's own rules and managing one's own organizational processes. In this regard, we also refer to the francophone studies in the sociology of work and organizational theory emphasizing that even within the employment relation, working often entails that groups of workers produce autonomous rules that serve organizational effectiveness and efficiency, as do the rules produced by the employer (Terssac 2003; Reynaud 1988). Unlike organizational autonomy, organizational discretion indicates room for action in a regulated process where the subject is obliged to decide and choose from a set of alternatives predetermined by heteronomous rules (Maggi 2003/2016).

Considered as dichotomous analysis dimensions, organizational autonomy and organizational discretion can be combined so as to identify four ideal types of "organization personality" (Barnard 1938)—i.e. four ways for the individual to contribute to the organizational process (Table 10.4).[14]

Table 10.4 Ideal types of "Organization Personality" (OP)

		Organizational discretion	
		Absent	Present
Organizational autonomy	Absent	1) Other-directed OP	2) Discretionary OP
	Present	4) Mainly autonomous OP	3) Relatively autonomous OP (cooperative autonomy)

The remainder of this section describes the above-mentioned ideal types and uses them to analyse the main theoretical and empirical studies[15] on smart-working practices to date with the aim of disentangling the implications for the regulation of work in terms of organizational autonomy, organizational discretion, and control.

Other-Directed Organization Personality: Neither Autonomy nor Discretion

Individual contributions to the organizational process are governed by the imposition of detailed, previous and heteronomous rules as well as by interim verification of their rigid application by individuals.

This ideal type is approximated by cases in which the use of portable communication tools is associated with the implicit imposition on workers to be on call, and connected to work everywhere and at any time, so as to meet requests for rapid response and problem solving expressed by colleagues, superiors and clients (Cavazotte et al. 2014). In this case, workers have no possibility to exercise discretion over where and when to answer incoming work-related queries. This ideal type is also approximated by the use of systems to support managers' decision-making that combine big data and data visualization technologies, which can be downloaded onto mobile devices. They allow all the managers involved in a decision-making process to have access to the same information simultaneously. At the same time, they rigidly predetermine some key steps of the process, such as the identification of anomalous events, the search for information, the evaluation of the situation, and identification of the nature and causes of the problem as well as of potential solutions (Davenport 2013).

Discretionary Organization Personality: Discretion Without Autonomy

Many studies in the literature that have emphasized the new opportunities for workers' autonomy opened up by smart working have actually referred to situations in which workers are allowed to make discretionary decisions about where, when and how to work.

Organizational discretion over the place of work refers to the possibility for the individual to work in spaces other than the company's premises on the condition that his or her choice respects the constraints imposed by the management, who pre-establishes or authorizes admissible alternatives and often imposes limitations on the frequency with which workers are allowed to work outside the company's workplace (Smart Working Observatory 2014b, 2015, 2016).

Discretion over working time refers to the opportunity for workers to choose between several working schedules determined by the organization or to adapt their working hours within certain limits set by the formal organizational rules in accordance with the restrictions imposed by legal regulations (Smart Working Observatory 2012, 2015). It also includes discretion corresponding to the implicit expectation that workers are able to schedule when they perform their tasks, always prioritizing the most urgent ones and taking customers' and supervisors' needs, and the interdependencies between their tasks and those of colleagues, into due consideration. In this regard, some studies have shown that the opportunities enabled by digital devices may be enacted in a context of implicit expectations for workers' constant accessibility. Thus, workers' room for manoeuvre to determine their working time and workplaces is reduced, leading to an imposition on them to work everywhere/all the time (Azad et al. 2016; Cavazotte et al. 2014; Mazmanian et al. 2013).[16] The consequences may include, among other things, the diminished ability to concentrate and to stay focused and thus to discretionarily manage one's own time and priorities effectively (Vendramin and Valenduc 2016).

Discretion over the ways to get the work done firstly concerns the possibility for the individuals to choose the device with which they communicate and work from remote locations from a set of devices that are bought and made available by the employer. Discretion over digital devices may also result from the transformation of workers' autonomy over the device deemed suitable to get their work done into discretion awarded to employees by the management.[17]

Moreover, discretion concerns how each individual should perform his or her job in the context of a structure of activities that are predetermined by the management.[18] At this level, digital devices are adopted and used for the following main ends: communicating information to coordinate workers in the performance of their tasks, sharing formerly developed ways to solve problems, and making sources of information and knowledge visible, so that operators may have access to them while performing their jobs (Wellman et al. 1996; Lehdonvirta and Mezier 2013). In other words, digital devices are adopted and used to increase the available resources for operators to make discretionary decisions.

In addition, new technologies allow managers to collect and analyse data about individuals' and process performance, thereby opening up new opportunities for the management to adopt a way of controlling performance which is alternative to direct supervision and consists of comparing individual work outcomes with individual performance targets. The latter, in turn, are related to process objectives, and both are predetermined by the management. Outcome control allows the management to control individuals' behaviours and workers' discretionary efforts, even though work is spatially and temporally "disembedded".

Cooperative Autonomy: Both Discretion and Autonomy

The actual regulation of work results from the combination of previous and heteronomous rules and autonomous rules. Autonomous rules are produced by a group of workers who can be identified as such only ex post facto. In addition, they are produced either previously to or simultaneously with the execution of tasks in order to solve problems that can jeopardize the effectiveness of the process and cannot be solved by already-developed procedures (Reynaud 1988; Terssac 1992).

It is assumed that operators accept heteronomous rules, and the implicit obligation to produce new rules to solve or anticipate problems, as this opens up the opportunity for them to develop new competences. The latter, indeed, are sources of power, identity and recognition within their own work group as well as of employability and visibility in the external labour market. In addition, it is assumed that the management accepts operators' autonomy as this is a source of new competences and organizational learning that boost work process effectiveness. Producing autonomous rules involves communications on ill-defined matters that are difficult to make explicit (i.e. problems, individual knowledge, and competences). For this reason, such communications require face-to-face interactions. Therefore, one could hypothesize that the extensive use of organizational solutions based on the spatial and temporal distance and standard communications between workers may prevent organizations from nurturing workers' competences and ability to produce autonomous rules. Indeed, there is some evidence showing that interactions involving demanding negotiations continue to be based mainly on informal and face-to-face communications, even in work processes where communications with colleagues, superiors and clients are increasingly mediated by digital devices and distance and mobile work is highly frequent (Azad et al. 2016; Vartiainen and Hyrkkänen 2010; Wellman et al. 1996).

Aspects of work over which smart workers (are required to) exercise their autonomy will be analysed in more detail in a later subsection (entitled "Applying the Typology to Research Data"). Here, we mention that there is some evidence showing that employers often have the implicit expectation that smart workers will be able to take personal responsibility for growing their own competences and building a network of professional relations, providing them with new resources to perform their activities (Schneckenberg 2009; CIPD 2014). Some ways for the individual to achieve those ends are working in co-working centres or in temporary work projects within virtual enterprises, which usually combine co-located and ICT-mediated interactions (Vendramin 2007; Vendramin and Valenduc 2016).

Mainly Autonomous Organization Personality: Autonomy Without Discretion

Individuals are able to produce their own rules to structure significant parts of their work processes, including operative goals. This type of organization personality is approximated by individual contributions to innovation processes, especially when completely new products are designed in collaboration with customers and suppliers, and it is almost impossible to state technical requirements in advance. Such innovations require coordination via mutual adjustment (Thompson 1967/2003), thereby ruling out the possibility that digital devices mainly mediate the necessary communication and that the involved individuals are spatially and temporally dispersed on a continuous basis. However, in some instances, the management adopts digital devices with a view to transforming this type of situation into one respectively characterized by discretion (see footnote 18) or cooperative autonomy. In the latter regard, we can consider the following example: The management adopts new technologies in a way that combines explicit rules and implicit expectations. The former rigidly prescribe the stages of the process and the order of their execution; the latter ask individuals to decide, in the daily work of innovation and according to the situation, what formal rules need to be followed and conversely which can be ignored or deliberately circumvented in order to ensure the success of the new product launch into the market (Pfeiffer et al. 2016).

Applying the Typology to Research Data

Now, we turn our attention to some studies on the best practices of smart working in Italy to date (Smart Working Observatory 2012, 2013a, b, 2014a, b, 2015, 2016, 2017). Our aim is to analyse the main aspects of work over which smart workers are required to exercise their autonomy and therefore to assess the extent to which the above-mentioned practices capitalize on employees' ability to innovate the organizational regulation of work.

In terms of best practices of smart working in Italy to date, organizational autonomy, which is a source of innovation, firstly concerns the place of work. In 2015, 36% of companies in the research sample (176 cases) reported accepting the fact that their employees worked at co-working centres, thereby capitalizing on their employees' ability to autonomously identify the potentially available options to work from outside the employer's premises. In 2016, the same answer was reported by 51%

of the large organizations that had put structured smart-working projects in place (63 cases) while a further 10% reported intending to adopt this new policy in the near future (Smart Working Observatory 2015, 2016).

In addition, organizational autonomy concerns the way of carrying out working activities, namely decisions about the devices for distant work and formal communication, as well as working procedures. The 2013 report foresaw that companies interested in promoting the autonomy of their employees in choosing their own devices and apps would have shifted, respectively, from 23% in 2013 to 33% in 2015 (devices) and from 15% in 2013 to 26% in 2015 (apps) (Smart Working Observatory 2013b). Likewise, in 2014, 19% of operators in the research sample (1,000 professionals) reported using autonomously selected devices and apps for which their own company had not predetermined any policy or service condition (Smart Working Observatory 2014a). As for working procedures, the findings from the 2016 survey administered to a sample of 1,004 employees in companies with more than 10 employees showed that the ability to anticipate problems[19] is one of the skills that mainly differentiated smart workers from other employees. The difference between smart workers and other employees in the possession of this skill was 14 percentage points. In addition, it was considered one of the most relevant skills by 56% of human resource managers from organizations with more than 10 employees (Smart Working Observatory 2016).

The above-mentioned research also highlighted that the ability to quickly identify key partners, both inside (i.e. colleagues) and outside the organization, and to succeed in building relations and sharing useful information with them was another skill that chiefly differentiated smart workers from other employees. The difference between the former and the latter group in the possession of this skill was 14 percentage points. The skill refers to exercising organizational autonomy over the sources of information needed for the execution of tasks and time for the generation, production and transfer of work-related information and communications.

In regard to other aspects of work, smart workers have organizational discretion over the time needed for the execution of primary tasks. Namely, they are required to decide when to start, to interrupt and to finish the execution of their working activities in the course of the working day by choosing from a set of alternatives predetermined by the constraints imposed by legal regulations, clients, superiors and the interdependence between their activities and those of their colleagues.

In addition, the tasks of each smart worker are usually part of a series of activities that can be separated, as they are related to each other by a pooled or sequential interdependence (Thompson 1967/2003), and for the most part are predetermined by the management. An exception in this regard is connected with the autonomy that smart workers enjoy in deciding their working procedures, the devices and apps used for distant work and formal communication, which results in the opportunity for them to autonomously innovate the content of their tasks and the required knowledge for performing them.

Finally, the smart worker's contribution to the process is governed by previous rules which determine the performance targets that he or she is expected to achieve mostly in a heteronomous way. Individual career paths are designed on the basis of evaluations of individual work outcomes. The findings from the 2017 survey showed that only 9% of large companies had adopted smart-working practices at the same time as new forms of work organization in which smart workers were involved in setting the objectives of their own work and encouraged to participate proactively in improving the organization as a whole (Smart Working Observatory 2017).

To summarize, in terms of best practices, organizational autonomy, which is a source of innovation, is mainly exercised at the micro level of the organizational process. It mainly concerns aspects of the social structure, the content of the tasks and the required knowledge to perform them. The best practices of smart working in Italy to date also allow workers to participate in setting the objectives of their own work and improving the organization. Therefore, they appear to require an organization personality that approaches the ideal type we have called "cooperative autonomy". Considering that, we argue that the best practices of smart working in Italy to date still fail to take full advantage of employees' ability to innovate the organizational regulation of work.

Moreover, the available empirical evidence (Vendramin 2007) has shown that the adoption of methods for controlling work and planning individual career paths based on the evaluation of individual performance may actually sharpen competition between organizational members. This, in turn, may reduce their willingness to share their own knowledge and competences, thereby limiting their opportunities, and those of their organization, to develop new organizational competences.

Digitalization, Occupation and Productivity

The current digitalization of social relations significantly affects labour relations and rekindles the traditional debate about the relationship between technical progress, economic growth, productivity and employment.

Mainstream theory on economic growth has posited that technological progress is a source of increased work productivity (Solow 1956). However, Solow also highlighted the problematic nature of the relationship between digital transformation and productivity, making a quip in 1987 that is today known as the "productivity paradox": "You can see the computer age everywhere but in the productivity statistics" (Solow 1987, p. 36). Askénazy and Gianella (2000) argued that productivity gains are not automatically achieved via the introduction of digital technologies. They "are a corollary of the organisational changes facilitated by technological innovations rather than the technologies themselves, and will be achieved only by companies which adopt new forms of work organisation at the same time as the new technologies" (Valenduc and Vendramin 2016, p. 15). In the same vein, Brynjolfsson and McAfee (2015) acknowledged that changes in the organization are inevitable antecedents for unlocking the potential of digital technologies. Thus, even the most apologetic literature nowadays has recognized the need for an organizational "qualification" of digital technologies—namely the need to design them as a function of work and production processes and to mould them to meet the needs of coordination that arise in their unfolding. In sum, organizational choices decisively affect the relationship between technological progress and productivity.

The impact of digitalization on work, in both quantitative and qualitative terms, is equally problematic and perhaps less predictable. The renewed interest in the Keynesian notion of technological unemployment[20] has revived and modernized old questions: Will machines replace humans? To what extent will the digitalization of production processes affect employment levels?

An example of a pessimistic scenario is described by Frey and Osborne (2013), who estimate that almost 50% of today's US jobs are at risk of computerization. Similarly, Hungerland et al. (2015) estimate that only 20% of the population will keep 80% of the value created and incomes earned for themselves. The somehow simplistic vein of these approaches has led many scholars to ascribe greater likelihood to a different scenario, in which employment goes through some relevant structural modifications: rather than reducing employment levels, digitalization will redistribute employment between sectors, occupations and tasks, although the way in which this redistribution will take place is difficult to predict. The "polarization" hypothesis (Autor and Dorne 2013) claims that jobs that bear the highest risk of extinction are those that are routine and non-manual (requiring mid-level skills), as it is more difficult to digitalize creative and relational work on the one hand (high skills) or manual and non-routine jobs on the other (low skills). Instead, the hypothesis of complementarity between capital and skills (Krusell et al. 2002) predicts that the demand for creative workers with high skills will increase at the same pace as digitalization but that workers with low skills will lose their jobs. Both hypotheses clearly point to vocational training and lifelong learning as fundamental policy tools for matching labour supply and demand.

Moreover, digitalization promises to affect the quality of work in an ergonomic sense. Risks related to the massive introduction of mobile ICT can be divided into two categories: indirect and direct effects (Barley et al. 2011). Indirect effects include those concerning work–life balance (see the next section). Direct effects, considered in this section, include all consequences of the introduction of ICT for the accomplishment of workers' tasks.

The consideration that ICT increases productivity at the macroeconomic level (Jorgenson 2001) collides with a now-extensive body of literature that has highlighted some criticalities at the level of individual productivity.

DigitAgile: The Office in a Mobile Device. Threats... 209

Table 10.5 Frequency of interruptions at work (very/fairly often): comparison between ICT-intensive and non-ICT-intensive employees, by country

| | ICT-intensive (%) | Non-ICT-intensive (%) | PP difference | 95% CI | | | |
				ICT-intensive (%)		Non-ICT-intensive (%)	
Italy	30	21	+9	25	35	18	24
Spain	38	29	+9	35	41	27	31
France	60	38	+22	56	64	35	42
Great Britain	62	43	+19	59	66	39	47
Denmark	56	39	+17	52	61	34	44

Source: Authors' own elaboration based on 2015 EWCS data (weighted by "W4")

Jobs in which communication is "pocketable, mobile, and continual" (Mazmanian et al. 2006, p. 3) require workers to carry out their tasks in a way that has been described as "polycronic" (Cotte and Ratneshwar 1999). Workers are required to carry out more than one task simultaneously and to be available to be continuously interrupted (Reinsch et al. 2008). The arrival of messages requires workers to interrupt the tasks they are currently performing to devote attention and time to those that arise unexpectedly. The potential of disturbance is high (Rennecker and Godwin 2005) and very frequent, as shown by the EWCS data (Table 10.5).

A study conducted in the early stages of ICT penetration highlighted that workers were able to concentrate for a maximum of three minutes before being interrupted (Gonzalez and Mark 2004). One can predict that workers will undergo a latent period before regaining complete concentration on the suspended tasks. This has negative consequences not only for the worker, in terms of stress, but also for the organization. Indeed, the short-term benefits in terms of accelerated accomplishment of individual tasks enabled by ICT may be offset by a decrease in long-term productivity (Rennecker and Godwin 2003).

In addition, the greater opportunities for vertical, horizontal, synchronous, asynchronous and remote coordination enabled by companies' digital platforms supporting collaborative work may exceed the actual needs of production processes, thereby causing collaborative overload (Cross et al. 2016) and inefficiency.

Reconciling Work with Private Life

In order to explore the consequences of agile work and the use of digital devices for the reconciliation between working hours and life outside of work, we first refer to studies that have dealt with the effect of atypical forms of work on work–life balance. Atypical working hours, such as part-time contracts, flexible working hours, or the use of remote work such as teleworking, can potentially help reconcile working time with private life (Bertolini 2006).

In this context, the use of agile work and digital devices opens new opportunities for flexible working hours—or fixed working hours undertaken at a distance from the workplace—and, at least theoretically, may facilitate better reconciliation of work with private life. There are, first, the savings in travel time and, second, the opportunity to perform activities—such as housework—while working from home.

Data from the sixth EWCS in 2015 show differences in the opportunities to reconcile work with private life between employees[21] depending on the organization of working hours, which can be rigid (i.e. working hours are completely predetermined by the employer) or based on increasing degrees of flexibility. In general, workers with flexible working hours manage to find time for private life during their working hours much more easily (Table 10.6).

From the point of view of time management, workers with flexible schedules seem to enjoy certain advantages; thus, the relaxation of the boundaries between work and family life may allow better reconciliation

Table 10.6 Employees reporting that it is "very/fairly" easy to find time for themselves or their family during working hours, by country

	R (%)	F (%)	PP difference	95% CI			
				R (%)		F (%)	
Italy	71	84	+13	65	77	78	90
Spain	63	81	+18	60	66	77	85
France	51	76	+25	45	57	72	80
Great Britain	70	86	+16	65	75	83	89
Denmark	59	87	+28	51	67	84	90

Source: Authors' own elaboration based on 2015 EWCS data (weighted by "W4")
R rigid, F flexible

between the two spheres. However, these benefits come at a cost: the absence of a rigid work schedule could present the opposite risk, in which working time interferes with the sphere of private life. Research on the use of virtual offices at IBM stressed the risk of "workaholism" for teleworkers, precisely as a result of the increased fragility of the boundaries between work and family (Hill et al. 1998). Qualitative results from this study suggested that flexible workers were more likely than the other group to work longer hours. However, this is not always the case. Data from the EWCS regarding Great Britain and Denmark are not in line with this statement (Table 10.7).

The fact that in Denmark and Great Britain—unlike in Italy, Spain and France—the percentage of workers who often work more than 10 hours a day is almost similar in both groups[22] is likely to be related to the less stringent legal regulations of the employment relationship in the former two countries. However, the aforementioned research conducted at IBM showed some ambiguous results as well: it seems that the greater number of hours worked was more likely to be a perceived effect rather than a real consequence of the virtual office. Consequently, Hill et al. (1998) drew attention to the importance of providing training for remote workers also in terms of social and psychological issues.

Mobile devices, which enable employees to perform their own job from virtually any place and at any time, sometimes lead to contrasting effects. Such effects seem to depend on the workers' ability to draw boundaries between work and private life, which are increasingly permeable. An Australian study has shown that use of the Internet helps ensure

Table 10.7 Employees whose working day is never longer than 10 hours, by country

	R (%)	F (%)	PP difference	95% CI			
				R (%)		F (%)	
Italy	91	71	−20	87	95	64	78
Spain	80	56	−24	77	83	51	61
France	65	45	−20	59	71	40	50
Great Britain	56	53	−3	51	61	48	58
Denmark	55	44	−10	47	63	39	49

Source: Authors' own elaboration based on 2015 EWCS data (weighted by "W4")
R rigid, F flexible

work–life reconciliation only on the condition that employees are able to maintain boundaries between family and work roles (Wajcman et al. 2010). According to another survey conducted in Australia, workers are indeed able to decide when it is time to turn their phone off or stop looking at their emails, thereby exercising de facto control over when and how much work is allowed to interfere with their private life (Wajcman et al. 2008). However, a Dutch study has highlighted that there are indirect effects from the encroachment of work devices into private life (Derks et al. 2014). This study, based on the comparison between a group of workers who used smartphones for work and a control group, has shown that it is the flow of job-related information that invades the time reserved for family and leisure. This could compromise individuals' ability to manage their time, as well as the quality of family relationships and the ability to engage in recovery activities. Using smartphones makes it difficult to balance family and work because of the lack of control over the number of messages and moments at which they arrive. The literature has emphasized that for individuals this creates a coexistence in two places—work and home—and a coexistence of work and family roles that are often mutually incompatible. This, in turn, may lead to a "disengagement" from home activities. Using smartphones could also prevent individuals from participating in recovery activities, such as mentally detaching from work, engaging in relaxing activities, and deciding for themselves which activities to pursue in their free time and when. The cost of flexibility seems to be the colonization of private life by working life, which individuals partially manage to control but which causes some indirect effects, especially when colleagues' and superiors' implicit expectations reduce workers' organizational discretion in their choice of when and where they should be engaged with work-related communications. The permeability between the two areas might take place not only in the work–family direction but also in the opposite one, thereby bringing the concerns and burdens of one's private life into the work sphere. We have constructed two indexes: one regarding the interference of work with family life and the other one concerning the interference of family life with work (Table 10.8).[23] The findings indicate that flexible and non-flexible workers bring work home in equal measure. However, in Spain, France and Denmark, flexible workers suffer more than do other employees[24] from

Table 10.8 Index of interference of work with family life and of interference of family life with work, by country. (Scores ≥ average)

		R (%)	F (%)	PP difference	95% CI R (%)		F (%)	
Italy	LF	51	54	+3	44	58	43	65
	FL	46	54	+8	39	53	43	65
Spain	LF	48	44	−4	44	52	38	50
	FL	47	55	+8	43	51	49	61
France	LF	55	54	−1	49	61	49	59
	FL	39	48	+9	33	45	43	53
Great Britain	LF	56	50	−6	51	61	45	55
	FL	43	48	+5	38	48	43	53
Denmark	LF	52	50	−2	44	60	45	55
	FL	41	49	+8	33	49	44	54

Source: Authors' own elaboration based on 2015 EWCS data (weighted by "W4")
F flexible, *FL* interference of family with working life, *LF* interference of work with family life, *R* rigid

the fact that their family life worries and problems sometimes prevent them from giving the time they should to their job (Table 10.8).

The use of mobile devices provides workers with the opportunity to organize their working time in a more flexible way and this produces some benefits in terms of work–life balance. At the same time, mobile devices offer new opportunities to work anytime and anywhere, thereby reinforcing colleagues' and employers' expectations that individuals will always be available (Mazmanian et al. 2013). This issue also arises because mobile devices are easy to transport, leading many workers to carry them with them outside of working hours. As a result, the flow of work-related information invades the sphere of private life, and increasingly blurred boundaries between the two spheres cause interferences in the opposite direction as well.

Conclusions

Smart working provides a mixture of opportunities and risks to organizations and workers. It may certainly be advantageous to employees, organizations and also the environment to the extent that it allows a reduction in commuting time (except in the case that commuting time is transformed into working time). Moreover, as usually happens in employment contracts that allow a certain degree of working-time flexibility, the greater elasticity of working time and the opportunity to work without spatial constraints facilitate the reconciliation of working time with domestic and other time. However, the possibility of working anywhere and at any time can be a source of risks as well, as the worker may be unable to effectively control the encroachment of digital working devices into his or her private life, due not only and not always to an explicit request from the employer but also to an implicit expectation of accountability. This may result in distracting the employee from the necessary recovery time and thus in a negative impact on his or her health and safety.

Smart working has ambiguous consequences for companies as well. Positive consequences include the possibility of improving the organization's human capital. However, smart working may be an obstacle to organizational autonomy, which often is a key factor in the development of new competences. Organizational literature has clearly highlighted that organizational autonomy and competences develop in work groups whose members interact frequently and intensively, mostly through face-to-face interactions. Management can be encouraged to incentivize workers to exercise organizational discretion rather than organizational autonomy, thereby sharpening control and restraining any employee initiatives to innovate the organizational regulation of work in the long term. Moreover, ICT-mediated communications make it easier for workers to be exposed to frequent interruptions and this may lead to a downturn in productivity in the medium to long term. In addition, some devices, such as companies' digital platforms to support collaborative work, may offer opportunities for organizational members to coordinate and communicate with each other which can exceed the actual need in the company, thereby leading to inefficiency.

The potential risks associated with smart working, especially those resulting from the request that the employee be available anywhere and at any time, can be opposed at many levels and by several means. At the individual level, this can be realized by giving the employee training in exercising effective control over the potential of digital devices to encroach paid work into the spaces and time normally reserved for personal life. The goal can be achieved at the company level by limiting workers' access to the company's digital platforms during certain periods and at the government level by putting forth regulatory proposals that take into consideration its negative potentialities. In regard to this point, some initiatives have recently been undertaken in Europe: in 2016, France introduced the worker's "right to be disconnected" in the *"Loi Travail"*[25]; some German automobile companies (e.g. BMW, Daimler and Volkswagen) have implemented company-level collective agreements, including limitations on workers' access to the company's digital platforms during non-working hours. In Italy, conversely, the legal regulation on "Agile Work" does not appear to acknowledge the potential risks involved with this way of working and fails to provide for appropriate regulation, de facto remitting regulation to collective bargaining or, worse, to individual negotiation between the employee and his or her employer.

To conclude, we can outline a number of future research directions. First, studies can investigate how methods for controlling work and planning individual career paths based on the assessment of individual performance affect the collective development of autonomous rules and new organizational competences. Second, analyses can consider how mobile devices affect work organization and work–family balance in order to find ways to maximize benefits from the advantages they offer while managing the risks they involve.

Notes

1. Cloud technologies, collaboration tools (e.g. social networks, blogs and wikis), unified communication and collaboration services (e.g. instant messaging, videoconferencing and technologies for storing, co-authoring and sharing documents), big data software, mobile devices (e.g. palmtops, tablets and smartphones), and apps (e.g. dashboards and decision cockpits) that can be downloaded onto mobile devices, thereby allowing workers to have access to digital platforms anywhere and at any time (Smart Working Observatory 2012; Vendramin and Valenduc 2016).

2. The use of the term "agile work" is commonplace, especially in Italy, at least in reference to work carried out within the employment relationship. See chapter II, entitled "Agile Work", of Italian Law No. 81/2017 "Measures for the protection of self-employed non-entrepreneurial work and measures to facilitate flexibility in the place and time of work within the employment relationship".
3. Many of the considerations we have made so far are drawn from Pratt (2013).
4. Economic News Release: American Time Use Survey Summary, 24 June 2016. https://www.bls.gov/news.release/atus.nr0.htm.
5. A total of 90% of eWorkers use email, access intranet platforms and sometimes participate in web conferences during their working day (Gareis et al. 2006, p. 50). To become an eWorker, therefore, it is necessary to have a series of digital skills as well as suitable devices (e.g. laptops, smartphones and fast Internet connections) (European Centre for the Development of Vocational Training (Cedefop) 2015). Thus, digital inequalities in the access to the labour market, in addition to the traditional ones, are emerging.
6. For example, the surveys carried out in 2002 and 2003 within the Statistical Indicators Benchmarking the Information Society project, the 2002 General Population Survey, the 2002 Decision Maker Survey and the 2003 General Population Survey (http://sibis-eu.org/about/about.htm).
7. Home is excluded from the European Commission's definition of eWorker.
8. The format of the query changed in the sixth survey, so we were unable to display a trend as for the previous index.
9. www.osservatori.net/smart_working.
10. In 2016, the sample of SMEs totalled 315 cases and there were 207 large companies (Smart Working Observatory 2016, pp. 28–29).
11. According to the Observatory, the reorganization of physical workplaces and an objectives-based performance-management system are two other fundamental elements of a complete approach to smart working.
12. The 2016 report clarified that "[t]his calculation leaves out those who carry out operative activities tied to their physical workstations such as artisans, qualified labourers, farmers, plant conductors, workmen of static and mobile machinery, and vehicle operators who, at the current state of technology, cannot adopt smart working or, at least, not in the

forms we commonly consider ... Also, freelance professionals, entrepreneurs, and workers of public or private organizations with less than 10 employees are not considered as potential smart workers because the way their work is organized is already characterized by high flexibility and autonomy" (Smart Working Observatory 2016, p. 7, our translation).

13. The 2016 and 2017 reports do not make absolute values and confidence intervals available.

14. Roberto Albano put forward the present typology; then it was discussed at a seminar by the authors of the present paper.

15. The empirical research examined below is mainly exploratory, in particular case studies based primarily on interviews.

16. The consequences for individual and organizational productivity and for individuals' work–life balance will be addressed in detail in later sections of this chapter.

17. See, for example, the practices implemented by Amadori Group (Smart Working Observatory 2012) and Miroglio Group (Smart Working Observatory 2014a).

18. Matt Black Systems is a case in point. The Chartered Institute of Personnel and Development (CIPD) (2014) highlighted that in the company each engineering designer was responsible for the whole process of product development (i.e. processing customer orders and purchasing material, designing, manufacturing and testing, inspection, marketing, and dispatch). The work was supported by software that provided each operator with the overall framework for dealing with any aspect of the project but also allowed a degree of flexibility to adjust each template to the nature of each task. The software also contained information and training materials that were used by newcomers to develop their knowledge and skills within the real-time working environment.

19. In other words, the ability to assess, according to the situation, whether it is better to follow the formally prescribed or another existing and available procedure (in digital organization memories) in order to carry out one's own activities or whether it is necessary to develop new procedures.

20. According to Keynes, technological unemployment is "unemployment due to our discovery of means of economising the use of labour outrunning the pace at which we can find new uses of labour" (Keynes 1930/1963, p. 358).

21. We refer to employees who use ICT devices for at least three fourths of their working time.

22. In Denmark and Great Britain, the difference between rigid and flexible workers is not statistically significant.
23. We constructed the indexes through a mean-based dichotomous transformation of the scores resulting from a principal component analysis. The first index includes "… How often have you …", "Kept worrying about work when you were not working?", "Felt too tired after work to do some of the household jobs which need to be done?" and "Found that your job prevented you from giving the time you wanted to your family?". Explained variance: Italy 61.95%; Spain 64.68%; France 58.70%; Great Britain 62.32%; Denmark 57.28%. The second index includes "… How often have you …", "Found it difficult to concentrate on your job because of your family responsibilities?" and "Found that your family responsibilities prevented you from giving the time you should to your job?". Explained variance: Italy 78.28%; Spain 77.37%; France 72.65%; Great Britain 78.56%; Denmark 70.03%.
24. In Denmark, the differences are significant for $p < 0.1$.
25. Law 2016–1088 of 8 Aug. 2016 relating to work, modernization of social dialogue and safeguarding of professional careers.

References

Askénazy, Philippe, and Christian Gianella. 2000. Le paradoxe de productivité: le changements organisationnels, facteur complémentaire à l'informatisation. *Economie et Statistique* 339–340: 219–241.

Autor, David H., and David Dorne. 2013. The Growth of Low-Skill Service Jobs and the Polarization of the US Labor Market. *American Economic Review* 103 (5): 1553–1597.

Azad, Bijan, Randa Salamoun, Anita Greenhill, and Trevor Wood-Harper. 2016. Performing Projects with Constant Connectivity: Interplay of Consulting Project Work Practices and Smartphone Affordances. *New Technology, Work and Employment* 31 (1): 4–25.

Barley, Stephen R., Debra E. Meyerson, and Stine Grodal. 2011. E-mail as a Source and Symbol of Stress. *Organization Science* 22 (4): 887–906.

Barnard, Chester I. 1938. *The Functions of the Executive*. Cambridge, MA: Harvard University Press.

Bertolini, Sonia. 2006. La conciliazione per le lavoratrici atipiche. *Economia e lavoro* 1: 57–71.

Brey, Philip. 1999. Worker Autonomy and the Drama of Digital Networks in Organizations. *Journal of Business Ethics* 22: 15–25.

Brynjolfsson, Erik, and Andrew McAfee. 2015. *The Second Machine Age. Work, Progress, and Prosperity in a Time of Brilliant Technologies.* New York: W. W. Norton & Co.

Cavazotte, Flávia, Ana Heloisa Lemos, and Kaspar Villadsen. 2014. Corporate Smart Phones: Professionals' Conscious Engagement in Escalating Work Connectivity. *New Technology, Work and Employment* 29 (1): 72–87.

Chartered Institute of Personnel and Development (CIPD). 2014. *HR: Getting Smart About Agile Working.* https://www.cipd.co.uk/knowledge/strategy/change/agile-working-report. Accessed 14 Dec 2017.

Cotte, June, and Srinivasan Ratneshwar. 1999. Juggling and Hopping: What Does It Mean to Work Polychronically? *Journal of Managerial Psychology* 14 (3–4): 184–205.

Cross, Rob, Reb Rebele, and Adam Grant. 2016. Collaborative Overload. *Harvard Business Review*, January–February. https://hbr.org/2016/01/collaborative-overload. Accessed 14 Dec 2017.

Davenport, Thomas H. 2013. How P&G Presents Data to Decision-Makers. *Harvard Business Review*, April 4. https://hbr.org/2013/04/how-p-and-g-presents-data. Accessed 14 Dec 2017.

Davenport, Thomas H., and Keri Pearlson. 1998. Two Cheers for the Virtual Office. *MIT Sloan Management Review* 39 (4): 51–65.

Derks, Daantje, Lieke L. ten Brummelhuis, Dino Zecic, and Arnold B. Bakker. 2014. Switching on and off…: Does Smartphone Use Obstruct the Possibility to Engage in Recovery Activities? *European Journal of Work and Organizational Psychology* 23 (1): 80–90.

Eurofound. 2015. *New Forms of Employment.* Luxembourg: Publications Office of the European Union. https://www.eurofound.europa.eu/it/publications/report/2015/working-conditions-labour-market/new-forms-of-employment. Accessed 14 Dec 2017.

———. 2016. *What Do Europeans Do at Work? A Task-Based Analysis: European Jobs Monitor 2016.* Luxembourg: Publications Office of the European Union. https://www.eurofound.europa.eu/it/publications/report/2016/labour-market/what-do-europeans-do-at-work-a-task-based-analysis-european-jobs-monitor-2016. Accessed 14 Dec 2017.

European Centre for the Development of Vocational Training (Cedefop). 2015. *Matching Skills and Jobs in Europe. Insights from Cedefop's European Skills and Jobs Survey.* http://www.cedefop.europa.eu/en/publications-and-resources/publications/8088. Accessed 14 Dec 2017.

220 R. Albano et al.

European Commission. 2010. *The Increasing Use of Portable Computing and Communication Devices and Its Impact on the Health of EU Workers.* Luxembourg: Publications Office of the European Union. http://digitalcommons.ilr.cornell.edu/intl. Accessed 14 Dec 2017.

European Foundation for the Improvement of Living and Working Conditions. 2017. *European Working Conditions Survey Integrated Data File, 1991–2015* [data collection]. 2nd ed. Colchester: UK Data Service, SN: 7363.

Frey, Carl B., and Michael A. Osborne. 2013. *The Future of Employment: How Susceptible Are Jobs to Computerization?,* Oxford Martin School Working Paper. Oxford: University of Oxford. https://www.oxfordmartin.ox.ac.uk/downloads/academic/The_Future_of_Employment.pdf. Accessed 14 Dec 2017.

Gareis, Karsten, Stefan Lilischkis, and Alexander Mentrup. 2006. Mapping the Mobile eWorkforce in Europe. In *Mobile Virtual Work. A New Paradigm?* ed. J.H. Erik Andriessen and Matti Vartiainen, 45–70. Berlin: Springer.

Gonzalez, Victor M., and Gloria Mark. 2004. "Constant, Constant, Multi-Tasking Craziness": Managing Multiple Working Spheres. Proceedings of the 2004 Conference on Human Factors in Computing Systems, CHI 2004, Vienna, Austria, April 24–29, 6 (1): 113–120.

Hill, Edward. J., Brent C. Miller, Sara P. Weiner, and Joe Colihan. 1998. Influences of the Virtual Office on Aspects of Work and Work/Life Balance. *Personnel Psychology* 51 (3): 667–683.

Hungerland, Fabian, Jörn Quitzau, Christopher Zuber, Lars Ehrlich, Christian Growitsch, Marie-Christin Rische, Friso Schlitte, and Hans-Joachim Haß. 2015. *The Digital Economy. Strategy 2030—Wealth and Life in the Next Generation, No. 21e.* Hamburg: Berenberg and the Hamburg Institute of International Economics (HWWI). http://hdl.handle.net/10419/121322. Accessed 14 Dec 2017.

Jorgenson, Dale W. 2001. Information Technology and the U.S. Economy. *American Economic Review* 91 (1): 1–32.

Keynes, John M. 1930. Economic Possibilities for Our Grandchildren. In *Essays in Persuasion,* ed. John M. Keynes, 1963, 358–373. New York: W. W. Norton & Co.

Krusell, Per, Lee E. Ohanian, José-Victor Rios-Rull, and Giovanni L. Violante. 2002. Capital-Skill Complementarity and Inequality: A Microeconomic Analysis. *Econometrica* 68 (5): 1029–1053.

Lehdonvirta, Vili, and Paul Mezier. 2013. Identity and Self-Organization in Unstructured Work. *Dynamics of Virtual Work. Working Paper Series* 1: 1–35. Hertfordshire: University of Hertfordshire. http://dynamicsofvirtualwork.com/working-papers/. Accessed 14 Dec 2017.

Maggi, Bruno. 2003. *De l'agir organisationnel : un point de vue sur le travail, le bien-être, l'apprentissage.* Toulouse: Octarès (2016, 2nd ed. Bologna: TAO Digital Library).

Mazmanian, Melissa, Wanda J. Orlikowski, and JoAnne Yates. 2006. CrackBerrys: Exploring the Social Implications of Ubiquitous Wireless Email Devices. Paper Presented at the 22nd EGOS Colloquium, Bergen, Norway, July 6–8.

———. 2013. The Autonomy Paradox: The Implications of Mobile Email Devices for Knowledge Professionals. *Organization Science* 24 (5): 1337–1357.

Pfeiffer, Sabine, Daniela Wühr, and Petra Schütt. 2016. Virtual Innovation Work: Labour, Creativity, and Standardisation. In *Virtual Workers and the Global Labour Market*, ed. Juliet Webster and Keith Randle, 77–93. Basingstoke: Palgrave Macmillan.

Pratt, Andy C. 2013. Space and Place. In *Handbook on the Digital Creative Economy*, ed. Ruth Towse and Christian Handke, 37–44. Cheltenham/Northampton: Edward Elgar.

Reinsch, Lamar N. Jr., Jeanine Warisse Turner, and Catherine H. Tinsley. 2008. Multicommunicating: A Practice Whose Time Has Come? *Academy of Management Review* 33 (2): 391–403.

Rennecker, Julie, and Lindsey Godwin. 2003. Theorizing the Unintended Consequences of Instant Messaging for Worker Productivity. *Sprouts: Working Papers on Information Environments, Systems and Organizations* 3 (3): 137–168.

———. 2005. Delays and Interruptions: A Self-Perpetuating Paradox of Communication Technology Use. *Information and Organization* 15 (3): 247–266.

Reynaud, Jean-Daniel. 1988. Les régulations dans les organisations: régulation de contrôle et régulation autonome. *Revue française de sociologie* 29 (1): 5–18.

Schneckenberg, Dirk. 2009. Web 2.0 and the Empowerment of the Knowledge Worker. *Journal of Knowledge Management* 13 (6): 509–520.

Smart Working Observatory. 2012. *Smart Working: ripensare il lavoro, liberare energia.* Milan: Politecnico of Milan, Department of Management Engineering.

———. 2013a. *I Fattori Chiave dei Sistemi Informativi "Smart".* Milan: Politecnico of Milan, Department of Management Engineering.

———. 2013b. *La Diffusione e i Benefici dello Smart Working in Italia.* Milan: Politecnico of Milan, Department of Management Engineering.

———. 2014a. *Le Tecnologie Digitali Chiave a Supporto dello Smart Working.* Milan: Politecnico of Milan, Department of Management Engineering.

———. 2014b. *Smart Working Scenario.* Milan: Politecnico of Milan, Department of Management Engineering.

———. 2015. *Nuovi Modi di Lavorare: Una Panoramica sullo Smart Working.* Milan: Politecnico of Milan, Department of Management Engineering.

————. 2016. *(Smart) Work in Progress!* Milan: Politecnico of Milan, Department of Management Engineering.

————. 2017. *Smart Working: sotto la punta dell'iceberg.* Milan: Politecnico of Milan, Department of Management Engineering.

Solow, Robert M. 1956. A Contribution to the Theory of Economic Growth. *The Quarterly Journal of Economics* 70 (1): 65–94.

————. 1987. We'd Better Watch Out. *New York Times Book Review,* July 12.

Terssac, Gilbert de. 1992. *Autonomie dans le travail.* Paris: Presses Universitaires de France.

————. 2003. Travail d'organisation et travail de régulation. In *La théorie de la régulation sociale de Jean-Daniel Reynaud. Débats et prolongements,* ed. Gilbert de Terssac, 121–134. Paris: La Découverte.

Valenduc, Gérard, and Patricia Vendramin. 2016. Work in the Digital Economy: Sorting the Old from the New, *ETUI Working Paper 2016.03.* Brussels: ETUI. https://www.etui.org/Publications2/Working-Papers/Work-in-the-digital-economy-sorting-the-old-from-the-new. Accessed 14 Dec 2017.

Vartiainen, Matti, and Ursula Hyrkkänen. 2010. Changing Requirements and Mental Workload Factors in Mobile Multi-Locational Work. *New Technology, Work and Employment* 25 (2): 117–135.

Vendramin, Patricia. 2007. Les métiers des TIC: un nomadisme coopératif. In *Où va le travail à l'ère du numérique ?* ed. Anne-France Saint Laurent-Kogan and Jean-Luc Metzger, 89–104. Paris: Presses Des Mines.

Vendramin, Patricia, and Gérard Valenduc. 2016. *Le travail virtuel . Nouvelles formes de travail et d'emploi dans l'économie digitale.* Fondation Travail-Université and Confédération des Syndicats Chrétiens. http://hdl.handle.net/2078.1/174224. Accessed 14 Dec 2017.

Wajcman, Judy, Michael Bittman, and Judith E. Brown. 2008. Families Without Borders: Mobile Phones, Connectedness and Work-Home Divisions. *Sociology* 42 (4): 635–652.

Wajcman, Judy, Emily Rose, Judith E. Brown, and Michael Bittman. 2010. Enacting Virtual Connections Between Work and Home. *Journal of Sociology* 46 (3): 257–275.

Wellman, Barry, Janet Salaff, Dimitrina Dimitrova, Laura Garton, Milena Gulia, and Caroline Haythornthwaite. 1996. Computer Networks as Social Networks: Collaborative Work, Telework, and Virtual Community. *Annual Review of Sociology* 22: 213–238.

Thompson, James D. 1967. *Organizations in Action.* New York: McGraw-Hill (2003. New Brunswick/London: Transaction Publishers).

11

"Always-on": The Collapse of the Work–Life Separation in Recent Developments, Deficits and Counter-Strategies

Rüdiger Krause

Introduction

One of the most significant features of the industrial age is the separation of production and reproduction. Whereas in previous epochs both fields of social life were intermingled and households and farms served as a centre of both production and reproduction, since the nineteenth century the work organisation in the emerging industries has led to a sharp distinction between the working sphere within factories on the one side and the domestic sphere reserved for recreation and family life on the other side. Simultaneously, the role of time for production and reproduction has fundamentally changed (for the general development, see Borscheid 2004; Rosa 2005). Whereas in the preindustrial era people lived and worked in accordance with natural rhythms such as day and night or the seasons (Thompson 1967, p. 56), with the advent of

---

R. Krause (✉)
Institute for Labour Law, Georg-August-University Göttingen, Göttingen, Germany
e-mail: ruediger.krause@jura.uni-goettingen.de

© The Author(s) 2018
E. Ales et al. (eds.), *Working in Digital and Smart Organizations*,
https://doi.org/10.1007/978-3-319-77329-2_11

industrialisation time became a central element in the new production model. Against the background of a fundamentally new perception of time as linear, quantitative and independent from natural events (Genin 2016, p. 282), which emerged with the invention of precise mechanical clocks around 1700, beginning with the textile manufacturers (Rifkin 1987, p. 86), it became common to fix and measure working time accurately (Supiot 2001, p. 58: "The stop-watch made its way into the workshop", citing Coriat 1994) and thus to separate working hours from personal hours. The next two centuries were filled with numerous attempts from lawmakers, trade unions and works councils to reduce and regulate the working time as a realm of subordination in order to protect the personal time of employees as a realm of freedom at least for male employees (Lee et al. 2007, pp. 24 et seq.).

At the beginning of the twenty-first century, it appears that this social model of work organisation has come to a turning point, at least for a considerable number of employees. Information and communication technologies (ICTs) make it possible to exercise productive activities anywhere and at any time, in particular if the employee has access to the (fixed or mobile) internet ("production is necessary, factories are not!"). Thus, ICTs have annihilated space and time as the two basic and inseparable connected dimensions for each social system (Domingues 1995, p. 233; Lee and Sawyer 2010, p. 295). This goes along with changes in the content of work because economic value creation depends increasingly on immaterial information and communication rather than on a direct handling of material objects. This development has an ambiguous character. On the one side, ICTs enable employees to work more autonomously and to better align professional and personal demands (work–life balance). On the other side, ICTs induce the severe problem of an encroachment of work life on private life. Thus, the time for recreation, family life and other social contacts is at risk of being absorbed by work-related tasks.

This situation raises several questions: Are the existing working time regulations still appropriate for employees who are "always" online by using their mobile devices extensively during their leisure time or by being permanently in a standby mode? Is deregulation the right answer or, quite the contrary, are a stricter enforcement of existing law and new regulations necessary? In short, must the norms be adjusted to the facts or the facts to the norms? Are the social partners, particularly those at the plant level, the right parties to reconcile flexibility and the need for a distance from work in order to protect the mental stability of employees?

This chapter proceeds as follows: In the second section, it analyses the current factual situation in detail referring to surveys and empirical studies from different countries, including the impact on the affected employees. Then, in the third section with a focus on the European level, it turns to working time regulations as a traditional instrument to limit the extension of work. In the forth section, it raises the question as to why working time regulations have obviously lost their effectiveness for so many workers. In the fifth section, counter-strategies by way of legislation or by way of collective bargaining at the plant level which aims to tackle the "Always-on" phenomenon are portrayed and assessed. A summary closes the chapter.

Current Factual Situation

An accurate assessment of empirical data appears useful for two reasons. First, any policy recommendation should rely on a firm basis. Second, the interpretation of existing law not only is a hermeneutic endeavour but also must be underpinned by a clear analysis of the factual situation the law aims to structure (Cotterell 1998, p. 171). The relevant data show that working or to be reachable for work at home or whilst on the move with the help of ICTs is not only an abstract option but a reality for a growing number of employees. In the past few years, a huge number of surveys and reports have analysed that development. Some of the studies do not distinguish precisely enough between the different periods that are affected (e.g. evening, weekend or leave) or between the question of how often the employees are actually contacted by a superior, a colleague or a customer. However, the trend that there is an increasing invasion of work-related issues into the private life of workers cannot as such be challenged. According to a recent study conducted by the German Federal Ministry of Labour and Social Affairs, 5% of the surveyed employees phoned or answered e-mails with a work-related content in their off time "daily", 15% of them "several times per week", 20% "several times per month", 25% "several times per year" and 35% "never" (Bundesministerium für Arbeit und Soziales 2015a, pp. 11 et seq.; likewise Bundesanstalt für Arbeitsschutz und Arbeitsmedizin 2016, pp. 75 et seq.). In regard to the affected periods of the free time, a study of BITKOM (the inter-trade organisation for the digital economy in Germany) showed that 30% of the employees surveyed are reachable "in the evening", 11% also "at the weekend", 6% "at night" and 3% "during the leave" (BITKOM 2013, p. 29). The same study of BITKOM, asking whether employees check their e-mails "autonomously", revealed the following result: 5% "during breaks", 25% "in the evening after work", 10% "in the morning before work", 10% "at the weekend", 7% "at night", 6% "during the leave" and 13% "always" (BITKOM 2013, p. 30). Employers often facilitate this behaviour of employees. According to a recent survey of the German Federal Statistical Agency (Statistisches Bundesamt), 83% of medium enterprises (50 to 249 employees) and 94% of enterprises (250 or more employees) offer mobile work to their staff. In 80% of these enterprises the employees have access to the firm's e-mail system, in 44% of the enterprises the workers have access to and can change business documents and in 36% of the enterprises the employees can use the firm's software from outside (Statistisches Bundesamt 2016). Of course, this development is not limited to German employees. Studies from the US (Middleton 2008, p. 209), Canada (Duxbury et al. 2006, p. 305) and France (Mettling 2015, pp. 12 et seq.) confirm that this trend is part of every modern economy (Joint ILO-Eurofound 2017, pp. 23 et seq.). Work extension is indeed a worldwide phenomenon ("Morbus BlackBerry"; for the general growing concern about unregulated overtime, see Eurofound 2016) notwithstanding that the average working times have decreased in the past 50 years (Lee et al. 2007, pp. 25 et seq.).

It is perfectly clear that the rapid development of ICTs is one of the key factors in this trend (Joint ILO-Eurofound 2017, p. 9; Bailyn 1988, p. 143). Thus, ICTs functions as work extending technologies. However, it would be too simple to conceive of the changes in the organisation of work only as a result of the technological progress. Indeed, the general changes in management strategies—i.e. management by objectives, the compression of work and the implementation of market mechanisms within the employment relationship—should not be ignored. In that respect, ICTs enable and fuel new kinds of human resource management methods which are driven mainly by economic forces.

This development has some serious consequences. First, as leisure time is increasingly interrupted by "work splitters", the necessary recreation time away from work is endangered. Several studies (Pangert et al. 2016) show that working beyond the regular working times and permanent accessibility can reduce the ability of the employees to organise their leisure time and can be detrimental to family life and social contacts. Moreover, in many cases, work extension can lead to internal restlessness, insomnia and even psychosomatic troubles. Therefore, about a third of those workers who are often or always accessible suffer from a great deal of stress. A recent representative study has impressively assessed the negative outcomes of permanent accessibility for the social relations as well as the physical and mental condition of employees (Hassler et al. 2016; for the negative consequences of working times which exceed 48 hours per week, see Tucker and Folkard 2012, pp. 16 et seq.).

Legal Framework at the European Level

This development, tellingly labelled "time porosity" (Genin 2016, p. 280), counters the trend of limiting working times which has been a significant feature of labour law since the beginning of the nineteenth century. This is done in order to better protect employee health from excessive working and to enlarge the space in which the employee is not the subordinate of his or her employer but has personal time for recreation, social contacts and self-fulfilment (for a comprehensive overview on the development, see Ramm 1986, pp. 77 et seq.). Thus, the legal framework on working times as an institutional limitation to separate the work life from the private life of employees comes into view. Although legal regulations are not the only tool to tackle an aberration in the field of employment, law is still one of the most important governance instruments. Therefore, it is of utmost interest whether a "governance gap"

228   R. Krause

exists at the level of regulations because social reality has "escaped" the existing legal framework or whether there is "only" a deficit at the level of an effective enforcement of the legal framework at hand.

General Remarks

From a legal point of view, different aspects have to be distinguished at the outset. On the one side, there is the dimension of working time regulations as public law. In that respect, the law determines the maximum hours of working. On the other side, the concrete working hours of employees are determined by contractual arrangements or by collective agreements. In their own way, both kinds of governance (in a broad sense including not only collective agreements but individual contractual employment conditions as well) of the employment relationship deal with the same topic, i.e. the fundamental distinction between working time as a sphere of subordination and personal time as a sphere of autonomy, although this traditional "Fordist" dichotomy neglected the gender perspective (Supiot 2001, pp. 60 et seq.). From another angle, the two kinds of governance serve different purposes (following the taxonomy of market governance sketched by Gereffi and Mayer 2005, p. 42). Public laws on working time issues reflect the democratic decision, to what extent employees are shielded against exorbitant work with the goal to protect their health as a means in itself and as a means to protect their permanent ability to work. Contractual arrangements and collective agreements reflect market forces and in doing so the question to which extent employees as individuals or as members of trade unions are willing to perform work as a quid pro quo for remuneration from the employer, notwithstanding that contractual arrangements do not always reflect employees' preferences but the dominant will of the employer. The concrete working time even of full-time employees is regularly lower than the maximum working time allowed by public law which is in part the merit of the European trade unions and their traditional bargaining strategy to reduce weekly working time (e.g. in Germany in 2012, the average working time of full-time workers was 41.9 hours weekly, whereas the average working time provided in collective agreements was 37.7 hours weekly, cf. Absenger et al. 2014; for a European survey, see Eurofound 2016, pp. 33 et seq.). Given this, it is important to distinguish between the different kinds of work extensions, namely those extensions which violate public law and those extensions which violate "only" contractual obligations or collective agreements. Moreover, the protection of employees against extended working as such must be distinguished from the question of whether this work is paid. However, this issue is linked with the problem of delimitation of work because an obligation for the employer to pay for additional work would create a strong incentive not to take this work for granted but to limit it. Nevertheless, owing to the limited space of this chapter, the following considerations will focus on the European working time regulations.

At the European level, as is well known, the Working Time Directive 2003/88/EC (WTD) plays the central role. In accordance with its predecessor Directive 93/104/EC and backed by Article 31 paragraph 2 of the European Charter of Fundamental Rights, the main goal of this regulation is to protect the health and safety of workers with regard to the organisation of working time. This is expressly provided in Article 1 paragraph 1 WTD as well as in numerous Recitals of the WTD (cf. Recitals 1, 2, 3, 4, 7, 9, 10 and 11 WTD) and was emphasised from the very beginning as its rationale (but see also Adnett and Hardy 2001, pp. 117 et seq., arguing that there are three rationales: work sharing, incomplete employment contracts, and family-friendly employment policies). The Court of Justice of the European Union (CJEU), then known as the European Court of Justice, has affirmed that position several times (CJEU 1996, paragraphs 45, 75 et seq.; 2000, paragraph 49; 2003, paragraph 50; 2004, paragraph 82) and has in particular endorsed a broad understanding of health and safety referring to the preamble of the Constitution of the World Health Organization (CJEU 1996, paragraph 15; 2003, paragraph 93). Moreover, Recital 4 of the WTD expressly states that health and safety at work are objectives which should not be subordinated to purely economic considerations. Thus, the question arises of whether the concrete regulations of the WTD suffice for this ambitious goal when it comes to ICTs as work extending technologies.

Limits and Entitlements

For the purpose of this chapter, it is sufficient to sketch those elements of the WTD which are relevant for "time porosity". First, Article 6 WTD as a basic rule of particular importance of European Union social law (cf. CJEU 2007, paragraph 23; 2010, paragraph 33) provides that the average working time for each seven-day period, including overtime, must not exceed 48 hours. The notion of "overtime" is not defined but it seems evident that it is to be the opposite of "normal working time". Therefore, in regard to the maximum weekly working time, not only the normal working time but also exceptional overtime shall be taken into account. According to Article 16(b) WTD, Member States can extend the reference period up to a length of four months. Second, the WTD establishes minimum entitlements to rest periods. Article 3 WTD provides a minimum daily rest period of 11 consecutive hours per 24-hour period. According to Article 4 WTD, the worker is entitled to an in-work rest break where the working day is longer than six hours. Last, but not least, Article 5 WTD states that every worker is entitled to a minimum uninterrupted rest period of 24 hours in addition to the daily rest period of a minimum of 11 hours. This means that the worker has a right to 35 consecutive hours of rest once a week. However, according to Article 16(a) WTD, Member States have the option to lay down a reference period not exceeding 14 days. In this context, the term "entitlement" does not mean that the worker is free to choose whether or not he or she works during the rest period. Rather, the CJEU has made clear that Member States must ensure that the rights conferred on workers by the WTD are fully effective and so Member States are under an obligation to guarantee that each of the minimum requirements is observed (CJEU 2006, paragraph 40). The German Federal Labour Court (Bundesarbeitsgericht) has gone a step further and ruled that the employer is also responsible for the compliance of employees with the German Working Time Act (Arbeitszeitgesetz) and thus has to organise his or her operations in a way which is compatible with the provisions of the Act (BAG 2003).

Concept of Work

Any limitation of working time and any entitlement of rest periods require a concept of working time or work (or both) as a reference point. If a Member State or even the employer or the employee could autonomously define the notion of "work", the whole working time regime would collapse like a house of cards.

Concerning the concept of working time, the first important feature is the binary conception of the WTD. According to Article 2 point (1) and (2) WTD, there are only two categories, namely "working time" and "rest period". Every time has to be classified in one of these categories. There is no third category. In accordance with this, the CJEU has ruled, in numerous decisions, that "working time" and "rest period" are "mutually exclusive" (CJEU 2000, paragraph 47; 2003, paragraph 48; 2005, paragraph 42; 2007, paragraph 24; 2011, paragraph 42). Thus, in its current version, the WTD ignores that there are "grey periods" (cf. AG Bot 2015, paragraph 29) between full work under the control of the employer on the one end of the scale and full free time of the employee without any constraints on the other end. The second important feature is the fact that the WTD defines positively only "working time". As regards "rest period", the definition is negative. According to Article 2 point (2) WTD, rest period means simply any period which is not working time. Therefore, the conception of working time is key for the application of the WTD.

The definition of working, provided in Article 2 point (1) WTD, contains three criteria. Thereafter, working time means any period (i) during which the worker is working, (ii) at the employer's disposal and (iii) carrying out his or her activities or duties in accordance with national laws or practice or both. In spite of the reference to Member States' laws or practice or both (remarkably the reference point differs in the different language versions of the WTD, cf. Franzen 2015, pp. 409 et seq.), the CJEU has ruled that the definition constitutes a conception of Union law because only an autonomous interpretation secures the full effectiveness and the uniform application in all Member States (CJEU 2003, paragraph 59; 2005, paragraph 44; critical Anzinger 2005, p. 9, who has represented Germany as an official in the negotiations of the WTD; also sceptical Franzen 2004, pp. 1043 et seq.). When the first few cases were submitted to the CJEU in the 2000s, the question arose of whether these three elements are cumulative or disjunctive in order to classify a specified period as working time (Barnard 2012, p. 547). Two Advocates General have argued that, according to the concrete situation, it can be sufficient that only two criteria are met in order to ensure a broad interpretation of the WTD (AG Saggio 1999, paragraphs 34 et seq; AG Colomer 2003, paragraphs 28 et seq.). In the landmark Simap decision, the CJEU did not follow this approach and ruled that all three elements have to be met (CJEU 2000, paragraphs 48 et seq.; for the interpretation of Simap, see Fairhurst 2001, p. 240). However, the Court has interpreted the third element in particular in a very broad sense and has reiterated this approach in numerous subsequent decisions (CJEU 2001, paragraph 34; 2003, paragraphs 53 et seq., 75 et seq.; 2004, paragraphs 93 et seq.; 2005, paragraphs 46 et seq. For the transposition of the interpretation of Directive 93/104/EC to Directive 2003/88/EC, see CJEU 2007, paragraph 29). Hereby, the Court eventually achieved the same outcome as the Advocates General with their diverging approach. According to the CJEU, all three criteria are met if the employee is required to be present at the workplace and to be available to perform his or her duties according to the circumstances. Thus, the Court came close to the definition in the Commissions' proposal of a WTD in 1990 which Article 2 point (1) reads as follows: "'working time' means hours of work … during which the employee is at the disposal of the employer at the work-site" (European Commission 1990). Recently, Advocate General Bot delivered a plausible interpretation of the unclear wording of Article 2 point (1) WTD and stated that the definition of working time contains (i) the spatial criterion (to be at the workplace) (this aspect is often misinterpreted; cf. Riesenhuber 2012, pp. 391 et seq., who argues that standby workers are not actually "working" in the meaning of the first criterion disregarding the fact that they are undoubtedly "at work"), (ii) an authority criterion (to be at the disposal of the employer), and (iii) a professional criterion (to be carrying out his or her activity or duties) (AG Bot 2015, paragraph 31; similar AG Colomer 2003, paragraph 31). In its judgement, the Court has not expressly adopted this conception but its reasoning is very similar to this approach (see also European Commission 2017, pp. 16 et seq.).

Consequently, the CJEU classified standby time where the employees are required to be physically present at the workplace as working time. In contrast, on-call time where the workers are required to be contactable but are not obliged to stay at a place specified by the employer is not regarded as working time but rather a rest time according to the WTD. Only those times in a on-call period in which the employee is actually working are regarded as working time. The Court argues that an employee who is only obliged to be at the disposal of the employer but can pursue his own interests and stay in his or her family and social environment is less constrained than an employee who cannot decide where to stay. Thus, as the authority criterion is in the two situations nearly equally met, the spatial criterion appears to be the decisive factor as regards the distinction between standby time and on-call time. Moreover, owing to the strict "two pillar approach" (cf. AG Bot 2015, paragraph 29) of the WTD and the lack of any intermediary category between working time and rest periods (CJEU 2005, paragraph 43; 2007, paragraph 25; 2011, paragraph 43), the fact is neglected that during on-call times the employee is less free and faces some constraints that he or she does not in those times in which the link to the employer is fully cut (Davies 2017, p. 498). Indeed, in a recent decision the Court has modified its approach ruling that on-call time must be regarded as working time, even if the worker spends the time at home but has the duty to reach his or her place of work within eight minutes because this duty limits significantly the opportunities for personal and social activities (CJEU 2018, paragraphs 63 et seq.).

Classification of "Free Time Work"

If an employee is preparing a PowerPoint presentation, writing a report or just checking his or her work e-mails late in the evening or on the weekend, it can be questioned whether all of those activities constitute working time. Against the background of the definition of working time in the WTD and its interpretation by the CJEU, the professional criterion is definitely met. However, at least at first sight, the other two criteria, namely the spatial criterion and the authority criterion, are problematic. As regards the spatial criterion, in these situations there is no duty of the worker to stay at a par-

234 R. Krause

ticular place designated by the employer. Moreover, the worker can stay in his or her personal environment and manage his or her free time, e.g. watching a movie in a cinema and afterwards writing a report after midnight. However, the simple fact that the employee can stay at home or work mobile cannot hinder the classification of the time where he or she performed the work as working time. As Advocate General Saggio has put it, it would not fit into the purpose of the WTD to exclude the periods where the worker is not at his or her usual workplace (AG Saggio 1999, paragraph 34). If the employer and the employee have agreed on a home-office day, there can be no doubt that the period where the employee is working has to be classified as working time. Thus, as far as the spatial criterion is concerned, it can make no relevant difference if the employee begins working in his or her office at the worksite and then continues the work at home even if the employer has not specified the place where the work is performed.

The authority criterion is harder to assess. In this context, Advocate General Colomer has stated that even the performance of work does not constitute working time if the employee is doing so on his or her own initiative, altruistically and outside the employer's sphere of influence (AG Colomer 2003, paragraph 29). Indeed, if the employee is working only on his or her own accord (e.g. checking the firm's e-mail account again and again out of pure curiosity), this "work" can hardly be classified as working time (Bayreuther 2016, § 11 paragraph 22). However, if the employee is charged with a huge number of tasks which cannot be accomplished during the regular working time so that he or she is forced to work at night, it would not fit to the purpose of the WTD to exclude those times with the argument that the employer has not directly ordered the worker to do so. In that respect, at least implicit orders must suffice for the authority criterion. Correspondingly, the European Commission has stated that the WTD does not recognise the notion of "voluntary work" and has emphasised that the Directive lays down that Member States shall take the measures necessary to ensure that the average working time for each seven-day period, including overtime, must not exceed 48 hours (Diamantopoulou 2000).

Apart from that, it would be contradictory if the employer accepts the results of the work performed, for example, between midnight and 2 a.m. on the one side and challenges that the employee has accomplished his or her tasks only because he or she is subordinated on the other side. The alternative, namely that the employee has worked as a "friend" of the employer in an altruistic manner, is fairly unrealistic. Consequently, working during times which are regularly free must be classified as working times with the consequence that the delimitation of maximum working time and the entitlements to rest periods are applicable. This is especially problematic with regard to the daily and the weekly rest period. It is questionable whether any interruption of the rest period (e.g. checking and answering an e-mail in five minutes) has the consequence that the 11-hour rest period starts again. In this regard, some German authors have proposed that short interruptions be neglected (cf.—but disregarding European law—Bissels and Meyer-Michaelis 2015, p. 2333; Wirtz 2014, p. 1401). On the grounds of the existing law, this approach is not convincing since it is very unclear whether an interruption is "short" (likewise assessment by Ulber 2016, § 6 paragraph 128). However, it is discussable to legally define short interruptions and come to a solution *de lege ferenda* by changing the WTD so that a widespread factual behaviour of employees coincides with the normative framework. Aside from this question, a strict approach for the classification of "free time work" as working time is preferable.

In this context, there is only one caveat. If the employer does not know that the employee is working beyond the regular working times and his or her ignorance is not based on negligence, he or she cannot be sanctioned with a fine for the violation of working time regulations if the conduct of the employee is revealed afterwards. It is not the task of the employer to intrude into the private sphere of the employee and check whether the employee works in the evening or on the weekend. However, it is a duty of the employer to organise business operations in such a way that the workers are able to accomplish the tasks without violating working time regulations.

Classification of "Permanent Availability"

Concerning the availability of employees, there are several problems. First of all, "availability" (or "accessibility") covers very different situations. On the one hand, there are situations in which an employee who stays at home is obliged to consistently keep track of how a machine functions via ICTs. On the other hand, there are situations in which an employee is available for the employer, colleagues or customers, but the possibility to contact him or her is largely theoretical because the option is rarely used and the employee is aware of this. In short, there is a broad spectrum between the different kinds of availability.

Coming back to the approach of the WTD and the CJEU, the extent of constraints of the employee is the decisive factor to distinguish working time from rest time. For the Court, a period can be classified as working time only if there are relatively strong constraints regarding the spatial criterion. If the employee is free to choose the place where to stay, his or her performance is regarded as only an on-call time which does not constitute working time. However, even on the grounds of the existing law, this approach seems too narrow when it comes to situations where the employee is required to supervise the functioning of machines via notebook from home without interruption or only with short breaks or mobile or he or she is permanently phoned and must immediately accomplish the conferred tasks. If there is no agreement on on-call work, it can be considered whether constant uninvited phone calls from the employer or superiors have to be qualified as intrusions into the private sphere of the employee protected by Article 7 of the European Charter of Fundamental Rights and Article 8 of the European Convention on Human Rights. In any event, under a working time perspective which is at stake here, such cases do not differ much from the situation of working on the premises of the employer, which would without any doubt justify the classification of this time as working time (Bayreuther 2016, § 11 paragraph 22). In both constellations, the worker is at the disposal of the employer as a core criterion to distinguish between working time and personal time. In other words, in such a case, the workplace has shifted from the premises of the employer to the home of the employee. This view is consistent with the argument of the CJEU in Tyco that a worker who is no longer carrying out his or her duties at a fixed place of work but rather during the journey to or from a customer has to be regarded as working during that journey (CJEU 2015, paragraph 43).

However, there are cases in which the freedom of the employee to manage his or her personal time is less constrained. In such situations during this time, the worker can to some extent pursue personal purposes. But it is important to realise that even in these cases the employee is not completely free, because he or she has to be available and must conduct him- or herself in such a manner that he or she can immediately react and start to work, e.g. not to drink alcohol or go swimming. Moreover, availability is a vague concept in another dimension. On the one hand, there can be an explicit obligation for the worker to be contactable by the employer or by other persons. On the other hand, there can be an implicit expectation of the employer that the worker is available and vice versa an impression of the employee that being available is expected and being not available can be detrimental at least regarding his or her further career. In particular, in situations with a lack of clear contractual arrangements, the features of ICTs promote the existence of grey areas of implicit expectations of both sides which are not easy to grasp.

Deficits and Reasons

In summing up the aforementioned considerations, it becomes evident that "Always-on" basically covers two different situations: first, the performance of work by using ICTs beyond the regular working times and also often during those periods which are protected by the maximum limit of working time or the entitlement of daily or weekly rest time; second, the availability via ICTs in the evening or on the weekend (the specific problem of working and being available during paid leave shall not be discussed here). Thus, in general, the collapse of the work–life separation has two different faces and, although they are intermingled, it is necessary to treat them differently because the legal problems are not exactly the same.

Additional Work Beyond Work Time Regulations

As regards working beyond the regulations of the WTD, there is no lack of norms. It is fully clear that there are limitations for working times but often enough they are neglected. The reasons for this phenomenon are diverse. From the perspective of the employer, the extension of work as

238 R. Krause

such is generally welcome because he or she receives more labour input in exchange for the remuneration. In many cases, the employer may not be fully aware of the extension because it is often out of his or her perception whether the employee is working at home or mobile beyond the regular working times. Even though the employer is obliged to control compliance with legal working time regulations, this obligation is often violated because there is an understandable lack of interest in doing so. Labour inspection is notoriously underfinanced and lacks enough staff to enforce the law effectively. Therefore, disregarding the law is often without any risk of detection.

The perspective of employees is multifaceted. In principle, each worker could simply refuse to work beyond the working time stipulated in individual or collective agreements and *a fortiori* beyond public law. It is perfectly clear that the employer regularly has no right to demand additional work beyond the promised hours and in particular beyond working time regulations, e.g. that this work shall be performed during the daily rest. Any agreement on such work would clearly be void and unenforceable. However, this work is actually performed in a grey area. Partly the employees have the feeling that checking and answering e-mails at night or early in the morning is not "real work". Partly the employees have the impression that the employer, superiors, colleagues or clients expect such behaviour. Partly the employees are interested in pursuing or finalising a specific project, and there is economic pressure, financial incentives and so on. Mostly there is not a simple instruction from the employer to work more than agreed and allowed but a complex bundle of internal motives and external expectations to do so. Modern management strategies ("off a presence-culture towards a results-culture") foster the attitude that the observance of working times is less important. This comes along with the "system logic" of work in modern societies. Whereas in a tayloristic-style factory no worker would stay "voluntarily" longer at the assembly line in order to produce fenders (because this kind of work has very little to do with self-fulfilment), many modern knowledge and creative workers internalise the goals of the firm and act in an entrepreneurial manner. This is of course not to glorify traditional forms of work organisation. Nevertheless, it is important to realise that the trend of delimited work rests on different driving forces. Thus, on the one side, a strengthening of labour inspection which is in charge of observing whether the employer runs his operations in compliance with working time regulations is reasonable throughout in order to clarify that at least gross violation of the law on working time is no peccadillo. However, owing to the bundle of different motives and interests which are at stake, it can be assumed that no single measure and in particular an external governance instrument like labour inspection will solve all the problems immediately.

"Time Porosity" by Being Available

With regard to "time porosity" in the sense that the employee is not actually working but is available for the employer as a result of an obligation of factual expectations, the situation is different. In that respect, two problems can be distinguished although they are linked with each other. The first problem concerns the relevant law—to be more exact, the structure of the WTD at least in the interpretation of the CJEU with its strict dichotomy between working time and rest time. This lack of an interim category is often criticised. However, the focus should not be on the reduction of protection by distinguishing between active and non-active times of standby workers as intended by the European Commission (European Commission 2004, 2005, 2010). If employees must be physically present at a particular place designated by the employer, they are without any doubt at the disposal of the employer although the intensity of their work varies, very strongly dependent on the concrete circumstances. The focus should instead be on the workers who are free with regard to the place where they stay but who are obliged or at least expected to be available. This leads to the second problem, namely that this availability comes in very different grades of intensity which do not fit well into the logic of law with its binary structure of "lawful" and "unlawful". Thus, it should be clear that there are situations of on-call work which should not be classified as rest time, as Advocate General Saggio has argued in his opinion in Simap (AG Saggio 1999, paragraphs 38 et seq.). However, it would be too strict to exclude each kind of availability from rest periods and classify it without any differences as working time.

Counter-Strategies

Although a more effective labour inspection is desirable, some other instruments should be examined. In a number of firms, there is an increasing awareness of the risks of an "Always-on" attitude. Many employees are not satisfied with this development but see no way to tackle the problem at an individual level. So, in particular at large car manufacturers or suppliers (BMW, Bosch, Daimler and Volkswagen), different schemes have become public to limit the times where employees have to work or to be accessible beyond their regular working time. These schemes are regularly concluded as works agreements between the employer and the (central) works council and provide, for example, the shut-down of servers on the weekend at least for rank-and-file workers. For instance, at the factory of Volkswagen in Wolfsburg, there is a works agreement on the handing-over of official smartphones to employees below the (superior) management level. According to the wording of this works agreement, the apps of the smartphones are blocked if the worker is not at the premises of Volkswagen. During the time slot between 6:15 p.m. and 7 a.m. and on the weekend, only the telephone function is working whereas other apps are off. Moreover, the employees are obliged to leave the official smartphones at the workplace except those employees who have on-call duties. Unfortunately, no further details became known either in respect to the technical dimension or in respect to the real impact and proper functioning of this works agreement. One might say that this works agreement is far from perfect because a superior could simply use the private telephone number of a subordinate and call him or her in the evening or on the weekend. However, this first step to tackle the problem should not be underestimated since it raises the awareness of the problem and tries to find a feasible solution. Moreover, it can be assumed that the inhibition threshold to call a private number is higher than to call the official smartphone number of an employee. Therefore, by "channelling" the communication, the obligation to leave the smartphones at the workplace might contribute to the reduction of an "Always-on" mentality. Other arrangements are more complex and provide that the employee has the right to fix (in matching with his or her

"Always-on": The Collapse of the Work–Life Separation... 241

superior or team) certain times in which he or she should be free from any telephone calls, e-mails, etc. (many examples are listed in Bundesministerium für Arbeit und Soziales 2015b).

These strategies at the plant level lead one to question whether actions at the legislative level can underpin these efforts. The new legislation in France which came into force on 1 January 2017 has recently introduced in Article L2242-8 7° Code du Travail a right to disconnection ("droit à la déconnexion") in order to protect the well-being and the private life of the employees against an increasing invasion by ICTs. However, the concrete implementation of this right is primarily a task for the social partners on the plant level and, lacking a collective agreement, secondarily a duty of the employer. This new piece of legislation shows that only a policy mix of different instruments on different levels has the potential to be successful. The legislator can steer the general direction and signal that a negative trend as such shall be stopped. But it needs a concrete implementation of this general rule at the plant level at least for two reasons: First, in every plant, the situation is different and a "one-size-fits-all solution" would not be feasible. Second, the effectiveness of such a policy depends mainly on the acceptance at the plant level. If the social partners create specific solutions regarding a right to disconnection in order to reconcile social and economic demands, it is much more likely that such an agreement will effectively influence what happens at the workplace in comparison to an act, that would potentially remain only law in the books. From a theoretical point of view, a "regulated self-regulation" seems the most promising way to achieve any progress. If the lawmaker stimulates the social partners or, in the lack of well-equipped trade unions or work councils, obliges the employer to regulate the use of ICTs in the daily operations of the firm, this kind of reflexive law would answer to the demands of the majority of affected employees (according to a study of the French think tank Eléas, 62% of the professionals using ICTs demand a regulation of this issue, cf. Ministère du Travail 2017) and appears to be more effective than a mere public law or individual rights approach (Rogowski 2013, pp. 31 et seq., 97 et seq.).

Another issue is the question of adjusting the WTD to the challenges of an increasing use of ICTs and thereby a growing number of on-call situations of employees. In that respect, one idea could be to introduce a "third time" as a new category between working time on the one side and rest periods on the other side. To conceptualise such a "third time" means to pick it out of the grey area and to make it a subject of regulation. Indeed, there are provisions at the European and national levels which can be used as a model for future regulation. At the European level, Article 3(b) Directive 2002/15/EC mentions periods of availability and defines them as periods during which the mobile worker is not required to remain at his or her workstation but must be available to answer any calls to start or resume driving or to carry out other work. In detail, this Directive prescribes that these periods and their foreseeable duration shall be known in advance by the mobile worker. What follows if the employee is not sufficiently informed in advance on the period of availability is not explicitly regulated but it can be assumed that in such a case this period has to be classified as regular working time (Buschmann 2011, p. 49). However, this regulation provides only a procedural and not a substantive protection because it ensures only transparency for the worker.

In contrast, at the national level, we find some regulations which have substantive character. For instance, in the Vorel case, a Czech provision is mentioned according to which the employer may agree to on-call duty with the employee for a maximum of 400 hours per calendar year. One might argue that this regulation concerns actually only standby work and cannot be applied to real on-call work. However, the provision deals not only with the situation that the employee has to perform standby work at the normal workplace but also at another place agreed upon with the employer (CJEU 2007, paragraph 12). It is true that such an agreement binds the worker with regard to the place where he or she is presently staying to a greater extent than in regular on-call situations. But even if the worker does not have to stay at a particular place agreed with the employer in advance, he or she is bound because he or she has to be available and cannot act according only to his or her own will. Thus, as the essence of the Czech regulation is to limit the extent to which the worker is contractually bound in regard to standby work regardless of whether he or she has to be physically present at the workplace, this approach can in principle be used as a model for the limitation of on-call work as well. Yet an Austrian regulation appears a bit clearer. According to Section 20a of the Austrian Working Time Act (Arbeitszeitgesetz),

"Always-on": The Collapse of the Work–Life Separation...   243

on-call work outside of regular working time must not exceed 10 days per month. Furthermore, there are specific regulations for the case that the employee is actually working during a period of on-call work.

When compiling these models, one approach could be that on-call work may be demanded and expected to be performed by the employee only if it is expressly agreed upon. This kind of formalisation would secure clarity and transparency and hinder the creeping intrusion of work-related issues into private life. Second, the frequency and duration of on-call work should be limited in order to protect employees against an "Always-on" culture with all the detrimental consequences for health but also for family life and social life. It is true that such a regulation runs the risk of being only law in the books. However, the rampant disregard of working time provisions is of course no valid argument to abstain from any regulation in this field of employment law. In contrast, a regulation of on-call work signals that this development does not stand outside of the law even if it provides only minimum requirements. Furthermore, it would contribute to the awareness that a collapse of the separation between work time and personal time is not a desirable expression of the autonomy of employees but rather will have negative consequences for the workers and for society as a whole in the long run.

Summary

The unregulated extension of work and the blurring of the separation between work life and private life cause serious and multifaceted problems for employees and for society as a whole. A policy mix of combined instruments at different levels seems most promising to tackle these problems. As far as work beyond the limitations of working time regulations and during mandatory rest periods is concerned, the problem is not the lack of regulations but the lack of an effective enforcement of the existing regulations. In this regard, a more vigorous labour inspection is desirable, but the effect of external governance should not be overestimated. In contrast, with regard to on-call work, there is at present a lack of regulation at the European level as this kind of work is simply classified as rest period although in a considerable number of cases the worker is constrained in his or her will to manage personal time. Therefore, a procedural and a substantive regulation would be desirable. But even if a right to disconnection were introduced, the question of enforcement would remain because of the inequality of power in the individual employment relationship and because of the diverse motives of employees to be permanently available for work-related issues. Thus, legislative actions have to be accompanied by concrete measures of social partners mainly at the plant level in order to make the abstract regulations workable and to ensure the compliance with protective regulations in the day-to-day operations of firms. So, as in other fields of employment law, a strong institutional representation of employees by trade unions and works councils is still an indispensable instrument for pursuing the interests of the workers.

References

Absenger, Nadine, Elke Ahlers, Reinhard Bispinck, Alfred Kleinknecht, Christina Klenner, Yvonne Lott, Toralf Push, and Hartmut Seifert. 2014. Arbeitszeiten in Deutschland, Entwicklungstendenzen und Herausforderungen für eine moderne Arbeitspolitik. *WSI Report 19*. Düsseldorf: WSI.

Adnett, Nick, and Stephen Hardy. 2001. Reviewing the Working Time Directive: Rational, Implementation and Case Law. *Industrial Relations Journal* 32: 114–125.

Anzinger, Rudolf. 2005. Das Bereithalten zur Arbeit am Beispiel des ärztlichen Bereitschaftsdienstes. In *Arbeitsrecht im sozialen Dialog: Festschrift für Hellmut Wissmann*, ed. Wolfhard Kohte, 3–14. Munich: Beck.

Bailyn, Lotte. 1988. Freeing Work from the Constraints of Location and Time New Technology. *Work and Employment* 3: 143–152.

Barnard, Catherine. 2012. *EU Employment Law*. 4th ed. Oxford: Oxford University Press.

Bayreuther, Frank. 2016. Arbeitszeit. In *Enzyklopädie Europarecht, Europäisches Arbeits- und Sozialrecht*, Band 7, ed. Monika Schlachter and Michael Heinig, 499–526. Baden-Baden: Nomos Verlagsgesellschaft.

Bissels, Alexander, and Isabel Meyer-Michaelis. 2015. Arbeiten 4.0—Arbeitsrechtliche Aspekte einer zeitlich-örtlichen Entgrenzung der Tätigkeit. *Der Betrieb* 40: 2331–2336.

"Always-on": The Collapse of the Work–Life Separation...   245

BITKOM. 2013. *Arbeiten 3.0—Arbeiten in der Digitalen Welt.* Berlin: BITKOM.

Borscheid, Peter. 2004. *Das Tempo Virus: Eine Kulturgeschichte der Beschleunigung.* Frankfurt a.m: Campus Verlag.

Bundesministerium für Arbeit und Soziales. 2015a. *Mobiles und entgrenztes Arbeiten.* Berlin: bmas.

———. 2015b. *Zeit- und ortsflexibles Arbeiten in Betrieben.* Berlin: bmas.

Bundesanstalt für Arbeitsschutz und Arbeitsmedizin. 2016. *Arbeitszeitreport Deutschland 2016.* Dortmund: BAuA.

Buschmann, Rudolf. 2011. Europäisches Arbeitszeitrecht. In *Recht—Politik—Geschichte: Festschrift für Franz Josef Düwell,* ed. Martin Wolmerath, 34–52. Baden-Baden: Nomos Verlagsgesellschaft.

Coriat, Benjamin. 1994. *L'atelier et le chronomètre.* Paris: Collection Choix-essais.

Cotterell, Ryan. 1998. Why Must Legal Ideas Be Interpreted Sociologically? *Journal of Law and Society* 25: 171–201.

Davies, Anne C.L. 2017. Getting More Than You Bargained For? Rethinking the Meaning of 'Work' in Employment Law. *Industrial Law Journal* 46: 477–507.

Diamantopoulou, Anna. 2000. Answer Given on Behalf of the Commission, OJ 2000 No. C 46 E/153.

Domingues, José Mauricio. 1995. Sociological Theory and the Space-Time Dimension of Social Systems. *Time & Society* 4: 233–250.

Duxbury, Linda, Ian Towers, Christopher Higgins, and John Thomas. 2006. From 9 to 5 to 24/7: How Technology Has Redefined the Workday Law. *Information Resources Management* 19: 305–332.

Eurofound. 2016. *Working Time Developments in the 21st Century: Work Duration and Its Regulation in the EU.* Luxembourg: Publications Office of the European Union.

European Commission. 1990. Proposal for a Council Directive Concerning Certain Aspects of the Organization of Working Time. COM(90) 317 final, OJ 1990 No. C 254/4.

———. 2004. Proposal for a Directive of the European Parliament and of the Council Amending Directive 2003/88/EC Concerning Certain Aspects of the Organisation of Working Time. COM(2004) 607 final.

———. 2005. Amended Proposal for a Directive of the European Parliament and of the Council Amending Directive 2003/88/EC Concerning Certain Aspects of the Organisation of Working Time. COM(2005) 246 final.

246 R. Krause

———. 2010. Report from the Commission to the European Parliament, the Council, the European Economic and Social Committee and the Committee of the Regions on Implementation by Member States of Directive 2003/88/EC ('The Working Time Directive'), COM(2010) 802 final.

———. 2017. Interpretative Communication on Directive 2003/88/EC of the European Parliament and of the Council Concerning Certain Aspects of the Organisation of Working Time, OJ 2017 No. C 165/1.

Fairhurst, John. 2001. SIMAP—Interpreting the Working Time Directive. *Industrial Law Journal* 30: 236–243.

Franzen, Martin. 2004. Die arbeitsrechtliche Einordnung des Bereitschaftsdienstes durch den EuGH. *Zeitschrift für Europäisches Privatrecht* 12: 1034–1067.

———. 2015. Überlegungen zur geplanten Revision der Arbeitszeitenrichtlinie. *Zeitschrift für europäisches Sozial- und Arbeitsrecht* 14: 407–413.

Genin, Émilie. 2016. Proposal for a Theoretical Framework for the Analysis of Time Porosity. *International Journal of Comparative Labour Law and Industrial Relations* 32: 280–300.

Gereffi, Gary, and Frederick Mayer. 2005. Globalization and the Demand for Governance. In *The New Offshoring of Jobs and Global Development*, ILO Social Policy Lectures, 39–59. Geneva: ILO.

Hassler, Melanie, Renate Rau, Jens Hupfeld, and Hiltraud Paridon. 2016. *iga. Report. Auswirkungen von ständiger Erreichbarkeit und Präventionsmöglichkeiten.* Dresden: Zukunft der Arbeit GmbH.

ILO-Eurofound. 2017. *Working Anytime, Anywhere: The Effects on the World of Work.* Luxembourg: Publications Office of the European Union.

Lee, Heejin, and Steve Sawyer. 2010. Conceptualizing Time, Space and Computing for Work and Organizing. *Time & Society* 19: 293–317.

Lee, Sangheon, Deirdre McCann, and Jon C. Messenger. 2007. *Working Time Around the World, Trends in Working Hours, Laws and Policies in a Global Comparative Perspective.* London: Routledge.

Mettling, M. Bruno. 2015. *Transformation numérique et vie au travail.* http://www.ladocumentationfrancaise.fr/var/storage/rapports-publics/154000646.pdf. Accessed 14 Dec 2017.

Middleton, Catherine. 2008. Do Mobile Technologies Enable Work-Life Balance? Dual Perspectives on BlackBerry Usage for Supplemental Work. In *Mobility and Technology in the Workplace*, ed. Hislop Donald, 209–224. London: Routledge.

Ministère du Travail. 2017. *Droit à la déconnexion.* http://travail-emploi.gouv.fr/grands-dossiers/LoiTravail/quelles-sont-les-principales-mesures-de-la-loi-travail/article/droit-a-la-deconnexion. Accessed 14 Dec 2017.

Pangert, Barbara, Nina Pauls, and Heinz Schüpbach. 2016. *Die Auswirkungen arbeitsbezogener erweiterter Erreichbarkeit auf Life-Domain-Balance und Gesundheit*. 2. Auflage. Dortmund: BAuA.

Ramm, Thilo. 1986. Laisez-faire and State Protection of Workers. In *The Making of Labour Law in Europe*, ed. Bob Hepple, 73–13. London: Mansell.

Riesenhuber, Karl. 2012. *European Employment Law: A Systematic Exposition, Ius Communitatis*. Cambridge: Intersentia.

Rifkin, Jeremy. 1987. *Time Wars: The Primary Conclict in Human History*. New York: Simon & Schuster.

Rogowski, Ralf. 2013. *Reflexive Labour Law in the World Society*. Cheltenham: Edward Elgar.

Rosa, Hartmut. 2005. *Beschleunigung: Die Veränderung der Zeitstrukturen in der Moderne*. Frankfurt a.M: Suhrkamp.

Statistisches Bundesamt. 2016. *61 % der Unternehmen in Deutschland ermöglichen mobiles Arbeiten*. https://www.destatis.de/DE/PresseService/Presse/Pressemitteilungen/2016/12/PD16_443_52911.html. Accessed 14 Dec 2017.

Supiot, Alain. 2001. *Beyond Employment*. Oxford: Oxford University Press.

Thompson, Edward Palmer. 1967. Time, Work, and Industrial Capitalism. *Past & Present* 38: 56–97.

Tucker, Philip, and Simon Folkard. 2012. *Working Time, Health and Safety: A Research Synthesis Paper, ILO, Conditions of Work and Employment Series No. 31*. Geneva: ILO.

Ulber, Daniel. 2016. Arbeitszeit. In *Europäisches Arbeitsrecht*, ed. Ulrich Preis and Adam Sagan, 334–411. Köln: Otto Schmidt.

Wirtz, Andreas. 2014. Gestaltungsmöglichkeiten bei der Verlängerung der täglichen Arbeitszeit nach dem ArbZG. *Betriebs-Berater* 23: 1397–1401.

Decisions and Opinions

Advocate General Bot. 2015. Opinion in Case C-266/14—Tyco, ECLI:EU:C:2015:391.

Advocate General Colomer. 2003. Opinion in Case C-151/02—Jaeger, ECLI:EU:C:2003:209.

Advocate General Saggio. 1999. Opinion in C-303/98—Simap, ECLI:EU:C:1999:621.

Bundesarbeitsgericht. 2003. Case 1 ABR/13/02, BAGE 106, 111.

Court of Justice of the European Union. 1996. Case C-84/94—United Kingdom v. Council, ECLI:EU:C:1996:431.
———. 2000. Case C-303/98—Simap, ECLI:EU:C:2000:528.
———. 2001. Case-241/99—CIG, ECLI:EU:C:2001:371.
———. 2003. Case C-151/02—Jaeger, ECLI:EU:C:2003:437.
———. 2004. Joint Cases C-397/01 to C-403/01—Pfeiffer and others, ECLI:EU:C:2004:584.
———. 2005. Case C-14/04—Dellas and others, ECLI:EU:C:2005:728.
———. 2006. Case C-484/04—Commission v. United Kingdom, ECLI:EU:C:2006:526.
———. 2007. Case 437/05—Vorel, ECLI:EU:C:2007:23.
———. 2010. Case C-243/09—Fuß I, ECLI:EU:C:2010:609.
———. 2011. Case C-258/10—Grigore, ECLI:EU:C:2011:122.
———. 2015. Case C-266/14—Tyco, ECLI:EU:C:2015:578.
———. 2018. Case 518/15—Matzak, ECLI:EU:C:2018:82.

12

Into Smart Work Practices: Which Challenges for the HR Department?

Teresina Torre and Daria Sarti

Introduction

Authors have defined Smart Working (SW) as an innovative approach to work organization. It is characterized by an explicit responsibility towards results by workers, associated with more flexibility in working conditions (place, time, and tools) in a context in which the evolution of advanced information technologies (AITs) is influencing working vision, work content, and work relationships themselves, thus enabling the diffusion of this specific phenomenon. According to some researches this approach is also referred to as agile working (CIPD 2008; Boormsa et al. 2011;

T. Torre (✉)
Department of Economics and Business Studies, University of Genoa,
Genoa, Italy
e-mail: teresina.torre@economia.unige.it

D. Sarti
Department of Economics and Management, University of Florence,
Florence, Italy
e-mail: daria.sarti@unifi.it

© The Author(s) 2018
E. Ales et al. (eds.), *Working in Digital and Smart Organizations*,
https://doi.org/10.1007/978-3-319-77329-2_12

ENEI 2014; Chiaro et al. 2015), flexible work arrangement (McNall et al. 2010) or activity-based working (Telsyte 2015)—entails a focused organizational policy (that means also new styles of leadership, skills, attitudes and behaviours) together with digital supports. Moreover, the first empirical studies highlight that a relevant number of enterprises have begun to participate in proposing initiatives and projects classifiable under this title and are organizing themselves to use the potential of SW approach, facing the inevitable problems that a change of so much relevance may introduce (Mazzucchelli 2014).

SW attracts enterprises because it seems to offer answers to two specific questions that they consider increasingly relevant. The first issue is that SW helps managers to develop a stronger goal orientation, coherent with the most recent strategic approaches, which ask for more attention to objects, suggesting to redesign the relationships between managers and co-workers. The second is about its ability to create favourable conditions for reducing the trade-off between work and life, which nowadays is the principal challenge for the social agenda. By the way, both problems belong to the traditional area of competence of the HR department.

Following previous research (Sarti and Torre 2017) focused on the comprehension of the SW model from the theoretical point of view and on the analysis of its first application in some Italian enterprises, we are now interested in studying how these enterprises are organizing themselves to support SW introduction, diffusion and stabilization. We observe that an important role is played by the HR department, which is one of the main players (perhaps the most significant one, as we will show) in the preliminary phase of definition of the condition to use SW and then in the phase of its organization and implementation. With our research, we focus on the whole process and on one specific organizational role, which is exactly the one played by the HR department in supporting such an organizational and "mind-set" revolution. Given the impact of SW in working environments, a new perspective for HR departments has to be considered. More in detail, a change in the HR "playing field" is requested, and more and different competences are needed for professionals operating in it.

We target on verifying whether and how its traditional tasks, as expressed in a number of studies on HR management literature, have to evolve

Into Smart Work Practices: Which Challenges for the HR...   251

(and in which direction) to support this new way of organizing work. In accordance with the explorative nature of our study, we examine in depth some case studies chosen among enterprises that were the foremost users of this form, following the idea that their experience is precious to understand evident and hidden transformations. Even if they differ a lot by sector, dimension and seniority, they use SW for the same reasons and face similar problems, so that the responsibility of the HR department seems to be akin in supporting the creation of favourable conditions for an appropriate recourse to SW.

Smart Working: The Definition and the Process for Its Implementation

There is a large consensus in academia and among practitioners about the fact that successful organizations are moving towards new organizational principles. Among these, collaboration (Vlaar et al. 2008), autonomy (Leonardi 2011) and responsibility (Hamel 2007) are indicated as the most important conditions for having workers satisfied with their working conditions and engaged with the tasks they are required to do. It is also acclaimed that the quality of working context directly influences the quality of work, which in turn is related to the quality of products and services (Birkinshaw 2010; Birkinshaw et al. 2008).

In this scenario, SW has been proposed as a new non-conventional organizational model to work organization (Boorsma et al. 2011; CIPD 2008; Lee 2013) in which the basic principles just mentioned find the possibility to be put together and strengthened (Grantham 2000).

One of the first and most mentioned definitions proposed to identify SW orientation is "an approach to organising work that aims to drive greater efficiency and effectiveness in achieving job outcomes through a combination of flexibility, autonomy and collaboration, in parallel with optimizing tools and working environment for employees" (CIPD 2008, p. 4). According to this clarification, SW is a challenge to gather and face in any organizational context and not simply a model to introduce and make working.

The identification of the key variables becomes the central question for understanding SW usefulness in organizational rethinking.

SW supporters suggest that this new approach to work is based essentially on the contemporary and correlated presence of three important pillars: flexibility, discretion (which is a more appropriate concept than autonomy) and responsibility (Gajendran and Harrison 2007).

The first element of SW is *flexibility* in working conditions (in terms of place, time and tools) managed directly by workers according to their needs and their personal preferences, agreed upon with the boss in a way that tasks and goals could be pursued.

A greater *discretion* in working activities is the operational condition: it is requested that the quality of work and its final result be determined by the way in which workers do what they are expected to do (and not by the physical presence in the organization).

A greater discretion has to be associated with an increasing *responsibility* of employees towards results, they are asked to provide and on which they are directly and personally engaged.

Beyond these pillars, the successful introduction of SW asks for other relevant and crucial conditions, which have to be built. Undoubtedly, the first concerns the cultural dimension. The specific characteristics of SW require a transformation of managers' traditional behaviours and a change in the relationships between managers and co-workers (CIPD 2014). Collaboration and trust become essential ingredients for an effective coordination of workers and, first of all, of teams, that may be situated in multiple locations, may have different availability for working activities, coherent with flexible arrangements they have defined, and they have to be led towards wished and shared results (Gastaldi et al. 2014). Still, the detachment of employees from unique and predefined working "places" (in terms of time and physical space) and their integration within the new virtual dimension of communication networks lead to changes in power distribution and in the authority relationships (Brewer 2000). This change oversteps the traditional organizational boundaries, which we are used to since the major changes that this "smart" approach is introducing involve every aspect and dimension of peoples' own lives.

Finally, the design of the work environment is also touched by this revolution. In the new approach, work is possible anywhere: the novelty of the present time is the diffusion of a sort of "continuous place" where people can work (Scornavacca 2014). So, in accordance with mobile and wireless conditions that enable system portability, work location and work time are no longer the basic elements of the job. Once again, the focus has to be put on expected results and not on the way or on the location where they are pursued.

New technologies represent a basic aspect in the SW model. So it is evident that without the recent evolution in the environmental technological context, this approach would not exist. The development of technologies towards the so-called AITs—and the way they are considered and normally used and much more positively sought by people in work and life—is a necessary part of the reasoning. Also, the new configuration of technology as a "portable" system (Scornavacca 2014) represents a condition for SW. The development and diffusion of those technologies, supporting communication, collaboration and social networking, along with the pervasive dissemination of powerful and easy-to-use mobile devices, can support organizations in developing the SW system (Ahuja et al. 2007).

Given its characteristics listed so far, SW implementation within a company can be considered a real process of organizational change (OC). Therefore, like any OC that overthrows the status quo, the process needs to be properly managed in this case also. Indeed, it is suggested that its acceptance and application may encounter some barriers among individuals and groups within the organizations, and may lead to negative consequences, if no attention is paid to prevent them.

According to scholars, OC has some specific aspects that need to be examined in depth. Those of specific interest in the present study are the different stages of the process and the different roles and interventions played by the various internal actors within the whole OC process (Lippitt and Lippitt 1975; Schein 1969).

Moreover, as previously suggested, SW is a new working practice, which can be seen as an innovative way of work organization, while its implementation may be considered in terms of organizational development. In this work, based on well-known masterworks in innovation and organizational development theories, the key phases of the SW process as well as the important roles for its implementation are identified. By linking those two main streams of literature, the path towards SW design and implementation can be analysed (Tagliaro and Ciaramella 2016).

As recommended by the literature on the topic, the OC process is usually defined by single main steps starting from the "initial entry", passing though the "problem diagnosis and roles definition", "taking action" and, in the end, providing "assessment of the process and feedback" (Lippitt and Lippitt 1975; Schein 1969). According to authors, the OC process also involves a mix of two important actions: on the one hand, it asks for organizational plans and objectives based on rationality; on the other hand, it requires the emotions and motivations of the individuals involved (March 1981). In this perspective, the critical stage of value sedimentation represents the final and essential step.

Following the innovation literature, two broad activities characterize the process: initiation and implementation (Rogers 1995). In short, the first is related to the gathering of information, the conceptualization, the realization of the need for innovation and the planning for the adoption of a specific innovation. Through this stage, the positions are created and the decision on implementing it (or not) is made. The second phase of the process is referred to as the implementation one; it includes all of the actions involved in putting the innovation into use and necessary to the organization to integrate it within its current organizational processes. So whereas often the initiation phase of the innovation is pursued by a single member or a small group of actors, the subsequent phase of implementation of the innovation usually concerns a much larger group of organizational members (Wynekoop and Senn 1992).

The initial part of the whole process is further divided into sub-steps. First, there is the phase in which the premises for an intervention to be carried out within a company are verified and through which the *knowledge-awareness* of the need for such intervention arises. Part of this first phase is the *diagnosis-analysis* stage. *Diagnosis* is related to the observation and recognition of a critical aspect of evidence of it; *analysis* means the discovery and detailed study of the observed phenomenon. The combined action of diagnosis and analysis can be seen as a cognitive process of a complex nature (Dutton and Duncan 1987) which may lead to the final decision of implementing or not implementing the innovation, according to the two just-mentioned levels: a rational one and an emotional one.

The implementation part of the process is also divided into two substeps: the *initial stage* in which there is a sort of pilot experimentation of the process to be implemented and the subsequent effective final process implementation. Finally, the intervention is concluded and an assessment of the whole process is carried out.

During the development of this stage, the innovation literature suggests the need for training focused on the attitude towards innovation among the organization members. In this sense, individual openness towards innovation and the connected enabling factors (i.e. trust) in its usefulness need to be verified in order to proceed with the whole process of implementation (Zaltman et al. 1973).

According to this general and acknowledged course of activities arising from both innovation and OC domains, we described the core stages of SW implementation identifying a three-step workflow process, which starts from the decision to verify whether conditions for SW are present in a specific situation, to the stage of the introduction and preliminary development of the solution (including sub-stages related to the analysis to develop and which partners to involve). Then it is necessary to reach the final stage of the implementation of the decision, including the role of accompanying the company during SW preliminary development and in the final assessing of the overall process. The model presented in Fig. 12.1 will be recalled later and used in the empirical analysis.

Moreover, the innovation literature recognizes the existence of a number of role players in the context of the organizational innovation process. For example, the start of an innovation is usually attributed to the efforts of an individual called the *innovator* (Schoen 1963); often, this is someone with power and prestige to emerge and take control as needed and this role is played by an organizational *sponsor* (Rogers 1995) or *champion*. Later, as the innovation process starts, the implementation stage makes demands for changes in the behaviour of organizational members; in this case, the role of *change agent* is needed. The task of the change agents is to communicate the innovation and its relevance to organizational members and positively influence their behaviour towards the innovation itself (Rogers 1995).

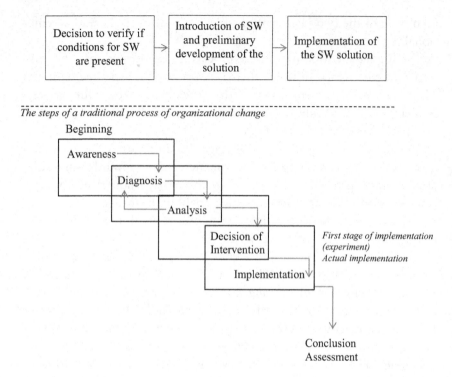

Fig. 12.1 SW implementation as a process of innovation and organizational change. (Source: Our representation based on Schein (1969), Zaltman et al. (1973))

At the Heart of the SW Introduction and Functioning: The HR Department

In the last decade, HR departments have been engaged in acquiring and increasing legitimacy on the managerial board. This effort risks to be frustrated if they do not succeed in facing new challenges, first those connected with the evolution of technologies and their influence on the HRM activities.

Being aware of the complexity of managing a work system that is a set of differentiated and related sub-systems makes them act as the integrator (or one of the integrators). On the other side, there is a chance to interpret this role with different aims and perspectives, which are different ways in which the role might be interpreted.

In this sense, currently the role that the HR department decides to play in any OC and in any innovation process might be considered a highly relevant move. This—especially in this kind of challenge in which a new way of organizing work, which is what SW is—forces the organization to deal with a multitude of HR-*specific* aspects which are not only technical (device, software and so on) but also managerial (appropriate training) as well as cultural (relationship between managers and workers).

In this vein, in order to represent the organization in a systemic view as an interrelation of sub-systems, we adopt the socio-technical approach (Emery 1990). According to this stream, any work system is composed of two interdependent sub-systems: the social one and the technical one. The second concerns process, tasks and technologies, whereas the first is related to people, relationships between them and authority structure (Chen and Nath 2008), thus highlighting the two souls of an organization—*hard* and *soft*—and stressing the need for a sort of mechanism able to integrate all of these different, but highly integrated, components. As a matter of fact, we would like to propose the HR department as the "main coordination mechanism", playing the role of glue and balancer of the different (and sometimes contrasting) interests and goals of each of the components. Moreover, it can represent the diverse identities and knowledge bases they may have, so that it has to aspire to become the orchestrator and the facilitator of any OC. Fig. 12.2 represents the system of relationships.

The strategic HRM view suggests that HR departments and HR professionals may play different roles, at different times or the same time, depending on the internal and external contingencies arising. This can be referred to as the *multiple roles* of HR departments, as suggested by Ulrich (1997). According to the author, four different roles can be identified as characteristic of any professionals in the field of HRM from the perspective of a business partnership between the enterprise strategies and HR priorities to consider for an effective relationship. They are defined as employee champion, administrative expert, change agent and strategic partner. The scholar briefly summarizes the essential features of each of these key parts—"employee champions deliver competent and committed employees, administrative experts deliver efficient HR practices,

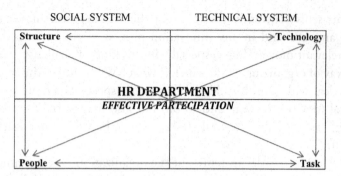

Fig. 12.2 The relationships activated by the HR department in the SW project. (Source: Adapted from Chen and Nath 2008)

change agents deliver capacity for change in individual behaviour and organisational culture, and strategic partners deliver business results" (Ulrich 1997, p. 25). He also indicates relative competences, a set of activities and evaluation measures in order to know how each task is pursued. Recently, a shift from a business partnership approach to a leadership HR approach was proposed by Ulrich and Brockbank (2005): the feature of this change is that the HR manager's role has to become less dependent on the business needs and more proactive towards employees and their motivations, so that he or she becomes able to develop effective capabilities in favouring engagement, the most crucial aspect in the whole management process. Fig. 12.3 describes the multiple-roles configuration.

The core idea on the basis of the model is the fact that HR professionals have to own excellent competences in both sides (business and people) working towards change with a future orientation and supporting the reinforcement of the organization's culture and of its strategic capabilities through effective and efficient development of its workforce (Ulrich and Beatty 2001) offering "useful" services; that means that those services are directly and precisely connected with productivity increase or with a measurable result.

In detail, it is proposed that five steps have to be developed. They are indicated in these terms: "1. define the basic organization design choices; 2. align the HR organization with the business organization; 3. organize to turn HR knowledge into client productivity; 4. clarify the responsibili-

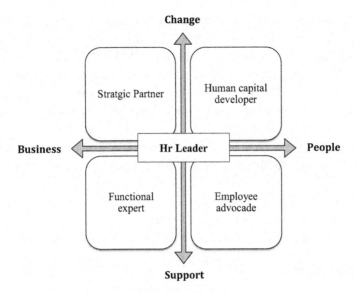

Fig. 12.3 The multiple roles of HR. (Source: Adapted from Ulrich and Brockbank 2005)

ties for each of the HR roles; 5. Create an engagement contract for how the HR roles will work together" (Ulrich and Grochowski 2012, p. 137).

It seems to us that the introduction of an SW project can be explained from this perspective, which indicates from an operational point of view what to do.

The innovations in the HR practices and in the organizational model—which have to be introduced with SW—represent a challenge both for the strategic orientation of the department and for daily activities. More exactly, many activities have to be rethought coherently with the new orientation (Cameron and Green 2015): for example, training programmes for the middle and top management, training for the end users, new communication plans, new ways to develop management by objective process systems, projects of cultural change, or processes' reorganization.

Other implications have to be considered for a complete introduction of SW; one is the usage of the working space and its layout, which can be oriented to increase employees' interactions and productivity. Therefore, particular office reconfigurations may lead to innovative ways of collaboration between workers, encouraging trust and cooperation in a context, like the SW approach, where control inevitably has to change its nature.

As introduced earlier, we expect that the HR department may play different roles at the single stages of the process. Indeed, as suggested by authors (Ulrich and Brockbank 2005), the HR departments may enact multiple roles in terms of both new challenges to face and new competences to care for and advance (Brockbank and Ulrich 2009).

Therefore, a deep change in working time and place is expected, a change which asks for different practices in managing co-workers, towards which the HR department has to address middle managers. In this sense, SW implementation may represent—as in any OC—an opportunity to radically transform organizational culture.

Our Research

The Aim of the Study

The goal of this work is to understand, first of all, which role (or roles) the HR department is expected to play for a positive introduction of SW and, then, what kind of support it is requested to offer at each phase of the whole process.

This study thus also aims to further investigate SW, which represents an under-researched field; many scholars, indeed, refer to the lack of studies in this domain. With regard to the Italian context, only the works by Politecnico (2012, 2015 and 2016) give an interesting representation of the phenomenon, presenting its characteristics and favouring its comprehension and diffusion.

Methodology and Data Collection

Therefore, a need for in-depth investigations calls for an explorative research, which is addressed here by using the multiple case study technique, which is suggested as the most appropriate according to the literature (Yin 2003).

The study focuses on a few experiences of Italian enterprises, which have adopted an SW implementation strategy for some years. In greater detail, we consider three enterprises—which have a sufficiently long experience in the adoption (even if, as known, we are discussing a recent phenomenon, the more ancient experimentation of which dates back to 2010) to be analysed with appropriate elements and sufficient documentation—and above all available to discuss their experimentation with a critical approach. Researchers consider this attitude to be really important, a necessary condition to contribute in developing knowledge of a trend, which risks becoming a "fad" to follow rather than a modern (but more important) and appropriate solution to use after a rigorous process of comprehension of its strengths and weaknesses and to personalize accordingly specific analysis.

Table 12.1 shows a synthetic overview of the organizations involved in the analysis presenting the industry, the dimension in terms of employees and the year of its foundation.

For the present study, a methodology relying on several sources of data was used (Eisenhardt 1989): face-to-face semi-structured interviews, phone conversations, and organizational secondary data (follow-up emails and archival data such as internal documents, press releases, websites, and news articles). In order to maximize the benefits from these sources of evidence and to better deal with reliability issues, two of the three principles suggested by Yin (2003) have been followed: the triangulation of data sources and their organization in an electronic and navigable case study database.

During the first phase, researchers have collected data on each enterprise (both general and specific information) in order to know, as much as possible, the organizational situation and the general context. In a fol-

Table 12.1 Organizations involved in the analysis

Organization	Industry	Number of employees (end 2016)	Year of foundation
A	Engineering	5800	1988
B	Banking	600	2007
C	Technological services	165	2000

Source: Our work

lowing step, direct analysis has been applied. The primary data sources for this study were some semi-structured interviews performed by the authors with the HR managers and with the people directly in charge of the project development of each firm involved in the research. Moreover, there were some interviews with a few trade unionists, who have participated in the definition of the arrangement and have direct experience (see Appendix for the list of proposed topics).

Potential informant bias has been addressed in several ways. First, the interviews collected both real-time and retrospective longitudinal data in several waves over seven months. According to Ozcan and Eisenhardt (2009), these kinds of data collection are ideal because retrospective data enables efficient collection of more observations (thus enabling better grounding) while real-time data mitigate retrospective bias (Leonard-Barton 1990).

Anonymity was guaranteed to the companies and the persons interviewed since this practice was suggested to favour candour and informational completeness. Also, open-ended questions have been used to give the informant the opportunity to express the wide scope of the concept they were questioned about (Koriat et al. 2000).

Interviews took place twice: a first group in June and July 2016 and a second one between November 2016 and January 2017. Normally, the duration of interviews was 45 minutes; in some cases—by the particular attitude towards storytelling by informants—interviews lasted between 60 and 90 minutes. All interviews were introduced by the presentation of the scope of the research and by thanking the informants for their availability to participate.

Data were collected at two levels. First, at a senior director level, semi-structured interviews were used to gain an understanding of pertinent challenges faced by the organization; the strategy, structure and practices within the organization; and how relationships with stakeholders are managed to maximize the communicational effect of the decision. Second, interviews were conducted at an operational level, which means with people who directly follow the process and organize the necessary activities to implement arrangements. The purpose of these interviews at the operational level was to gain insight into the "real reality" of the implementation of SW practices at any step, searching to go beyond the mainstream idea that "SW is beautiful". Interviews with trade unionists have the function of testing the other perspective, that of workers who practise SW (whose direct involvement represents the next step of the whole research project).

The three cases are introduced below in order to provide an outline of the nature of the organizations' experience with SW. Key questions will be drawn together in order to illustrate the most relevant elements, which offer useful insight about our topic and the implications for HR practices.

The Main Findings

Our three enterprises—even if very different in terms of industry, dimension and seniority—present a similar approach to our topic and some interesting differentiations about the role of the HR department. In the following, the results of this first investigation will be depicted.

The "Medium-Soft" Approach to SW: Some Common Features from the Three Case Studies

Looking at the general orientation, we see that, in all three cases, a "medium-soft" approach to SW enactment is pursued and this is coherent with the Italian context in which this model is taking its first steps. A few simple rules are shared among the three cases and characterize what we have called the "medium-soft" approach to SW: (1) the adherence to SW by workers is voluntary, (2) the approval of the manager is necessary, (3) the use is limited (at a maximum of 8 days per month) but, at the same time, (4) broader than possible diffusion of this possibility is favoured among workers in those departments, where it has been evaluated that the solution is possible.

The decision to implement SW in the three organizations has been motivated by the search for more organizational flexibility, the benefits of which are considered to be positive both for enterprise and for workers: this characteristic of SW is seen to be its principal strength.

Managing a Complex Process: The Roles of HR Departments in the Single Steps of SW Initiation and Implementation

As for the development of the whole process, the experiences we examined suggest that the process was as complex and time-consuming as any process of OC normally is. Complexity depends on the need to explore conditions of practicality in order to make well-structured proposals. Length is connected with the number of involved subjects to whom they are "selling" the project and, in the end, with whom they are reaching an agreement—top management, offices and departments whose activities can be easily managed in SW, pertinent managers and workers, and trade unions. Here, we propose Table 12.2, in which the tasks that have been carried out according the single three stages of the process in any of our cases are indicated.

Starting from these tasks and wishing to examine in depth the HR department involvement, we identified four different roles played by the HR department during the process of SW development. We propose to identify them as the *innovator*, when it is the starter or initiator (it has the idea and it wishes to understand whether and how); the *sponsor*, when it embraces other people's ideas and it doesn't move directly; the *supporter*, when it embraces other people's ideas and helps to study them; and the *developer*, when it realizes the content. In Table 12.3, we summarize the situation for each enterprise, derived from our recipients' information.

It is evident that there is a deep difference in attitudes and behaviours from one situation to another by the HR department. When it becomes a *promoter*, that means that it is really committed and available to invest in building a serious project even if few subjects are interested in it in the specific context. When it is a sponsor, that means that others are interested in SW and so it offers consultation on technicalities in order to allow the motivated person to continue; when it is a *supporter*, it is more involved both on the strategic level and on the operational one. In the end, the role of *developer*, even if it is very relevant because without this operational role any project does not work, may be less relevant in order to favour a real and deep change in the organization interested in SW.

Table 12.2 Main actions by the HR department during the process of SW development

	Case A	Case B	Case C
Preliminary analysis	Help to the ICT department to analyse conditions. Support to the definition of the pilot project. Participation in defining a plan of communication.	Search for information on SW in general. In-depth analysis of the internal situation. Support of external consulting. Presentation of the idea to top management. Involvement of trade unions. Definition of a pilot project.	Help in understanding whether and how just-diffused ways of organizing work are new ways. Definition of a mainframe. Interaction with general trade unions.
Introduction	Participation in the definition of a first formalized project. Participation in the definition of the conditions for an effective use. Informal communication.	Presentation of the pilot project. Training session for middle management (on SW functioning) and training session for potential involved workers. Definition of keys indicators.	Participation in the definition of a first formalized project. Participation in the definition of the conditions for an effective use. Informal communication. Definition of the general project, with the top management commitment.
Implementation	Improvement of new systems for assessing SWs. Chief Operating Officer's strong commitment. New organizational approach towards results. Communication plan shared with trade unions.	In-depth analysis of the **results** (in terms of satisfaction by users and managers and by eventual problems). Support to the departments interested in using SW to verify how to do it. Evaluation of the general situation to extend SW. Definition of the communication plan. Improvement of new systems for assessing SWs.	Predisposition of scheme of the operational implications. Formal communication. Definition of key indicators.

Source: Our work

266   T. Torre and D. Sarti

Table 12.3 Phases of the process and the role played by the HR department

	Preliminary analysis	Introduction pilot project	Implementation
Case A	*Innovator*	*Developer*	*Developer*
Case B	*Supporter*	*Supporter*	*Developer*
Case C	*Sponsor*	*Supporter*	*Developer*

Source: Our work

These different viewpoints can be read into Ulrich and Brockbank's model, offering an innovative interpretation to each of the elements of the scheme (Fig. 12.3) and confirming that the future orientation is an essential feature of the HR leadership. In light of the fact that any radical change, which is what SW can become if correctly used, needs strong competences on both the technical side and the relational one, the service orientation and the attention to the internal client's optimal solution are necessary conditions which have to characterize an HR department engaged in SW solution research. This substantial awareness is present in all three enterprises we consider. Furthermore, it is really interesting that the smallest company of this study, which had not had an HR department until that moment, after top management's suggestion to verify this opportunity, created it just to oversee the process from the perspective of change agent.

Changing HR Practices

The most significant outcome that is interesting to examine in depth accordingly to the chosen perspective is represented by the changes in HR practices. It is perhaps evident that change management actions for managing the SW model are a necessary condition. It does not matter which role the HR department plays—*promoter, sponsor* or *supporter*—in the first two phases (the initial part of the process). It assumes a big role in the implementation phase: the "exceptional initiative" begins in transforming into the normal way of doing things, first of all if the preliminary project has been well managed with regard to the cultural dimension of this new way of thinking. This moment is a key point. Indeed, even if different interpretations are reported in Table 3, a common attention to some aspects has been underlined in all of the cases examined. We refer to (1) care of the middle and top management, the interest of whom has to be reinforced; (2) specific training for the end users in order to maximize benefits they bring out; (3) support to develop new relationships between managers and co-workers; (4) new communication plans to explain the reasons and the importance of the project toward the inside of the organization (so that all the workers can understand) and towards any other stakeholder (as corporate social responsibility manifestation, too); and (5) projects of cultural change in general. As is known, this last is the crucial level of change: the way of thinking and acting has to be converted from a "control logic" to a "trust logic". This is possible only through a goals' orientation: a real use of this as a management tool is, according to our enterprises, one of the principal challenges to make SW the way of working of the future.

This aspect has been underlined in connection with another element. With reference to the whole process, we could find that the SW project has favoured a reinforcement of the global vision of the enterprise, the participation of all the players and new relationships among the various components. In detail, the challenge of reinforcing the connection between the two systems which form the global entity of the enterprise—the social one and the technical one—is emphasized with the introduction of SW. It sometimes happens that the technical dimension (processes task and technologies) and the social ones (attitudes, skills and values of working people) do not interact. On the contrary, with an SW project, they have to cooperate, so that effective participation becomes the key word for a real change.

Final Considerations

Preliminary results of our research offer some interesting conclusions about the topic we chose to focus on, regarding the elements characterizing the role of the HR department in the introduction and implementation of an SW model.

There is a general agreement among our representatives on the idea of the centrality of HR in the development of SW projects. This is not only because SW is essentially a different way of work organization but, first of all, because it asks for a diverse approach to work and its tasks and to the way it is run and controlled: this is why the HR department is at the centre of the question. With its multiple-roles characterization, the HR department is careful towards both people, who have to learn how to work and how to organize and manage work in new and evolving conditions, and business, which represents the main goal of any department.

Indeed, the analysis of our enterprises suggests that the two phases of initiation and implementation are crucial. Particular care has to be given to the first pilot projects, which introduce SW in a department or office. The definition of its real benefits, the engagement of middle managers and an appropriate training for users are central in the development of SW practices, coherent with the fact that it represents a real process of OC to manage properly. Equally, implementation has to be followed, guaranteeing a balanced and fair diffusion.

At the same time, a variety of experiences confirm that there is not a unique path towards effective implementation of SW: it has to be designed starting from a specific situation and with specific attention to the features of any organization. The roles that we identified help in understanding this aspect, clarifying that none fits better than another.

Another relevant outcome is connected to the confirmation of the importance of the cultural dimension of SW: a deep change is necessary in the minds of the key players: managers and workers, whose jobs and relative relationships have to change. From this perspective, the HR department assumes a leading role in creating preliminary favourable conditions in order to prepare not only the adoption of an SW model but a fruitful one. At the same time the HD department plays a determinant role in presenting the project to trade unions and in buying its sharing.

Moreover, the HR department has to intervene on the tools, paying attention to the context in which mobile and wireless support are used facilitating work relationship and so paying attention beyond the technological component. With reference to organizational support, its role is necessary for the process of analysis to find activities to transform in SW possibilities and to guarantee fairness as an internal condition. So the definition of a framework of simple and clear rules for the individual adoption and for a shared organization has taken up these subjects, offering the opportunity to look at a long period of orientation, in which SW becomes part of a new strategy to sell to workers.

The match is open, but the first evidence shown by our research leaves a good hope for future developments.

Appendix

Interview Questions for HR Managers

SW: Reasons/Objectives and Results

Main reasons that lead (at the beginning) to invest in SW initiative. Main benefits expected from SW.
Year of beginning to think about SW implementation.
Year of implementation of first initiatives on SW.
After how much time did you see first results? What was the first result observed? Was it among your expectations that result and that level of result? Unexpected positive results?
Today level of achievement of previous stated objectives/benefits?
Current percentage of smart workers related to the whole workforce. How was it at the beginning? What is your final target and how much time you planned to reach it?
What is needed in your organization in order to have success with mobile workers? (this includes technical, managerial, organizational and cultural issues)*.

*Chen and Nath (2008, p. 45)

Idea, Implementation and Actors/Functions Involved

Who had the idea? Who followed and implemented it (instrument interfunctional team, one function/department)? Functions involved (at different stage) or different stakeholders (unions)?

What was the role of CEO in all this? (from the very beginning he or she was the initiator, he or she immediately approved and sponsored the idea when communicated by the one who wanted first to promote it, it took a little bit of effort to convince CEO ...).
What was the role of Middle management in all this?
What was the role of Line in all of this?
What was the role of HR department?
What was the role of other important actors (e.g. trade unions)?

Main Obstacles and Concerns

Individuals' perspective—What are the main concerns of mobile workers (e.g. technology-related concerns, work related concerns, time committed concerns, expectations to be reachable anytime anywhere etc.)*.

Technological perspective—What are the main technical issues your organization faces in supporting mobile workers (e.g. security, bandwidth and connectivity)? How are they addressed?*.

Social perspective—Has the proliferation of mobile workforce raised any significant issues between the worker and his or her supervisor(s)?*

* Chen and Nath (2008, p. 45)

Smart Workers and Job Design

What different types of mobile workers are supported?*.
What are the specific tasks being supported (e.g. virtual team work, remote access form the field etc.)?*.
What changes in the level of each job responsibility and goals, number and kind of tasks, formalization and training?
What changes in the level of goal definition, control and supervision, assessment and reward?
Are there diversity issues? Gender, age, tenure etc.

* Chen and Nath (2008, p. 45)

Investments Made in Different Organizational Systems

Field		Reference
HR	Change management actions implemented in the organization: 1. Training for the middle and top management 2. Training for the end users 3. Communication plans 4. New MBO systems 5. Projects of cultural changes 6. Processes' reorganization	De Kok (2016)
Space organization and layout	Redesign of the workspaces, supporting a different work organization	Elsbach and Pratt (2007)
ICT	Extent to which employees telework (% teleworkers and time per week) Extent to which employees use ICT personal devices (PC, tablet etc.) Extent to which employees use external ICT services (e.g. Skype, Twitter) at any time from an place	Martinez-Sanchez et al. (2007)

Corporate Level Policies (Managerial Systems)

Does your organization have any formal process by which mobile workers receive appropriate training (both technology related and nontechnical such as work–life balance, danger, antisocial behaviours, distraction)*.

Is the way workers are evaluated and rewarded changed?

How do you measure success for your mobile work programme (e.g. efficiency, effectiveness, retention, job satisfaction, ROI etc.)*.

*Chen and Nath (2008, p. 45)

Culture and Top Management Support

Do you think that your organization's culture is conductive of effective mobile work? How was it improved? How can it be improved?*

*Chen and Nath (2008, p. 45)

Interview Questions for SW Responsible in Charge

When do you hear anything about SW for the first time? Do you agree with the decision to introduce SW in your enterprise?

Which is personal your experience with SW?

How much freedom do you have in using SW for your colleagues?

Which are the most relevant problems you met with? Which the most significant benefits?

Which kind of support do you ask for managing SW?

Are you satisfied with SW experiences?

What do you ask to HR department for a better use of SW?

Are you ready to manage smart workers? What competences do you need to develop?

What are you interested in learning about SW?

What do you think is the future of SW? in your unit?

Interview Questions for to Trade Unionists

Which was trade unions role in SW decisions?

What do you think about SW in your enterprise?

Which benefits? Which problems?

How do workers accept SW? Which is you role in favouring SW introduction?

Is SW sufficiently supported in your enterprise? Which role did HR department play?

How strong has the Top management support been?

Which future for industrial relationships?

References

Ahuja, Manju K., Katherine M. Chudoba, Charles J. Kacmar, D. Harrison McKnight, and Joey F. George. 2007. IT Road Warriors: Balancing Work-Family Conflict, Job Autonomy, and Work Overload to Mitigate Turnover Intentions. *MIS Quarterly* 31 (1): 1.

Birkinshaw, Julian. 2010. *Reinventing Management*. San Francisco: Jossey-Bass.

Birkinshaw, Julian, Garry Hamel, and Michel Mol. 2008. Management Innovation. *Academy of Management Review* 33 (4): 825.

Boorsma, Bas, R. Bulchandani, C. Jr. Gerard, Peter Drury, Philip Grone, Tony Kim, Shane Mitchell, Michelle N.D. Slinger, and Patrick Spencer. 2011. *Work-Life Innovation, Smart Work—A Paradigm Shift Transforming: How, Where, and When Work Gets Done.* San Jose: Cisco Internet Business Solutions Group (IBSG). Retrieved April 30, 2013.

Brewer, Ann M. 2000. Work Design for Flexible Work Scheduling: Barriers and Gender Implications. *Gender, Work & Organization* 7 (1): 33.

Brockbank, Wayne, and Dave Ulrich. 2009. The HR Business-Partner Model: Past Learnings and Future Challenge. *People & Strategy* 2 (2): 5.

Cameron, Esther, and Mike Green. 2015. *Making Sense of Change Management: A Complete Guide to the Models Tools and Techniques of Organisational Change.* London: Kogan Page Publishers.

Chartered Institute for Personnel and Development. 2008. *Smart Working. The Impact of Work Organisation and Job Design*, Research Insight. CIPD, London.

———. 2014. *HR: Getting Smart About Agile Working, Impact of Work Organisation and Job Design*, Research Report. CIPD, London.

Chen, Leida, and Ravi Nath. 2008. A Socio-Technical Perspective of Mobile Work. *Information Knowledge Systems Management* 7 (1): 41.

Chiaro, Gianluigi, Giacomo Prati, and Matteo Zocca. 2015. Smart Working: dal lavoro flessibile al lavoro agile. *Sociologia del lavoro* 138: 69.

De Kok, Arjan. 2016. The New Way of Working: Bricks, Bytes, and Behavior. In *The Impact of ICT on Work*, ed. Jungwoo Lee, 9–40. Singapore: Springer.

Dutton, Jane E., and Robert B. Duncan. 1987. The Creation of Momentum for Change Through the Process of Strategic Issue Diagnosis. *Strategic Management Journal* 8 (3): 279–295.

Eisenhardt, Kathleen M. 1989. Building Theory from Case Study Research. *Academy of Management Journal* 14 (4): 532.

Elsbach, Kimberly D., and Michael G. Pratt. 2007. The Physical Environment in Organizations. *The Academy of Management Annals* 1 (1): 181.

Emery, Fred E. 1990. Characteristics of Socio-Technical Systems. In *The Social Engagement of Social Science*, ed. Eric E. Trist and Hugh E. Murray, vol. 2, 177–208. Philadelphia: University of Pennsylvania Press.

Employers Network for Equality and Inclusion-ENEI. 2014. *Agile Working, a Guide for Employers*, Report. ENEI, London.

Gajendran, Ravi S., and David A. Harrison. 2007. The Good, the Bad and the Unknown About Telecommuting: Meta-analysis of Psychological Mediators and Individual Consequences. *Journal of Applied Psychology* 92 (6): 1524.

Gastaldi, Luca, Mariano Corso, Elisabetta Raguseo, Paolo Neirotti, Emilio Paolucci, and Antonella Martini. 2014. *Smart Working: Rethinking Work Practices to Leverage Employees' Innovation Potential.* In 15th International Continuous Innovation Network (CINet) Conference Operating Innovation–Innovating Operations 337.

Grantham, Charles E. 2000. *The Future of Work: The Promise of the New Digital Work Society.* New York: McGraw-Hill.

Hamel, Gary. 2007. *The Future of Management.* Cambridge: Harvard Business Review Press.

Koriat, Asher, Morris Goldsmith, and Ainat Pansky. 2000. Toward a Psychology of Memory Accuracy. *Annual Review of Psychology* 51 (2): 481.

Lee, Jungwoo. 2013. Cross-Disciplinary Knowledge: Desperate Call from Business Enterprises in Coming Smart Working Era. *Technological and Economic Development of Economy* 19 (1): S285.5.

Leonard-Barton, Dorothy. 1990. A Dual Methodology for Case Studies: Synergistic Use of a longitudinal Single Site with Replicated Multiple Sites. *Organisation Science* 1 (3): 248.

Leonardi, Paul M. 2011. When Flexible Routines Meet Flexible Technologies: Affordance, Constraint and the Imbrication of Human and Material Agencies. *MIS Quarterly* 35 (1): 147.

Lippitt, Ronald, and G. Lippitt. 1975. Consulting Process in Action 1. *Training and Development Journal* 29 (5): 48.

March, James G. 1981. Footnotes to Organizational Change. *Administrative Science Quarterly* 26: 563.

Martinez Sanches, Angel, Manulea Pérez Pérez, Carnicer Pilar de Luis, and Maira Josè Vela Jimenez. 2007. Teleworking and Workplace Flexibility: A Study of Impact on Firm Performance. *Personnel Review* 36 (1): 42.

Mazzucchelli, S. 2014. Lo Smart Working Come Benefit: pratiche innovative di welfare aziendale, in: Welfare aziendale. La risposta organizzativa ai bisogni delle persone. *I Quaderni di Sviluppo & Organizzazione* 20: 91.

McNall, Laurel A., Aine D. Masuda, and Jessica M. Nickin. 2010. Flexible Work Arrangements, Job Satisfaction and Turnover Intentions: The Mediating Role of Work-to-Family Enrichment. *The Journal of Psychology* 144 (1): 61.

Ozcan, Pinar, and Kathleen M. Eisenhardt. 2009. Origin of Alliance Portfolios: Entrepreneurs, Network Strategies, and Firm Performance. *Academy of Management Journal* 52 (2): 246.

Politecnico di Milano. 2012. *Smart Working: ripensare il lavoro, liberare energia,* Rapporto 2012. Osservatorio Smart Working. Milano: Politecnico di Milano.

———. 2015. *Smart Working: scopriamo le carte!,* Rapporto Osservatorio Smart Working. Milano: Politecnico di Milano.

————. 2016. *(Smart) Work in Progress*, Materials Presented at the Conference on Smart Working, Octobre 12 ottobre.

Rogers, Everett M. 1995. Lessons for Guidelines from the Diffusion of Innovations. *The Joint Commission Journal on Quality Improvement* 21 (7): 324.

Sarti, Daria, and Teresina Torre. 2017. Is Smart Working a Win-Win Solution? First Evidence from the Field. In *Well-being at and Through Work*, ed. Tindara Addabbo, Edoardo Ales, Ylenia Curzi, and Iacopo Senatori, 231–251. Torino: Giappichelli Editore.

Schein, Edgar H. 1969. *Process Consultation: Its Role in Organization Development*. Reading: Addison-Wesley Publishing Co.

Schoen, Donald A. 1963. Champions for Radical New Inventions. *Harvard Business Review* 41 (March–April): 77–86.

Scornavacca, Eusebio. 2014. *Incorporating System Portability into Technology Acceptance Models*. Paper presented at the International Conference in Mobile Business-ICMB. https://aisel.aisnet.org/icmb2014/10.

Tagliaro, Chiara, and Andrea Ciaramella. 2016. Experiencing Smart Working: A Case Study on Workplace Change Management in Italy. *Journal of Corporate Real Estate* 18 (3): 194.

Telsyte. 2015. *Activity Based Working Is Driving*, Whitepaper. Telsyte, Sydney.

Ulrich, Dave. 1997. *Human Resource Champions: The Next Agenda for Adding Value and Delivering Results*. Cambridge, MA: Harvard Business School Press.

Ulrich, Dave, and Dick Beatty. 2001. From Partners to Players: Extending the HR Playing Field. *Human Resource Management* 40 (4): 293.

Ulrich, Dave, and Wayne Brockbank. 2005. *The HR Value Proposition*. Boston: Harvard Business School Press.

Ulrich, Dave, and Joe Grochowski. 2012. From Shared Services to Professional Services. *Strategic Human Resource Review* 11 (3): 136.

Vlaar, Paul W.L., Paul C. van Fenema, and Vinay Tiwari. 2008. Cocreating Understanding and Value in Distribuited Work: How Members of Outside and Offshore Vendor Team Give, Make, Demand and Break Sense. *MIS Quarterly* 32 (2): 227.

Wynekoop, Judy L., and James A. Senn. 1992. CASE Implementation: The Importance of Multiple Perspectives. *Proceedings of the 1992 ACM SIGCPR Conference on Computer Personnel Research*. ACM.

Yin, Robert K. 2003. *Case Study Research Design and Methods*, Applied Social Research Methods Series. Thousand Oaks: Sage Publications.

Zaltman, Gerald, Robert Duncan, and Jonny Holbeck. 1973. *Innovativeness and Organizations*. New York: John Wiley and Sons.

13

Conclusion

Ylenia Curzi

This book has presented original pieces of theoretical and empirical research from different disciplines (i.e. labour law, organization and human resource management, labour economics) with a view to contributing to the current debate on the major implications of digitalization on work and work relationships.

The digitalization of work is a far-reaching phenomenon and its exact impact on work and work relationships is still uncertain. There is widespread agreement among scholars that an in-depth understanding of the complex trajectories of today's transforming work relationships cannot be developed by one single scholarly discipline alone. This in turn raises the question of how various disciplines can concretely contribute to the study of work and its changes.

This concluding chapter reflects the continuous discussion with the other editors of this book. It goes without saying that the sole responsibility for the ideas expressed hereby rests with the author.

Y. Curzi (✉)
Marco Biagi Department of Economics, University of Modena and Reggio Emilia, Modena, Italy
e-mail: ylenia.curzi@unimore.it

© The Author(s) 2018

E. Ales et al. (eds.), *Working in Digital and Smart Organizations*,
https://doi.org/10.1007/978-3-319-77329-2_13

For the purposes of this chapter, we will assume (like Maggi 1991) that there are at least three distinct ways or approaches in which various disciplines can contribute to the study of work changes: the monodisciplinary, multidisciplinary and interdisciplinary approach.

What is involved in the monodisciplinary approach is that, in the study of the same phenomenon (e.g. the digital transformation of work, work relationships and the major implications), scholars from different disciplinary backgrounds draw attention to aspects, set the problems to be dealt with, and frame the research questions in accordance with the typical analytic perspectives of their own disciplines. In addition, it entails that scholars use theoretical concepts, analytic techniques, methodologies, languages, and rules that are suitable for their own disciplines in order to address problems, issues and research questions. Almost all of the essays collected in this book reflect, at least in part, this kind of approach. However, the monodisciplinary analysis is not the arrival point of the present volume. In fact, the combination of various theoretical and research studies, which are rooted in different disciplines, has offered the opportunity to broaden the investigation of the digital transformation of work and work relationships beyond the boundaries of the single disciplines. The aim of the present chapter is to summarize the suggestions for multidisciplinary reflections in the present volume to highlight the central question that cuts across almost all of the studies in this volume and to shed light on the way in which it can be addressed from an interdisciplinary perspective.

Let us start with the first issue, namely the suggestions for multidisciplinary reflections offered by the present book. As mentioned before, the present volume combines various research and theoretical studies that, for the most part, remain embedded in the perspective of analysis, theoretical concepts, analytic techniques, and methods that are typical of their own particular disciplines. Even if the concepts are expressed through the same terms (e.g. autonomy), they do not necessarily have the same meaning as they are stipulated in theories belonging to different disciplinary environments. Despite that, it is possible to identify some connections or correspondences between them. On this basis, the comprehensive analysis of the various studies collected in the book reveals that they point to some long-term processes in the development of the digital transformation

Conclusion **279**

of work, which converge on the same direction. Thus, they outline some common trends regarding how work and work relationships may change in the era of digital transformation. Before we deal with this point in more detail, it is noteworthy to highlight that the studies in the present book clearly converge at another, more challenging level. In fact, they share the view that the concrete implications of the digitalization for work and work relationships in a given (i.e. spatial and temporal situated) socio-economic and organizational context are not simply the result of new digital technologies themselves and their technical features. Put another way, far from being the determining factor, the latter are just one of the many conditioning factors that interact with one another, thereby shaping the final outcome of the transformation in a non-deterministic way. Among the "other" conditioning factors mentioned by the studies in the present book are the following:

- corporate strategies; role, responsibilities, competences, basic attitudes and behaviours of HR department staff; the ways in which workers (are required to) contribute to the wider organizational process, the way the work performance integrates itself within and coordinates itself with somebody else's organization (Ales Chap. 2; Fabbri Chap. 3; Albano et al. Chap. 10; Torre and Sarti Chap. 12);
- the dynamics of interaction and conflict between different and competing rationalities both at the company and at the sectoral level, and the relative ability of the involved parties to influence the "rules of the game" of the digital transformation of work (Cattero and D'Onofrio Chap. 8; Avogaro Chap. 9);
- the characteristics of national economies and institutional settings, the role of broader ideologies in shaping political choices, the way in which policymakers orient themselves with respect to different value-laden goals, and which choices they make to balance competing value-laden goals (Paba and Solinas Chap. 4)

From this perspective, Fabbri (Chap. 3), Paba and Solinas (Chap. 4) and Albano et al. (Chap. 10) point to some evidence calling into question the hypotheses of the mainstream economic theories that technological advances will automatically increase productivity, improve the quality of work, and lead to a fair income distribution. Drawing on a meta-analysis of available empirical research in different countries, Paba and Solinas (Chap. 4) argue that the extensive use of digital technologies is more likely to change the employment structure than reducing the levels of employment via computerization and automation of work. However, they also point to the negative externalities that, in terms of increased economic insecurity and social inequalities, the digital transformation of work is likely to impose on workers and society as a whole in the transition phase. In particular, they argue that the creation of new jobs and the demand for new skills are likely to be associated with increasing inequalities without appropriate policies for workers' retraining and requalification. Similarly, Menegatti (Chap. 5) points to evidence showing that, irrespective of the level of their skills, those working in the new occupations that have recently emerged in the digital era (Workers on demand via Application) have to face a very high risk of economic uncertainty.

In a similar vein, in contrast to the dominant managerial discourse claiming that digital technologies are the key factor for the spread of new ways of working in which workers would be free to choose where, how and when to perform their work, several studies in this book highlight that the extensive use of digital technologies can open up new room for management to increase their control over workers' performance and for companies operating digital platforms to significantly influence the structure of the relationship between clients and service providers (Ales Chap. 2; Fabbri Chap. 3; Menegatti Chap. 5; Ingrao Chap. 6; Cattero and D'Onofrio Chap. 8; Albano et al. Chap. 10). Taken together, the above-mentioned studies also highlight that management's and platform's control over work and workers' performance can have a different extent and be exercised in different ways. On the one hand, it can find expression in rules that leave no space for workers to decide when or for how long to work, which tasks to perform and by which methods of work, as in the case of logistic work processes performed in Amazon's fulfilment centres (Cattero and D'Onofrio Chap. 8) or Uber taxi drivers (Ingrao Chap. 6). On the other hand, management's and platform's control can find expression in rules that try to regulate work activities from outside while delegating workers' discretionary decisions about where and when to work or even admitting workers' autonomy (Fabbri Chap. 3; Menegatti Chap. 5;

Albano et al. Chap. 10). The case study of Amazon (Cattero and D'Onofrio Chap. 8) provides updated evidence for a well-accepted conclusion: the rigid and comprehensive predetermination of work, which today can capitalize on the new digital technology-enabled opportunities, severely affects workers' well-being. In a similar way, other studies in this book highlight that we cannot take for granted that digital work patterns, which increase the scope of workers' autonomy and discretion, always have positive consequences for well-being at work. Indeed, workers' autonomy or discretion (or both) over some key aspects of work (e.g. place and methods of work and tasks to be performed) may go along with an implicit request for them to perform supplemental work or to be permanently available (Fabbri Chap. 3; Albano et al. Chap. 10; Krause Chap. 11). This, in turn, may eventually result in work intensification, interference of work time with private time in both directions, and negative consequences for work–life balance and individual well-being.

The above-mentioned trends are still preliminary hypotheses, which ask for future research and additional demonstrable evidence. However, they clearly give rise to the fundamental question cutting across almost all of the studies in the book: how to regulate the digital transformation of work relationships with a view to representing, promoting and protecting the interests and needs of all the parties involved. That is, not only the needs, interests and rights of those who exercise control over the strategic decision-making process underlying the (organizational) structuration of digital work but also those of digital workers.

Finding an answer to this question requires drawing knowledge from all of the scholarly disciplines represented in the present book (i.e. organization and HR management, labour law, and labour economics) and in particular requires moving from a multidisciplinary towards an interdisciplinary approach to the study (and regulation) of the digital transformation of work.

Like other scholars (De Bartolomeis 1991; Maggi 1991; 2011; Fabbri 2013), we assume that the interdisciplinary study of whatever phenomenon (thus, also the digital transformation of work) rests on two basic conditions. First, scholars from different disciplines should converge on consistent epistemological premises. Second, starting from consistent "views of the world", they should identify some shared, bridging analytic categories that allow them to cooperate on an equal basis to achieve a common goal, in this case finding appropriate regulatory solutions from the perspective of digital workers' protection.

In light of the above-mentioned research question, the first condition involves labour economists and organizational theorists moving away from the mainstream view in their disciplines, which considers economic efficiency the main (if indeed not the only) criterion of rationality guiding organizational behaviours, to embrace a rather different view. A view which is capable of taking into consideration a broader range of value-laden rationality criteria, including, for example, those that are traditionally considered by labour law, namely health and safety at work, equal access to the labour market and decent work opportunities, human dignity, personal reputation, fair income distribution, and so on. From the economic point of view, this means conceiving firms as social institutions, which are permanently characterized by an inner conflict between different and competing value-laden criteria of rationality (Albano et al. 2016). Such a conflict is inevitable and represents the key driver of the capability of whatever social institution (including therein a company) to change continuously over time. The conflict between the different value-laden criteria of rationality, that coexist within companies at any given time, cannot be eliminated because the relationship between the competing criteria of rationality has the character of a trade-off, and thus it is impossible to optimize all of them at the same time. The implication for policymakers should be clear: Protecting and promoting workers' needs, interests and rights involve imposing on companies a precise responsibility towards workers and thus imposing constraints on the rationality criterion of efficiency. The above-mentioned conception of social institutions and firms is consistent with a particular conception of organization underlying some organization theories, namely the conception of organization as a process of actions and decisions, which is guided by bounded rationality towards ever-changing, different and competing goals and values (Simon 1947; Thompson 1967) and develops over time through cooperation, competition, conflict and compromise (Terssac 1992, 2003, 2011).

In the same vein, as pointed out by Fabbri (2013), the interdisciplinary study of work relationships (and their changes) also requires that labour law scholars move away from the epistemological stance that has recently

Conclusion   **283**

dominated their discipline, namely the view that considers legal rules as univocally determined by socio-economic-organizational dynamics. That is, the view that considers the *Sein* (i.e. the realm of things that are) the key determinant of the *Sollen* (i.e. the realm of norms, including therein the law). Labour law scholars, in contrast, are required to embrace the rather different view that, considering the *Sein* and the *Sollen* as analytical plans, focuses on the recursive relationships between them (Fabbri 2013).

As we have just mentioned above, a second necessary condition for the interdisciplinary study of the digital transformation of work is the identification of some shared, bridging analytic categories that allow scholars to communicate across different disciplinary boundaries.

In this regard, it is worth mentioning that labour law studies in this book highlight that finding appropriate regulatory solutions in the perspective of digital workers' protection asks that labour law scholars experiment with innovative categories to overcome the shortcomings of the traditional notions of their discipline. The latter indeed make it difficult to apply labour law provisions in situations where digital work is performed in a way that appears neither as autonomous as self-employed work nor as subordinated as work performed within employment relationships and thus does not fit completely with either autonomous or subordinated work (Ales Chap. 2; Menegatti Chap. 5; Cavallini Chap. 7; Avogaro Chap. 9). In similar situations, which are actually the most frequent ones, difficulties arise mainly because the application of labour law provisions is deeply embedded in a mono-dimensional interpretation of work relationships (i.e. employment/self-employment, working time/non-working time, etc.) (Ales Chap. 2; Menegatti Chap. 5; Cavallini Chap. 7; Avogaro Chap. 9; Krause Chap. 11). In this regard, however, some are sceptical about the creation of new intermediate categories between the opposite poles of the above continuum, claiming that this attempt to break the above-mentioned impasse is likely to fail to solve the problems for digital workers while running the risk of creating new ones for "regular" employees (Menegatti Chap. 5). Other scholars argue that it is necessary to carry out an overall revision of the typological approach to work regulation that has been adopted by labour law since the beginning of its existence. According to that approach, the formal and general qualification of workers as employees or self-employed workers always prevails on the way in which a specific work is performed. Therefore, the revision of the above approach should entail, first, shifting attention to the way in which the work performance is coordinated with somebody else's organization (Ales Chap. 2), and second, the identification of a non–mono-dimensional framework for the interpretation of the regulation of work relationships. From this perspective, cooperation between labour law and organizational scholars can prove useful but requires the identification of some shared, bridging analytic categories that allow scholars to talk together. We believe that the concepts of regulations and rules can prove useful to this end.

In the conception of organization (and work) as a process of actions and decisions, which is guided by bounded rationality towards ever-changing, different and competing goals and values and develops over time through cooperation, competition, conflict and compromise, the regulation is the order of that process (Albano et al. 2016). Such an order consists of rules that can be autonomous and heteronomous (Maggi 2003/2016). Heteronomous rules include legal norms—i.e. rules or obligations with a particular cogency that try to regulate the organizational process as a whole from outside. The order of the process finds expression in different ways of controlling and coordinating tasks and people who perform them. The latter, in turn, can be analysed by means of appropriate typologies—e.g. the one that distinguishes between four different types of coordination: standardization of the work performance, standardization of professional competences, feed-forward regulation, and mutual and autonomous regulation (Albano 2013, pp. 50–51). What is interesting to note is that the third and fourth types allow workers to make autonomous decisions about aspects of their work but that the second obliges workers to make discretionary decisions and the first does not admit any discretion and autonomy at all. The analysis of the organizational regulation of work based on the above-mentioned concepts and typology, rather than on the "autonomous/subordinated" work continuum, could represent the new point of reference for the application of labour law provisions. In fact, the above-mentioned concepts and typology allow the analysis of the source that produces the rules shaping the ways of controlling and coordinating work, making it possible to distinguish if they are autonomous or heteronomous with respect to workers'

Conclusion **285**

actions. They also allow the analysis of the ways of controlling and coordinating work, making it possible to judge whether they offer workers the opportunity to make autonomous decisions. The above analysis could therefore prove useful to decide whether to apply labour law rules to ensure adequate protection for digital workers' interests and rights. In addition, it may be of help to support the legislative intervention aiming at differentiating the distribution of protecting measures depending on the way in which the digital work(er) is controlled and coordinated.

What has been proposed in the above is just a preliminary outline of some basic analytic categories that could prove useful for addressing, from an interdisciplinary perspective, the key issue of how to regulate the digital transformation of work relationships so as to guarantee adequate protection for digital workers.

Further research is needed for refining the above categories. At the same time, the above-mentioned issue is only one of the many raised by the digitalization of work. The latter indeed is a complex and rapidly evolving phenomenon that is likely to pose additional interpretative challenges in the future. Given that, more research is needed to come to the elaboration of a wider analytical framework, which cannot but require the contribution of experts from a broader range of disciplines. However, we believe we have taken some preliminary steps in this direction by showing how it is possible to "create a communication channel" between different disciplinary backgrounds.

References

Albano, Roberto. 2013. Razionalità e regolazione organizzativa. In *Organizzare il servizio sociale. Nodi Interpretativi e strumenti di analisi per gli assistenti sociali*, ed. Roberto Albano and Marilena Dellavalle, 19–56. Milano: FrancoAngeli.

Albano, Roberto, Ylenia Curzi, and Tommaso Fabbri. 2016. *Organizzazione: parole chiave*. Torino: Giappichelli.

De Bartolomeis, Francesco. 1991. Formazione e pedagogia. Un'intervista. In *La formazione: concezioni a confronto*, ed. Bruno Maggi, 187–204. Milano: Etaslibri.

Fabbri, Tommaso. 2013. Le relazioni di lavoro come questione interdisciplinare: implicazioni per la ricerca e la didattica. In *Regole, politiche e metodo. L'eredità di Marco Biagi nelle relazioni di lavoro di oggi*, ed. Francesco Basenghi and Luigi Enrico Golzio, 126–150. Torino: Giappichelli.

Maggi, Bruno. 1991. Le concezioni di formazione. Un quadro per il confronto. In *La formazione: concezioni a confronto*, ed. Bruno Maggi, 7–33. Milano: Etaslibri.

———. 2003. *De l'agir organisationnel: un point de vue sur le travail, le bien-être, l'apprentissage*. Toulouse: Octarès (2016, 2nd Edition). Bologna: TAO Digital Library.

———. 2011. Théorie de l'agir organisationnel. In *Interpréter l'agir: un défi théorique*, ed. Bruno Maggi, 69–96. Paris: Presses Universitaires de France.

Simon, Herbert A. 1947. *Administrative Behavior*. New York: Free Press.

de Terssac, Gilbert. 1992. *Autonomie dans le travail*. Paris: Presses Universitaires de France.

———. 2003. Travail d'organisation et travail de régulation. In *La théorie de la régulation sociale de Jean-Daniel Reynaud. Débats et prolongements*, ed. Gilbert de Terssac, 121–134. Paris: La Découverte.

———. 2011. Théorie du travail d'organisation. In *Interpréter l'agir: un défi théorique*, ed. Bruno Maggi, 97–121. Paris: Presses Universitaires de France.

Thompson, James D. 1967. *Organizations in Action*. New York: McGraw-Hill.

Index[1]

A

Abuse of economic dependency, 124, 127
Accidents, 20, 123, 170
Active involvement of a third party, 16
Adjustment, 3, 4, 12, 15, 48, 204
Agency work, 16, 19, 130
Agile work, 7, 13, 193, 194, 210, 215, 216n2
Agreements, 7, 17, 41, 80, 84, 126, 129, 131n3, 145, 149–159, 171–177, 179, 181–183, 185, 186, 215, 228, 229, 236, 238, 240–242, 264, 267, 277
Algorithm, 15, 30, 100, 102–104, 106
Algorithmic, 96, 97, 99–101, 103–104, 106n1

Allocation of prerogatives and responsibilities, 13, 17
Alternative work arrangements, 84
"Always-on" mode, 21
Amazon, 6, 95, 120, 130n1, 141–160, 280, 281
Amazon web services (AWS), 160, 161n8
Anonymity, 262
Antitrust laws, 69, 81, 84
Approval of the manager, 263
Artificial intelligence (AI), 39, 42, 44, 48, 51–54, 58
Atypical working hours, 210
Authority relationships, 252
Automation, 7, 12, 29, 31, 39, 43, 45–47, 51, 54, 60n4, 141, 143, 144, 155, 160n1, 280
Automation tax, 54

---

[1] Note: Page numbers followed by 'n' refer to notes.

© The Author(s) 2018
E. Ales et al. (eds.), *Working in Digital and Smart Organizations*,
https://doi.org/10.1007/978-3-319-77329-2

287

288 Index

Automatization, 167, 168
Autonomous, 15, 24, 25, 27, 31–34, 98, 100, 127, 152, 168, 200, 203, 231, 283, 284
Autonomous rules, 8, 199, 202, 203, 215
Autonomy, 7, 15, 23, 32–34, 36, 115, 118, 146, 150, 155, 160, 173, 194, 199–207, 214, 217n12, 228, 251, 252, 278, 280, 281, 284

B

Behaviours, 94, 107n2, 108n3, 124, 166, 202, 226, 235, 238, 250, 252, 255, 258, 264, 271, 279, 282
Best practices, 3, 184, 204, 206
Big data, 42, 142, 160, 166, 200, 215n1
BMW, 181–182, 215, 240
"Boosted" subordination, 24, 27, 123
Business, 2, 11–17, 27, 33, 43, 44, 49, 68–73, 75, 76, 80, 85n5, 86n11, 94, 96, 98, 102, 109n9, 117, 119, 122, 133n30, 150, 153, 160, 161n6, 182–184, 198, 226, 235, 257, 258, 268
Business to business service, 77

C

Call centre, 118, 120–121
Castel S. Giovanni, 156, 157
CGIL, *see* Italian General Confederation of Labour

Challenge, 3, 4, 12, 14, 18, 20, 23, 26–27, 80–84, 113–115, 118, 124, 130, 151, 181, 234, 241, 249–269, 285
Change, 4, 5, 11, 14, 24, 27, 31, 40–43, 46–49, 51, 58, 59, 73, 95, 98, 104, 118, 119, 166, 167, 169, 170, 173, 179, 181, 183, 184, 194, 207, 224, 226, 250, 252, 253, 255–260, 264, 266–268, 270, 271, 277–280, 282
Changes in the HR practices, 257, 266–267
CISL, 158, 173
Client, 17, 19, 20, 25, 32, 74–77, 79, 82, 96, 102, 104, 116, 122, 124–127, 175, 197, 200, 203, 206, 238, 258, 266, 280
Co-determination, 48, 152, 153, 169, 180
Co-determined, 151
Collaboration and trust, 33, 252
Collective agreement, 7, 80, 81, 84, 129, 130, 149–159, 171–174, 176–177, 179, 181, 182, 184–186, 215, 228, 229, 238, 241
Collective autonomy, 150, 160
Collective bargaining, 20, 26, 80, 141–160, 169, 174, 179, 181, 184, 185, 215, 225
Colonization of private life by working life, 212
Co-managerial prerogatives, 15
Co-managers, 15, 17
Competences, 8, 150, 167, 202, 203, 207, 214, 215, 250, 258, 260, 266, 272, 279, 284

Index **289**

Complexity, 2, 4, 7, 30, 36, 41, 179, 256, 264
Conception and execution, 145, 146
Conflict, 4, 143, 147, 150, 151, 155, 158, 160, 183, 186, 279, 282, 284
Continuity, 72, 73, 76, 119, 120
Continuous education, 167, 176
Continuous place, 253
Contract law, 114, 124, 125, 129
Contractual integration, 123
Contractual label, 122
Control, 6, 7, 14, 15, 20–22, 30, 32–34, 70–77, 81, 84, 86n11, 95–100, 105, 106n1, 108n3, 108n9, 114, 119, 126, 129, 142, 145–148, 172, 176, 178, 180, 194, 199–207, 212, 214, 215, 231, 238, 255, 260, 270, 280, 281
Control test, 72–74, 106n1
Cooperative autonomy, 200, 202–204, 206
Coordinated condition, 22
Coordinated self-employment, 17, 24
Costumers' rating, 15, 16
Critical aspects, 180, 254
Crowdwork, 67, 113–130
Cultural dimension, 252, 266, 268
Cyber-physical systems (CPS), 42, 166, 167

D

Data controller, 103, 105, 106
Data Protection Authority, 101, 102, 109n10
Data subject, 101–106, 109n12

Deactivating, 124
Deactivation, 70, 74, 98, 107n2, 115, 124, 125, 128
Dematerialisation
of the company, 13, 16
of the workplace, 4, 12–14, 18, 20–23
Dependency, 25, 71–75, 81, 85n5, 119, 168
Dependent contractors, 75, 84, 116
Developer, 264, 266
Didi Chuxing, 123
Different approach, 128, 180
Diffusion, 47–49, 54, 55, 141, 165, 176, 198, 249, 250, 253, 260, 263, 268
Digitalisation, 2–7, 12–17, 20, 21, 26, 29–37, 48, 113, 141, 142, 148, 155, 159, 207–209, 277, 279, 285
Digital revolution, 5, 40, 42–44, 46–48, 50, 58, 59
Digital Taylorism, 145
Digital technologies, 2, 11, 12, 42, 48–50, 53–55, 98, 143–145, 148, 155, 179, 193, 207, 279–281
Digital transformation and digitalisation, 4, 12–17, 21–23
of business, 13
Dignity, 3, 26, 56, 79, 83, 99, 102, 103, 151, 282
Directive n. 95/46/CE, 100, 103
Discretion, 7, 32–34, 36, 37, 146, 198–207, 212, 214, 252, 281, 284
Discretionary decisions, 201, 202, 280, 284

290 Index

Discretionary organization personality, 201–202
Discretion over digital devices, 201
Discretion over the ways to get the work done, 201
Discretion over working time, 201
Diseases, 148, 180, 181, 184
Distance work, 14
Distortion of competition, 80
Distribution of rights, 78
Duty of the employer, 19, 235

E

E-commerce, 6, 12, 142, 160
Economic and legal entity, 13
Economic damages, 106
Economic dependence, 75, 77
Economic dependency, 25, 116, 119, 133n30
Economic development, 169, 178
Economic reality test, 72, 73, 106n1
Education, 44, 57, 170–173, 175–179, 181–183, 185, 186
Electronic panopticon, 145, 146
Employee-like persons, 75, 84
Employees, 3, 14, 35, 68, 96, 114, 167, 195, 224, 252, 283
Employee's monitoring, 97
Employers' renounce to performance's assessment responsibilities, 22
Employment
as legal typology, 23, 24
levels, 44, 178, 208
relationship, 5, 16, 17, 19, 22, 23, 70, 80, 88n31, 98, 101, 107n1, 118–120, 124, 127,

150, 154, 211, 216n2, 227, 228, 244, 283
tests, 71, 74, 84, 118
Empowerment and in the responsibilisation of costumers, 15, 17
Encroachment of work devices into private life, 212
Enlarged labour law, 27
Enrichment, 4, 12, 16, 22, 23
Establishment, 13, 18, 19, 72, 149, 153, 160
Evaluation, 3, 6, 100–102, 105, 124, 200, 206, 207, 258, 265
eWork, 195
eWorkers, 195–197, 216n5
Explorative research, 8, 260

F

Feedback, 15, 16, 93–106, 125
Feedback systems, 6, 93–106, 108n3
FILT-CGIL, 157, 158
Find an equilibrium, 186
Firm-level, 152, 158, 159
Flexibility, 2, 3, 5, 25, 35, 59, 77, 98, 114, 145, 167, 171, 180–182, 184, 185, 210, 212, 214, 216n2, 217n12, 217n18, 225, 249, 252, 263
Flexibility, autonomy and collaboration, 251
Flexible schedules, 210
Flexible working hours, 210
Foodora, 75, 116, 118, 119, 131n2
Fourth Industrial Revolution (4IR), 5, 39–59, 148
Framed, 17, 22, 23

Index   **291**

Framing of the provision of services, 12
Freedom to provide services, 69, 82, 99
Free movement of services, 82–85
Fulfillment centers, 142–149, 152, 154–156, 159, 161n4
Functioning of the business, 15
Future orientation, 258, 266

G

Gebhard formula, 82, 85
Germany, 3, 41, 45, 48, 49, 75, 141–160, 166, 168, 181, 185, 226, 231
Gig-economy, 5, 6, 67–69, 73, 78, 79, 84, 93–105, 108n4, 114, 118, 128, 130n1, 168
Good faith, 124, 125
Guarantee of a certain standard of service, 16

H

Heteronomous rules, 199, 202, 284
Homework, 14, 15, 19
HR department, 8, 249–269, 279
Human being friendly first, 27
Human dignity, 26, 79, 83, 99, 102, 103, 282
Hypothesis of complementarity between capital and skills, 208

I

ICT-based mobile work, 193, 195
ICT-based system, 143

IG Metall, 3, 7, 166, 169, 177–185
Immaterial safety, 18
Impact of digitalization on work, 207
Impact of the Fourth Industrial Revolution (4IR), 40, 44, 47
Imperative requirements, 82
Implementation, 5, 8, 142, 184, 227, 241, 250–255, 260–262, 264–270
Incentives, 49, 50, 54, 153, 166, 229, 238
Independence, 5, 25, 59, 77, 115, 168, 182, 184
Independent contractors, 5, 68–70, 79, 80, 83, 84, 85n1, 97, 98, 101, 114–116, 131n3
Individual agreement, 173
Individual productivity, 35, 208
Individual right, 171, 176, 182, 241
Individual, unilateral or bargained, modification, 26
Industrial policies, 5, 40, 41, 49, 52
Industrial relations, 4, 6, 150, 158, 159, 174, 176, 185
Industrial relations system, 152
Industrial robots, 44, 45, 48, 60n4
Industry 4.0, 4, 30, 49, 51, 141, 142, 159, 165–186
Initiation, 254, 264–266, 268
Innovative approach, 1, 249
Innovator, 255, 264, 266
Integration, 23–25, 41, 42, 49, 71–75, 80, 81, 166, 252
Integrator, 256
Interference of family life with work, 212, 213

292 Index

Interference of work with family life, 212, 213
Intermediate categories, 25, 69, 75–78, 84, 86n17, 116, 117, 283
Intermediators, 17
Intrinsically trilateral work relationship, 16
In-work poverty, 79, 83
Italian General Confederation of Labour (CGIL), 157, 158, 169, 173
Italian labour market, 169
Italy, 1, 3, 35, 43, 52, 72, 75, 116–120, 124–126, 141–160, 166, 168–177, 180, 183, 185, 194, 196, 197, 199, 204, 206, 209–211, 213, 215, 216n2

J

Job creation, 2, 58
Job loss, 45, 47
Joint committee, 176, 183
Juridical dimension, 13

L

Labor
  narratives, 148
  rights, 148
Labour exception, 80, 81
Lack of studies, 260
Leadership HR approach, 258
Lean manufacturing, 175
Learning places, 179
Legal subordination, 71, 73, 75
Length, 148, 230, 264

Lifelong learning, 170, 177–181, 208
Logistics, 6, 42, 143, 150, 280
Loi Travail, 128, 215
Low-skilled jobs, 144

M

Machinery, 81, 166–168, 170, 171, 175, 176, 178, 180, 185, 216n12
Mainly autonomous organization personality, 203–204
Management, 3, 12, 15, 29, 32, 33, 35, 37, 48, 108n3, 143, 144, 146, 148, 149, 151–154, 156–159, 173, 175, 178, 184, 201–204, 206, 210, 214, 226, 227, 238, 240, 258, 259, 264–267, 270, 271, 277, 280, 281
Managers' control, 199
Mandatory minimum fees, 82
Material safety, 18
Maximise control, 70
Mechanical engineering industry, 169, 176–177, 183
Medium-soft approach, 263
Middleman, 122
Minimum wage, 5, 26, 68, 69, 73, 75–84, 107n1, 116, 117, 129, 130
Misclassification, 78
Mobile devices, 8, 13, 30, 32, 165, 193–215, 224, 253
Multiple-roles of HR departments, 257, 260
Multiple test, 72

Multitude of HR-specific aspects, 257
Mutation of skills, 185
Mutual adjustment, 204
Mutuality of obligation, 72–74

N

New competences, 202, 203, 214,
 260
New non-conventional
 organizational model, 251
New normal, 177–181, 186
New organizational principles, 251
New structural features of the work
 relationship, 22
New work patterns, 26
Not a unique path, 268

O

Office reconfigurations, 259
On-demand economy, 93
Operators' autonomy, 203
Organisation
 of work, 35, 143, 159, 167, 169,
 175, 180, 185, 226, 229
 of working hours, 210
Organisational autonomy, 7, 194,
 199–207, 214
Organisational change (OC), 31,
 179, 207, 253–257, 260, 264,
 268
Organisational discretion, 36, 199,
 200, 205, 212, 214
Organisational model, 33, 114, 150,
 259
Organizational discretion over the
 place of work, 201

Organizational "qualification" of
 digital technologies, 207
Organizational regulation of work,
 199–207, 214, 284
Organizational safety, 18–21
Organization personality (OP),
 200–204, 206
Other-directed organization
 personality, 200
Outcome control, 202

P

Part-time, 151, 157, 171, 183, 210
Peer-to-peer, 94–99
Period of conflicts, 186
Personal data, 6, 95, 96, 100,
 104–106
Personal information, 100–103
Personalize accordingly specific
 analysis, 261
Personal work relations, 6, 78–80,
 82, 84
Physical as well as the juridical place
 where workers have (the right)
 to perform their duties, 13
Physical notion of workplace, 13
Physical presence, 13, 20, 96, 252
Physical risks, 18
Physical separation, 14, 15, 19
Poland, 155, 158
Polarization hypothesis, 208
Pony express, 118–120
Portability, 6, 104–106, 253
Positions, 34, 79, 128, 144, 149,
 170, 180, 183, 185, 196, 229,
 254
Posting of workers, 19

294   Index

Posture of the work relationship, 13, 17
Precariousness, 120, 180
Previous, and heteronomous rules, 200, 202
Privacy, 101, 102, 104
Privatization of the workplace, 12–14, 18, 20–23
Productivity, 2, 7, 31, 35, 36, 41, 44, 47, 50–52, 54, 55, 145–148, 165, 178, 179, 181, 185, 194, 207–209, 214, 217n16, 258, 259, 279
Professional levels, 170, 171, 176, 182, 185
Prosumer, 15–17, 22, 23, 94
Purposive approach, 79

Q

Quality and time check of the result, 21
Quality of work, 44, 170, 174, 208, 251, 252, 279
Quantification of the work performance, 20
Quantification of working hours, 20
Quantification of work performed outside employers' premises, 20
Quasi-subordinate, 77, 84, 116, 130
Quasi-subordinate workers, 25, 75, 116

R

Rating, 15, 16, 70, 74, 95, 96, 98, 100–102, 104, 105, 107–108n2, 108n3, 113, 114, 116, 125, 126, 154

and reviews, 95, 99–100
Reallocation
  of managerial prerogatives, 15, 17, 22
  of prerogatives and responsibilities, 15
Reconciliation
  of working time with domestic and other time, 214
  of working time with time, 194
  of work with private life, 210–213
Regulation, 3, 5, 6, 8, 12, 21, 22, 59, 99, 101, 103–104, 125, 126, 128, 143, 152, 170, 173, 194, 201, 206, 211, 215, 224, 225, 227–229, 235, 237–239, 241–244, 281, 283, 284
Regulation of work, 180, 199–207, 214, 284
Reinforce employers' control power on workers, 22
Reinstatement, 125, 127
Relationship
  between digital transformation and productivity, 207
  between technical progress, 207
  between technological progress and productivity, 207
Reliability, 70, 100–102, 261
Remote work, 12, 31, 166, 210
Remote workers, 195, 198, 211
Reputation, 16, 17, 94–96, 100, 102, 106, 282
Reputational mechanisms, 15, 17
Reputational profile, 101
Reputational rating, 102
Reputational service intermediator, 17
Reputational systems, 94, 114, 126

Index **295**

Reserved for non-working life, 194
Resources, 49, 54, 56, 83, 142, 146, 151, 153, 157–159, 202, 203, 205, 227, 277
Responsibilisation, 15, 17
Responsibility, 13, 17, 22, 37, 81, 94, 116, 123, 167, 168, 203, 218n23, 249, 251, 252, 259, 267, 279, 282
Result-oriented approach, 15, 21
Results, 12, 15, 16, 21, 23, 27, 30, 35, 37, 40, 45, 46, 51, 53, 56, 58, 71, 74, 85n5, 95–100, 124, 126, 142, 146, 151–153, 157, 159, 167, 170, 171, 176, 177, 179, 182, 183, 185, 186, 194, 201, 202, 206, 211, 213, 214, 226, 234, 239, 249, 252, 253, 258, 263, 265, 267, 279, 281
Right to access, 104
Right to data portability, 105, 106, 109n11
Right to disconnect, 8, 21, 168, 172, 173, 241, 244
Robots, 30, 43–48, 51–56, 60n4, 166, 167, 178, 179, 185
Robot tax, 53–55, 57
Run a loss, 74

S

Safe and healthy work environment, 18, 19
Safety obligation, 18–20
Seasonal or temporary worker, 155
Sector, 7, 40–44, 46–49, 120, 142, 149–151, 153, 157, 165, 168, 177–179, 185, 208, 251

Self-employed, 16, 23, 25, 74–76, 79–85, 96, 97, 121, 122, 124, 126, 128
Self-employed work, 6, 121, 123, 126, 127, 129
Semi-structured interviews, 261, 262
Sensitization, 184
Services, 6, 12, 15–17, 21, 22, 25, 29, 41–44, 46–50, 55–57, 67, 69–71, 74, 77, 79, 81–85, 87n22, 93–97, 99–102, 105, 107n1, 107n2, 114, 115, 117–119, 122, 127, 128, 131n2, 131n3, 133n30, 150, 151, 153, 157, 160, 166, 171, 173, 180, 184, 205, 251, 258, 261, 266, 280
Shared safety, 18, 19
Sharing economy, 68, 95, 101, 106, 128
Smart machineries, 166, 167, 170, 176
Smart unions, 173
Smart work, 3, 34–36, 173, 194, 249–269
Smart workers, 172, 197–199, 203–206
Smart working (SW), 8, 35, 172, 173, 177, 180, 193–201, 204–206, 213, 214, 216n11, 216–217n12, 249–269
Social control, 147
Social partners, 7, 8, 169, 172–174, 176, 178, 181, 183, 185, 186, 225, 241, 244
Social protection, 68, 83
Socio-technical approach, 257
Someone else's ownership of the workplace, 19

296   Index

Specialization, 7, 167, 170
Sponsor, 255, 264, 266
Standard setting of Labour Law, 18
Statutory minimum fees, 81, 82, 85
Strategies, 7, 37, 49, 74, 79, 116,
    117, 151, 153, 154, 157, 158,
    161n6, 168, 174, 181,
    223–244, 257, 261, 262, 269,
    279
Strategy of suggestions, 170
Stressful activities, 179
Strike, 128, 149, 152, 155, 157, 159
Subordinate agents, 19
Subordinate employment, 68, 71,
    74, 75, 78, 79, 118
Subordination, 19, 22–25, 27, 33,
    71, 72, 75, 85n5, 86n14, 115,
    118, 119, 122, 123, 224, 228
Subsidiary 'indicia,', 72
Supporter, 56, 57, 184, 252, 264,
    266
SW, *see* Smart working

T

Tailor-made, 167, 174
Tasks, 7, 19, 20, 25, 36, 44–47, 51,
    67, 117, 119, 120, 126,
    130n1, 144–148, 161n4, 167,
    168, 170, 175, 179, 180, 184,
    195, 201, 202, 205, 206, 208,
    209, 217n18, 224, 234–236,
    241, 250–252, 255, 257, 258,
    264, 267, 268, 270, 280, 281,
    284
Team leaders, 156
Team-work, 170, 175, 270
Technical subordination, 19, 72

Technological unemployment, 40,
    53, 58, 170, 208, 217n20
Technologies, 2, 11, 29, 40, 69, 93,
    142, 178, 193, 253, 279
Tempered technical subordination,
    19
Temporary, 54, 59, 69, 145,
    153–158, 203
Times of inactivity, 74
Track data performance, 98
Trade union, 4, 7, 26, 49, 51, 80,
    81, 128, 143, 148–153,
    155–160, 161n6, 165–186,
    224, 228, 241, 244, 264, 265,
    268, 270
Trade union rights, 128
Traditional notion of workplace, 13
Traditional work relationships, 12
Transition, 5, 12, 26–27, 54, 58, 59,
    169, 280
Triangulation, 70, 261
Trilateral relationship, 22, 27
Typological approach, 11–27, 283

U

Uber, 70, 73, 74, 76, 77, 96–101,
    105, 106n1, 107–108n2,
    108n3, 114, 116–119, 122,
    123, 126, 131n2
    drivers, 3, 12, 68, 74–77, 86n18,
    97, 104, 105, 106–107n1,
    116, 119, 280
UIL, 158
Undertaking, 13, 15, 18–20, 70, 75,
    80, 81, 87n22, 87n23, 115
Unemployment rates, 149, 154, 166
Unionization rates, 154, 157

Index **297**

Union list, 154
Union power, 160
Unitary exercise of managerial
prerogatives by the employer,
23
Universal basic income (UBI),
53–55, 57, 58

V

Ver.di, 149–151, 159, 160, 161n7
"Vertically integrated" platforms, 70,
75, 77
Virtual market place, 16, 22
Virtual supervisors, 74
Volkswagen, 181, 215, 240
Voluntary, 234, 263

W

Warehouses, 143, 144, 147, 149,
155–157, 159
Web, 47, 94–96, 109n10, 173,
216n5
Win-win collective agreements, 186
Work 4.0, 166–168, 174, 177–184
Work by platform, 113–130
Work-control devices, 15, 20, 22
Work environment, 13, 14, 17–21,
147, 168, 180, 184, 252
Worker life, 102
Worker profile, 106
Work–family balance, 8, 215

Working hour, 3, 18, 20, 21, 25, 36,
53, 160, 210, 215, 224, 228
based system of quantification of
working time, 20
Working time, 8, 14, 15, 20, 21, 23,
36, 37, 71, 72, 76, 107n1,
115, 121, 157, 176, 177,
180–182, 184, 185, 194, 196,
198, 201, 210, 211, 213, 214,
224–240, 242–243, 260, 283
Working-time flexibility, 214
Work-life balance, 7, 20, 21, 37,
168, 177, 180, 181, 186, 208,
210, 213, 217n16, 224, 271,
281
Work-life conciliation, 181
Work-on-demand via app, 67
Work organization, 5, 8, 31–33,
36–37, 141–149, 158, 159,
170, 201, 206, 215, 249, 251,
253, 268, 271
Workplace, 4, 12–14, 17–24, 45,
114, 142, 159, 166, 168, 174,
179, 182–184, 195, 196, 201,
210, 216n11, 232–234, 236,
240–242
Work processes, 29, 32, 33,
143–149, 159, 180, 203, 280
Works councils, 150, 152–154, 224,
240, 244
Work system, 256, 257
World Class Manufacturing (WCM),
175, 185

CPSIA information can be obtained
at www.ICGtesting.com
Printed in the USA
LVOW13*1946310518
579135LV00013B/283/P